HV 8143 .B87 1997
OCLC: 37226896
POLICE ASSOCIATION POWER,
POLITICS, AND CONFRONTATION

W9-CZA-718

DATE DUE

DEC 10 2000	
DEC 21 2000	
DEC 16 2005	
DEC 12 2005	

GAYLORD   PRINTED IN U.S.A.

THE RICHARD STOCKTON COLLEGE
OF NEW JERSEY LIBRARY
POMONA, NEW JERSEY   08240

POLICE ASSOCIATION POWER, POLITICS, AND CONFRONTATION

ABOUT THE AUTHORS

John Burpo is Assistant to the President for the 16,000 member Combined Law Enforcement Associations of Texas (CLEAT), and Director of the National Coalition of Public Safety Officers/Communications Workers of America organizing project. In a twenty-plus year career in the police labor movement, Mr. Burpo has organized law enforcement officers, negotiated collective bargaining agreements, represented groups and officers in arbitration proceedings, and been involved in many local referendums and other political campaigns. He is a graduate of the University of Tennessee (cum laude) and the Tennessee School of Law, and is a member of the State Bar of Arizona. Mr. Burpo wrote the seminal treatment of police labor organizations—*The Police Labor Movement: Problems and Perspectives.* (Charles C Thomas, 1971) Before becoming a labor advocate, Mr. Burpo worked as a consultant for the International Association of Chiefs of Police and as police legal advisor to the Tucson, Arizona Police Department.

Ron DeLord has been President of the Combined Law Enforcement Associations of Texas (CLEAT) for twenty years, and during that time, has become recognized nationally as an innovator who has brought fresh ideas into an often stagnant police labor movement. Mr. DeLord's major achievement has been to lead CLEAT from an idea into a multimillion dollar, high-powered labor organization that is the source of pride for more than 16,000 Texas law enforcement officers, and the model for other police labor groups across the country. He is a frequent speaker at law enforcement seminars, and a contributor of numerous articles to professional journals. He is a graduate of Lamar Tech, holds a Master's Degree in Criminal Justice from Sam Houston State University, and has received a Doctor of Jurisprudence from Southwestern College of Law. Additionally, Mr. DeLord has been a street police officer in Beaumont and Mesquite, Texas.

Michael Shannon is a Washington, D.C. based political consultant who has received numerous awards for his creative work in political campaigns. He represents federal, state, and local political candidates in their campaigns, and has assisted many police associations in local referendum contests. Mr. Shannon lectures frequently at professional political association programs, and writes for various journals, including Campaigns and Elections Magazine and Governing Magazine. He has been involved in international political training in Croatia, Bulgaria, Trinidad, and Tobago. He is a graduate of the University of Oklahoma (Phi Beta Kappa). Mr. Shannon has also been a writer for the Dallas Morning News.

POLICE ASSOCIATION POWER, POLITICS, AND CONFRONTATION

A Guide for the Successful Police Labor Leader

By

JOHN BURPO
RON DeLORD
MICHAEL SHANNON

CHARLES C THOMAS • PUBLISHER, LTD.
Springfield • Illinois • U.S.A

THE RICHARD STOCKTON COLLEGE
OF NEW JERSEY LIBRARY
POMONA, NEW JERSEY 08240

Published and Distributed Throughout the World by

CHARLES C THOMAS • PUBLISHER, LTD.
2600 South First Street
Springfield, Illinois 62794-9265

This book is protected by copyright. No part of
it may be reproduced in any manner without
written permission from the publisher

© *1997 by* CHARLES C THOMAS • PUBLISHER, LTD.
ISBN 0-398-06810-0 (cloth)
ISBN 0-398-06811-9 (paper)
Library of Congress Catalog Card Number: 97-26780

With THOMAS BOOKS *careful attention is given to all details of manufacturing
and design. It is the Publisher's desire to present books that are satisfactory as to their
physical qualities and artistic possibilities and appropriate for their particular use.*
THOMAS BOOKS *will be true to those laws of quality that assure a good name
and good will.*

Printed in the United States of America
RO-R-3

Library of Congress Cataloging in Publication Data

Burpo, John H.
    Police association power, politics, and confrontation :
a guide for the successful police labor leader / by John
Burpo, Ron Delord, Michael Shannon.
        p.   cm.
    Includes bibliographical references
    ISBN 0-398-06810-0. – ISBN 0-398-06811-9 (pbk.)
    1. Trade-unions–Police–United States. I. Delord, Ron.
II. Shannon, Michael. III. Title.
HV8143.B87   1997
331.88'113632'0973–dc21

CONTRIBUTORS

Mark Clark
Director of Intergovernmental Affairs
Combined Law Enforcement Associations of Texas
Houston, Texas

Joe Durkin
Director
Madison Professional Police Association
Madison, Wisconsin

Michael Fehr
Past President
San Jose Police Officers' Association
San Jose, California

Harold Flammia
Past-Past President
San Antonio Police Officers' Association
San Antonio, Texas

Larry Friedman
Legal Administrator
Peace Officers Research Association of California
California

Darryl Jones
Past President
Prince Georges County Fraternal Order of Police
Prince Georges, Maryland

Richard Ratliff
Past President
El Paso County Sheriff's Officers' Association
El Paso, Texas

Dedicated to the memory of Douglas E. Ward of Brownsville, Texas, a distinguished police officer, labor leader, caring husband and father, and a true friend. He made a difference, and will not be forgotten by those who knew him.

PREFACE

Any law enforcement officer who has ever served as the leader of a labor organization knows that the view from the top is a scary proposition. Yesterday, the officer was riding in a squad car, arresting thugs and doing all the other things that previous training had so ably prepared him or her to do. Today, that same officer is president of the police association, entrusted with the authority to make crucial decisions which affect the economic well-being and job satisfaction of fellow officers.*

The scope of a police labor leader's duties are vast. There is the negotiation of a collective bargaining contract over wages, other economic benefits, and working conditions; and enforcing that contract through the grievance procedure and arbitration. There is, or at least should be, interaction with the political and business leaders in the community. There is the business of managing the association and its financial assets, which, depending on the size the organization, can range anywhere from tens of thousands to multimillions of dollars per year. The leader must also keep the members reasonably happy (or, at least not unhappy!), deal with the news media, engage in an ugly confrontation with the employer from time-to-time... the list of imperatives goes on infinitely.

Sadly, there are few places where the police labor leader can learn how to fulfill these responsibilities. There are plenty of trade seminars and an abundance of literature on the raw mechanics of being a police labor leader—how to bargain a contract, what this Supreme Court case says about an officer's rights in an internal affairs investigation, or what that federal law says about overtime benefits. But there's no place that a police labor leader can go to find out how to effectively lead the

*AUTHORS' NOTE: As used throughout this book, the terms "police association" and "police labor leader" refer to any labor organization and its elected president, whether at the municipal, county, state, or federal level, which represent a membership of law enforcement officers over job-related issues.

organization so that the goals and aspirations of the membership are substantially achieved.

The reason that there's no resource for this kind of information is that there are very few people in the field of police labor relations who understand the driving forces that make the difference between a labor organization's success or failure. The prevailing view among police labor leaders today is that they can show up on the first day of collective bargaining, or make a presentation before the city council or commissioner's court on the issue of the day; and because they are representing cops—the "thin blue line"—the protectors of the community, that the wants and needs which are expressed on behalf of the membership will be instantly satisfied.

This approach would be as if the Dallas Cowboys (or if you're a really diehard fan, the Tampa Bay Buccaneers) had shown up on the day of the Super Bowl without having gone through pre-season and playing even one down during the regular season, and then expected to win the game. And how disappointed these Show-Up-On-Big-Game-Day police labor leaders have all been to discover that the world does not begin at the police or sheriff's department, or the door of the association hall.

The fact is that there are principles at work in every community today, which, if understood by police labor leaders, will allow them to drive their organizations to greatness, and to achieve the goals set by the group, whether that goal be more money, benefits, staffing levels, safety issues, or other matters of concern. These principles concern the accumulation and effective use of **power** as the primary means of achieving a police labor organization's goals. Without power, a police labor leader is at the mercy of politicians, government bureaucrats, community leaders, and community interest groups. On the other hand, these other people and groups become less important to the association's success when the organization learns how to accumulate and use power for the self-interest of the association's members.

The fact is that police associations should exist for one, and only one purpose – the accumulation and use of power. Ultimately, power becomes the source for enriching the lives and well-being of the police association's members.

This book is divided into six primary parts, each of which looks at one facet of power. Part 1 defines the concept of power; Part 2 discusses how a police association can build power; Part 3 looks at the ultimate source of association power—politics; Part 4 examines the use of confrontation as power tool; Part 5 discusses the importance of association-news media relations as a means to achieve power; and Part 6 evaluates ten different case studies to show how the book's principles actually work.

Additionally, there is a seventh part at the end of the book—a special addition, which provides a historical perspective of the police labor movement in this United States, and updates the state of the labor movement as of today by looking at the national organizations trying to organize the police. This addition is significant since there has been no published work in at least twenty years about the state of the police labor movement.

Unfortunately, there is always a price to pay in the quest for power. Any time that a police association starts claiming a larger slice of the economic pie, or a place at the table where community power is brokered, some persons or groups are going to start crying foul. That's because the police association is interfering with the traditional patterns of doing business, and others find this tactic frightening, especially when being exercised by workers who carry guns and have the power to arrest citizens.

The point is that when the police association seeks power, there's going to be a great deal of discomfort, an occasional amount of conflict, and even a smidgen of absolute chaos. That's why the author's have centered this book around the four quotes appearing at the beginning of the book. These statements are the guideposts for the ideas about power expressed throughout each chapter.

Saul Alinsky's statement that "Change comes from power, and power comes from organization," lies at the heart of this book. The authors truly believe that police labor leaders must be change agents, and that power is the only way to achieve that change. Frederick Douglass' comment that "Power concedes nothing without a demand" expresses the notion that police labor leaders can achieve nothing when up against the status quo power structure —those who have the power, without insisting upon what rightfully belongs to the membership.

Former Texas Agriculture Commissioner and populist figure Jim Hightower once defined precisely the essence of decisive leadership: "The only two things in the middle of the road are yellow stripes and dead armadillos." Simply stated, police labor leaders must get off the fence and make the tough, hard choices that will lead their organization to greatness. Finally, the authors' friend and colleague, long-time San Antonio police labor leader Jerry Clancy, said it best when talking about that point in any dispute when the leader must throw caution to the winds in an all-out battle against the enemy: "If all else fails, we'll drop the bomb and live in the ashes."

The authors make no claim to special insight—we are not the all-knowing, all-seeing gurus of the police labor movement. In fact, our collective credentials are in some combination of attorneys, union organizers, political consultants, and worst of all, Texans (two by birth, one by virtue of a dubiously acquired driver's license), qualities which might draw some people to be overly skeptical of the ideas expressed herein. We do, however, have a combined sixty plus years of experience in bargaining contracts, representing law enforcement officers, leading local and statewide political fights, and assisting police associations to achieve their goals. We have experienced the thrill of winning many a fight against an employer or political bogeyman, and we have been on the losing end of the stick a number of times as well. We've learned a great deal from our collective history, and believe that it would be not only useful, but essential, to give to those police labor leaders who experience the same failures year-in-and-year-out some insights into how they can put their organizations on the path to success.

The authors' lifelong work allows us to tell a story about what it takes for a police association, and the leader who guides that group, to make the organization a winner in the many battles that lie ahead. Except for Part VII on the historical perspective and analysis of the police labor movement, this book is not, and does not purport to be, a meticulous research project with precise authorities for every idea set out herein. In fact, we have begged and borrowed a large amount of the ideas discussed throughout the book (and tried as much as possible to give ample credit to others). Instead, this book is about real life, and the day-in-and-day-out struggles which can bring a police association to true greatness.

Change comes from power; and power comes from organization.
Saul Alinsky

Power concedes nothing without a demand. It never did, and it never will.
Frederick Douglass

The only two things in the middle of the road are yellow stripes and dead armadillos.
Jim Hightower

If all else fails, we'll drop the bomb and live in the ashes.
Jerry Clancy

CONTENTS

Part III

POLITICS - THE LIFEBLOOD OF A SUCCESSFUL POLICE ASSOCIATION

Part IV

POLICE ASSOCIATIONS AND CONFRONTATIONS

Part V

POLICE ASSOCIATIONS AND THE NEWS MEDIA

Part VI

CASE STUDIES ON POLICE ASSOCIATION POWER, POLITICS, AND CONFRONTATION

Part VII

SPECIAL ADDITION
DISORGANIZED LABOR: HISTORICAL PERSPECTIVE AND ANALYSIS OF THE POLICE LABOR MOVEMENT IN THE UNITED STATES

POLICE ASSOCIATION POWER, POLITICS, AND CONFRONTATION

Part I

THE ESSENCE OF POWER AND POLICE ASSOCIATION LEADERSHIP

Chapter 1

THE PRESSURES FACING A POLICE ASSOCIATION LEADER

There is a direct correlation between quality leadership and the effective accumulation and use of power. Powerful labor organizations are built and/or led by successful leaders. Unfortunately, there are pitfalls, misfortunes, and catastrophes awaiting even the most well-intentioned, capable leaders.

The police association is a constant pressurecooker for a leader. There are general meetings, board meetings, labor committee meetings, negotiations, political events, council meetings, budget workshops, conventions, seminars, and endless other demands on your time. The spouses and children of an association leader protest these impositions on the family lifestyle.

The absolute worst pressure comes from a small segment of the membership who are by nature suspicious, cranky, ungrateful, demanding, biased, and opinionated. Additionally, these same members are lazy when it comes to volunteering their time to make the organization a success. Unless you are having a meeting to discuss the abolishment of their extra jobs, or perhaps layoffs, forget about having these whiners and naysayers come to a general meeting.

Police Association Leaders Are Motivated by Two Interests

Police association leaders cannot let these pressures get them down. Remember that you are essentially motivated by two interests. First, you should not be afraid to admit that you have a self-interest in being a leader. You make sacrifices because of the enjoyment of being in a leadership position.

Second, you could have never been elected to a leadership position unless the membership believed that you had the best interests of the organization, and their interests, at heart. Leaders should want to advance the organization and leave their mark on the police profession.

Leaders Have Five Key Skills

In their book, *Leaders*, Bennis and Nanus point out five key skills of all leaders. First, the effective leader has the ability to accept people as they are, and not as they would like them to be. As a police association leader, you should therefore avoid trying to change the basic characteristics of people, especially police officers.

Second, the good leader approaches relationships and problems in terms of the present, rather than the past. You should never rehash old mistakes. Always remember that if you lead, you will invariably make mistakes. Therefore, it is a wise maxim to push forward with your ideas for change, and ignore the "middle of the road" crowd.

A third leadership skill is the ability to treat others who are close to you with the same courteous attention that you would extend to strangers and casual acquaintances. You should never take your spouse, children, friends, and close business associates for granted. It is amazing what you can learn from their observations.

Another skill is the ability to trust others, even if the risk sometimes seems great. You do not have to be on guard and suspicious all the time. The most successful leader will trust the police association board and general members, and give them responsible tasks to perform.

A last important ability is to act without the constant approval and recognition from other people. As a true leader, you must take risks; and risks will invariably alienate some people. Remember that you cannot be all things to each and every member. You must therefore set your goals and push the organization and its members toward those goals.

Some of the Challenges Facing Police Labor Leaders

It is a challenging task to organize police officers into a viable labor organization, sustain that organization over time, achieve substantial economic gains, build political muscle, and reach any type of consensus among the officers as to direction of the organization. Police officers are basically "nonunion" union members. Officers want all the benefits of union membership without being identified as a union member.

Although there are exceptions, many police officers have no "brand loyalty" toward their own police association. Associations are decertified by competing police labor organizations telling the members "we could have gotten you more." The primary police association may have one or more smaller police labor groups contradicting the "unified voice" to the public and council. Ethnic, fraternal, social, religious, and gender-oriented organizations are competing with the police labor organization to be the voice of the officers.

The pressures on police labor leaders are tremendous. The normal job pressures are multiplied many times over as new pressures from the members, the public, the politicians, and the police administration are added to your already busy schedule. Most leaders do not have "release time" from work, and therefore, they have to work 40-hours for the city and volunteer their time another 40-hours for the association. The loss of family time, overtime, and career opportunities wears on the leader. The members are rarely appreciative, and generally turn on the leader after a term or two.

Unlike the private sector unions where elected officials serve for decades, police labor leaders have very short tenures. Burnout causes police association leaders to drop out after one or two terms. There are very few long-tenured police leaders in the United States. If the association leader is not relieved of duty to conduct association business, the stress adds up even faster.

The antigovernment, no-more-taxes shift in the political voting patterns of the nation is impacting police budgets. Surprisingly, many police officers support the "no new taxes" movement, not understanding that no new taxes means less revenue for themselves as government employees. Police associations are just one of many special interests groups competing at the shrinking taxpayers' trough.

Political action should be the focus of every police labor organization. Every decision impacting the living and working conditions of a police officer is decided by a politician. Whoever has the power to influence the majority to vote "for" their position gets the lion's share of the budget pie. Unfortunately, police officers tend to be apolitical or extremely conservative in their political thinking. A part of the police labor leader's responsibility is to move the group toward the political arena and involvement with political officials and issues—it is the most fundamental principle of the police labor movement that political action most effectively advances the interests and agenda of the organization.

Police associations with binding impasse arbitration often believe that they do not have to be politically involved, and that kind of thinking is wrong. You can never break out of the pack by splitting the difference in arbitration. Periodically, a police association needs a big contract to get ahead of inflation. Without political power, the association is helpless to get the politicos' approval.

One of the greatest challenges facing any police association is to get the members to support the organizational goals of the association, i.e., better wages, benefits, and working conditions. Because no one knows the reason why an individual police officer may vote for a candidate, police association endorsements should not be reflective of how the members will vote individually. Individual misdirection from the organizational goals of the association stymies many a police association in making an organizational endorsement.

Finally, most police associations do not have a strategic plan for the future. If the leaders do not know where the association is heading and they have no vision for the association, how can they expect the ordinary member to follow them? Consensus building among the members and developing leadership skills is crucial to the future of the association.

Some Parting Thoughts for Association Leaders

Being a police association leader is a thankless task. Police officers are not generally known for their kind and appreciative nature. If you seek association office expecting accolades, you have made a big mistake.

As a leader of a police association, you are normally a volunteer who has committed a fixed period of time during your career to help improve the living and working conditions of your fellow officers. Do not hesitate to admit that you are selfish about your service. Every gain you make for the members helps you personally as a member.

Too many leaders are exhausted by the whiners and naysayers who taunt association leaders at every twist and turn. Never let these losers get you down. They are jealous of your position and too lazy to take on the task themselves. Don't waste your energy arguing with them.

There is one last, parting thought: you are only elected to serve a tour. The association is not the be-all and end-all of your life. You should work hard, be creative, challenge authority, force change, visualize the future, and inspire others to believe in the organization. When your tour is over, help those who follow you to lead the association into the future!

Chapter 2

SOME OBSERVATIONS ABOUT POWERFUL POLICE ASSOCIATIONS

This part of the book is focusing on the concept of power and how it relates to police associations. The fact is that every successful police association in this country–every organization that has been successful in improving members' economic conditions, protecting their rights, and improving professional standards, is an organization that has effectively accumulated and used power for the benefit of its members. It is absolutely certain that every powerful police association has the same basic components.

The powerful police association is constantly evolving as an organization. It manages to far outdistance its competitors. While controversy tends to follow the powerful police organization, that is an advantage more than it is a disadvantage. It is not a matter of if, but when, the next controversy will occur in the community.

The powerful police association confronts the issues that cause its enemies and competitors to seek cover. It seldom takes a middle-of-the-road position on any issue of concern to its members. Strong police associations keep the weaker members of the organization from herding together and seeking the path of least resistance.

The powerful police association must be prepared to fight in the political and social arena if it is to force change. The association cannot advance the police profession if it does not have a voice in the community. Police associations should never apologize for demanding a right to participate in the power structure.

Frederick Douglass said in 1849 that, "Power concedes nothing without a demand. It never did, and it never will." Every social and political change in this country has come after a struggle over power.

Government and its management bureaucracy exercises power over the police profession, and they will not relinquish it without a demand.

A sad commentary on this struggle of police organizations to gain the right to participate in the power structure is that many associations, their leaders, and their members have swallowed the management propaganda hook, line, and sinker that it is unprofessional to be a player in the power structure. The management propaganda machine controls the media and, many times, holds a more positive image in the public eye than does the association.

Because of management's place at the power table, it has perpetuated a negative public image of police unions, civil service, collective bargaining, arbitration, and political activity by police organizations. Weak police associations accept these negative images as truths, and avoid any appearance of being political or powerful.

It is always amazing that public employers go unchallenged when they protest negotiating contracts with their police associations, but have no qualms about letting millions of dollars in contracts go to their "friends" (translated as campaign contributors). Management, through its local media contacts, editorializes against police endorsements of candidates while playing the political power game itself.

Every police organization must walk before it can run. Some organizations just learn the power game faster than others. If your association wants to move from its humble professional origins to dominance in the power structure, it will take time, commitment, and courage. The powerful police association adopts a "no guts, no glory" attitude. The winning association challenges the conventional wisdom of the time day-in-and-day-out.

The weak police associations continuously seek the status quo. The powerful police organization pushes to the edge of the envelope by challenging the status quo. Anytime you push against the power structure and demand your rightful place at the table, there will be controversy.

What your police association is willing to do to change the status quo is what will determine whether it will be a winner or loser in the game. The power game will be played out every day in your community. The question is whether your association will be willing to pay the price of admission.

Chapter 3

WHO IS SAUL ALINSKY, AND WHY IS HE SUCH HOT STUFF?

The quote at the beginning of this book, "Change comes from power and power comes from organization," is from the writings of Saul Alinsky. Many readers are no doubt wondering: "Who the hell is Saul Alinsky?" and "What does this slogan have to do with police associations?"

The fact is that if any police association president is to succeed in making the association a potent force in the community, the principles of Saul Alinsky must be understood and used every day. And while many police labor leaders know little or nothing about Saul Alinsky, every time they set up a PAC, endorse a candidate, call for a demonstration or picket line, or otherwise shake up the power structure a little bit, they're doing things that would have brought a smile to Alinsky's face.

Who Was Saul Alinsky and Why Are His Ideas So Important?

Saul Alinsky was a Chicago native who left a promising career in criminology in the 1930s and became a social activist. His initial interest was in organizing poor people to fight for their rights as citizens so that their lives would be better. Alinsky indeed believed, just like the slogan says, that "change comes from power and power comes from organization." He ultimately received international acclamation for his success in forming urban community organizations which made a difference in the lives of poor people.

The central theme in all of Alinsky's work is that people on the lower end of the social and economic scale who have nothing (people he calls "the Have-Nots") must organize for the purpose of accumulating and using **power** to make their lives better. The heart of Alinsky's teaching is that **conflict** must be brought to bear on people who already have the money and power ("the Haves"), if the "Have-Nots" are to benefit.

Some of Alinsky's sayings about what a group should do when it doesn't have power and want it are real classics:

"The only thing you get is what you're strong enough to get, so you better organize."

"No issue can be negotiated unless you first have the clout to compel negotiations."

The Police Association Leader's "I'm-Not-a-Poor-Person-So-This-Stuff-Doesn't-Apply-to-Me" Syndrome (or, Why Alinsky Is So Important to Police Associations)

A very common reaction among police association leaders when first exposed to Saul Alinsky is: "I've got better things to do than listen to this nonsense!" But before you dismiss the wisdom of Saul Alinsky so lightly, you might want to read on a little bit further.

Late in his career, Alinsky saw that poor people weren't the only folks in America having the screws turned to them. He pointed out that middle-class people (the "Have-Some-and-Want-Mores," a category which most cops fall into) have been lulled into a false sense of security with their suburban homes, two-car garages, and bass boats. The people with the *real* power—the politicians and money people behind the politicians, have continued to act in their own self-interest, and thrown a few little crumbs to middle-class folks.

If you don't think this description of the power elite is accurate, take a better look at the world around you. Politicians at all levels of government continue to be protected by the power of incumbency, in large part due to the money provided by wealthy business contributors. Middle-class people, on the other hand, watch the buying power of their paychecks continually slide downward or they lose their job and get no paycheck at all!

Saul Alinsky won't have a whole lot of relevance to your world if you are from a community where wages and benefits for police officers are at the top of the scale, where every call for service is answered within one minute because there's cops falling all over each other, and the community thinks that the local police are the greatest thing since the invention of the VCR. But there are many cities and counties which only throw an economic bone to the cops every now and then, but only after all the swimming pools have been built, the Friends of the Library get every book they asked for in the budget, and the Arts Council pushed through that big pay raise for the ballerinas in your local dance company. These are the same communities where Widow Jones has to wait 30 minutes for a cop show up to find out whether that creep hanging around in the back yard is the milkman, a Peeping Tom, or a rapist; and the community do-gooders start screaming for civilian review every time one of the bad guys gets a torn thumbnail during a resisting arrest encounter. If your police association falls in the latter category, then you'd better read on!

Every frustration that the leader feels about how to achieve more for the police association and its members can be relieved by the teachings of Saul Alinsky. You can be assured that there's always an answer somewhere in Alinsky's collection of works about how to make that hard-headed council member move off of a position, or how to make the big-shot Chamber of Commerce guys and gals pay attention to the law enforcement needs of the community rather than which of the downtown business crowd is going to get the next sweet tax abatement from City Council.

And don't be fooled into thinking that just because your police association is in a state with the Best Collective Bargaining Law in the Universe, that you don't need to pay attention to Saul Alinsky. Even in states like Wisconsin, which has a model binding arbitration law, police associations like the Madison Professional Police Association have used Alinsky-like rough-and-tumble tactics in the 1990s in order to get the City Council's attention, because traditional bargaining methods weren't working as well any more (see Chapter 37 for a case study on the Madison Professional Police Association's experience).

If You're Gonna Make the Power Structure Squirm, You've Got to Leave All of Mama's Childhood Preachins' Outside the Front Door of the Association Hall

Think about the last time that as an association leader, you thought about a confrontation with your employer. For example, you've been given a low-ball offer at the bargaining table, so in order to get that big 10 percent pay increase, you think about putting pressure on city hall: officers will go out to the local airport and hand out "Traveller Advisory Warnings" to incoming and outgoing passengers about the out-of-control crime rate in your city...and you want to put every council member's home telephone number on the advisory so that visitors and residents out at the airport can give the council a piece of their minds about the crime situation.

You get all excited about this plan, and then all of a sudden, you're overcome with guilt because your parents told you many times long ago that nice folks don't speak or do ill to others. Or maybe you outline the plan at a membership meeting, and one hand-wringing member says, "I admire your ends (the 10% pay raise), but not the means to the end."

Alinsky warns us about the "means versus ends" argument. "If you're too delicate to exert the necessary pressure on the power structure," he says, "then you might as well get out of the ballpark." The point here is that so long as it's legal, you do what you gotta do to get where you're going!

A police association leader must throw out all those traditional notions of right and wrong and always beware of "means-versus-ends" members of the organization. When you start talking about the airport "Travel Advisory Warning" idea at your membership meeting, be prepared to overcome some of these responses:

• "That's unprofessional!" (or, "Police officers shouldn't do that!")
• "This isn't the time." (or, "Let's not rush into anything too quickly.")
• And here is the absolute biggest cop-out to worm out of a confrontation: "Let the lawyers take care of it."

Whenever your police association is faced with an issue that requires a heavy-handed response, Alinsky tells us that there are only three questions that the leadership needs to ask, and if there's a reasonable probability that these questions can be answered **YES**, then you need to move forward with your plan.

1. Is the end **achievable**? (Can we get the 10%?)

2. Is the end **worth the cost**? (Will the $20,000 we spend on a public campaign against the city council, and the heartburn it's going to cause even some of our close political allies, be worth the 10%?)

3. Will the means **work**? (Are those airport flyers plus the radio ads and other flyers handed out around town enough to make the council move off of its low-ball position and give us the 10%?)

The issues of ethics, morality, and means versus ends is important for police labor leaders to understand, because it helps to clarify their thinking in critical situations. The next chapter will explore this concept even further.

When You Become a Police Association President, You Need to Rethink Some of Those Words You've Always Thought of as "Bad"

There are certain words common to the world of Saul Alinsky that we think of in a negative way: words like "power," "self-interest," "conflict," and "compromise." We have come to view these terms as evil; whereas, Alinsky gets us to see them a more positive way.

Alinsky asks a very simple question about the word "power": "If power is such a bad thing, why are so many people and organizations seeking it?" **Every** organization, he says, should exist for only one reason—the accumulation of power in order to have the ability to act, or to produce a result. If your police association does not exist for this purpose, it probably has very little reason to exist at all.

"Self-interest" is another word that gets a bum rap according to Saul Alinsky. We all have self-interest, he says, and it's important to recognize the constant conflict between professed moral principles and self-interest. Police association leaders are constantly attacked by members who believe that the leader is gaining something from his or her tenure as an officer in the association. Hopefully, the leader sought the office at least in part to improve the living and working conditions in the department. But any association leader would be less than truthful if he or she denied that they had some self-interest at heart (e.g., attraction to power, being the head of an organization).

"Conflict" is seen as a good thing by Alinsky. Without it, he says, the *status quo* would never be changed. For example, without conflict, many police associations and other public employee labor groups would never have gotten bargaining laws passed, negotiated the attendant agreements with excellent wages and benefits, or achieved civil service rights. While most police officers see themselves as preservers of the *status quo* and therefore dislike conflict, it is conflict forced on the power structure that brings change to the system.

Finally, many people, and in particular police association members, view the notion of "compromise" with considerable suspicion. It is seen as weakness or betrayal. But Alinsky says that while conflict is important to move toward a better result, compromise is the only way you ultimately get there!

When You've Got to Go to the Mat with Your Employer, There's No Better Guide for Action than Saul Alinsky

If your police association gets in a fight with the city or county over wages, benefits, manpower, or that Big and Hot Topic of the nineties —civilian review, and if you're looking for ideas on what's going to make the government move closer to your position, the answer can be found in the teachings of Saul Alinsky. Here's an overview of some of Alinsky's more well-used power tactics that have worked time-and-again for police associations around the country:

1. **Power is not only what you have, but what your enemy thinks you have**. Remember that power is, sometimes in larger and other times smaller parts, an illusion. If it was something other than illusion, the Communists would still be in power in Eastern Europe, and there would still be a USSR today! So when your association "war chest" is in a healthy state for a looming fight with the city, or the PAC account has enough money to take on that mayor who has been a thorn in the association's side (and everyone in town knows about it!), the less likely it will be that the city council or commissioner's court will stand firm against your position on a particular issue.

2. **Always go outside the experience of the enemy**. Several years ago, a large western police association was in a fight against a city that was planning to lay off approximately 12 percent of the sworn officers. One of the association tactics was a short flyer explaining the problem to the citizens, along with each council member's home telephone number and a plea for people to turn out at the next council

meeting. After a barrage of telephone calls to council member's homes (Can you imagine your telephone ringing 20-30 times during a night), and a turnout of more than 500 citizens at a council meeting, the council backed off of its layoff plan. The plan worked because it caught the council off guard without any way to retreat.

3. **Never go outside the experience of your own people.** This concept is pretty obvious—you wouldn't want to call for a work slowdown or speedup in a police department where the biggest form of confrontation in the past twenty years was a letter to the editor of the local newspaper from the association president!

4. **Ridicule is man's most potent weapon.** There's a great deal of enjoyment to be had in poking fun at your enemy, particularly in these days and times where politicians are not on the list of 10 Most Respected People in America! For example, one Texas police association campaigned several years ago against a city bond issue for an Arts District after the city had reduced police and fire pension benefits, primarily using the tactic of ridicule. The association ran a series of newspaper and radio ads telling citizens that after the bond issue passed and they needed a police officer, they could call the ballet! The ads were humorous, and the bond proposal was defeated.

5. **A good tactic is one that your people enjoy.** There is a deputy association in the western part of the country which was in contract negotiations in the mid-eighties when there was considerable confusion over the Fair Labor Standards Act and overtime benefits. At the bargaining table, the sheriff contended that jailers were completely off the clock during their lunch hour and could leave the jail; in actual practice, jailers were being made to stay in the jail, go back to work before the lunch hour was up, and not be compensated for it. So during one bargaining session, the deputies' association held a free barbecue lunch underneath the window where the negotiations were taking place; jailers told their supervisors that the sheriff had said it was okay in negotiations to take a half-hour outside for lunch and they walked outside to eat! Supervisors knew they couldn't stop the exodus because all parties to the contract were at the site, the tactic caused a serious manpower problem in the jail, and it forced everyone involved to find a solution to the lunch versus overtime issue. The converse of this tactic is that **any tactic that drags on for too long becomes a drag**. If the association had kept the free lunch idea up day-after-day, the members would have quickly become bored and stopped coming outside.

6. **The threat is usually more terrifying than the thing itself.** In the deputy association negotiations mentioned above, the stumbling block to a settlement ultimately became the sheriff's position on disciplinary issues. At an association meeting, it was proposed that if there was no settlement by a certain date, there would be a picket line at the front door of the sheriff's department (right next to the sheriff's office), and that two of the sheriff's biggest supporters—organized labor and the NAACP—would be asked to participate in the picket. Word undoubtedly flowed back to the sheriff very quickly (isn't that always the case after an association meeting?), the picture of his closest political supporters and employees lining up outside his office window came to mind, and a settlement followed soon thereafter!

7. **Keep the pressure on.** Any time that the police association is in a fight with the city or county, the group must keep coming with a new tactic until the fight is over. One tactic in and of itself will not do the trick; there must be constantly changing actions that will drive the employer crazy to the point of capitulation.

In Closing, This Chapter Can't Even Begin to Cover Everything About Saul Alinsky, So Go Buy His Books

This chapter has only scratched the surface about Alinsky and what he means to police associations. If you want to know more about his ideas, you might consider purchasing his two books: *Reveille For Radicals* and *Rules for Radicals*. They are both published by Vintage Press (Random House) and can be ordered through your local bookstore. *Rules* was written later in Alinsky's life—it's a great deal more readable, and is more pertinent to social activism in modern times.

Chapter 4

THE ETHICS OF MEANS AND ENDS

We looked in the previous chapter at Saul Alinsky's eternal question, "Does the end justify the means?" Alinsky says the real question is, "Does this **particular** end justify this **particular** means?"

Simply stated, "The **end** is what you want, and the **means** is how you get it." Police leaders face many "moral" decisions every day; in particular, when the organization is facing a battle with the power structure of the city, county, or state. These leaders quickly discover, as Alinsky found, that "the real arena is corrupt and bloody."

An activist police leader, when faced with decisions, views the issue of means and ends in pragmatic and strategic terms. Ask yourself, what are my **actual resources**; and what are the possibilities of various **choices of action**? Ask of the ends only whether they are achievable, and are worth the cost. Ask of the means only whether they will work.

It is often unbelievable that a police association leader will make decisions that will affect the organization for decades without first asking himself the above questions. What are the **actual resources** of the association? How much does money does the organization have, and how much of that money is it willing to spend on this particular issue?

What are the possibilities of various **choices of action**? Is this a minor skirmish wherein you have an unlimited number of options, or is this the be-all and end-all of battles with just one avenue of response? Seek counsel from your closest advisors, board of directors, and friends removed from the issue, and then fashion a responsive action.

As we noted in the previous chapter, the means-and-end moralists and nondoers are recognized by verbal responses such as, "We agree with the ends but not the means," or "This is not the time." A police labor leader cannot allow himself to be swayed by weak souls who want to either analyze the real situation from a purely moral perspective, or to continuously avoid the fight because it is not the right time. If you must make every decision from a purely moral viewpoint, then become a preacher. Whiners, naysayers, losers, nondoers, and spectators never think it is the right time.

Alinsky says, "The most unethical of all means is the non-use of any means." Inaction is a course of action! If you vacillate long enough, most issues will resolve themselves. Of course, you may or may not have participated in the course of events, or become the prevailing party.

Eleven Rules Pertaining to the Ethics of Means and Ends

Saul Alinsky sets forth eleven rules pertaining to the ethics of means and ends. Let's take a brief look at each one.

RULE #1: One's concern with the ethics of means and ends varies inversely with one's personal interest in the issue.

Our morality is strongest on an issue by which we are not affected. A parallel rule is, *one's concern with the ethics of means and ends varies inversely with one's distance from the scene of the conflict.* Very few police unions supported the eighties strike by PATCO (representing air traffic controllers) because they had no personal interest in the strike, and they were removed from the scene of the conflict.

In fact, the PATCO strike is as historically important to police unions as the Boston Police Strike on 1918. The PATCO strike sent a signal to employers in both the private and public sector that unions were weak, divided, and lacked solidarity.

RULE #2: The judgment of the ethics of means is dependent upon the political position of those sitting in judgment.

As pointed out by Alinsky, the Declaration of Independence can be viewed from both the American and British perspective. History is made up of "moral" judgments based on politics. The opposition's means, used against us, are always immoral, and our means are (of course!) always ethical and rooted in the highest of human values.

The editorial board of the local newspaper is seldom going to support the police association when it fights the establishment over *power* issues. The newspaper's owner is a part of the power structure of the community. To combat the moralist position of the newspaper against your issue, an effective police leader couches the organization's issue with such terms as "protecting the community against drugs," "helping the families of officers who risk their lives for you," and "the thin blue line."

RULE #3: In war, the end justifies almost any means.

Alinsky writes about Churchill, a rabid anticommunist, having to support Russia after Hitler invaded in 1940. Churchill stated that his only purpose was to defeat Hitler, and that he would make favorable reference to the Devil in the House of Commons if Hitler invaded Hell.

It is often said that in politics there are no friends, only alliances. When an association is in an all-out war against the powers-that-be, it must remain focused on the purpose of the battle. The alliances of an organization may change as the battle intensifies.

At times, police leaders have to make alliances with diverse groups in order to win on an issue. For example, the ACLU oftentimes takes on the city over constitutional rights issues affecting the police (residency, polygraphs, right to counsel); and the association must publicly side with the ACLU. While this galls the uninitiated member, the means justify the end in this instance.

RULE #4: Judgment must be made in the context of the times in which the action occurred and not from any other chronological vantage point.

Alinsky makes several observations. Ethical standards must be elastic to stretch with the times. In the politics of human life, consistency is not a virtue. Men must change with the times or die.

Police labor leaders cannot make tough decisions based on how history will view their decisions. There will always be those who will criticize every decision, and others who will say they told you so. If you have all the facts and have thoroughly analyzed the situation, your actions are the best available at the times.

RULE #5: *Concern with ethics increases with the number of means available and vice versa.*

To the activist police leader, the first criterion in determining which means to employ is to assess what means are available. There is only one question: Will it work? Alinsky says moral questions may enter when one chooses among equally effective alternate means.

If you have but one choice, the lone means becomes endowed with a moral spirit. The cry becomes, "What else could I do?" The person with many means can evaluate each option on a moralistic basis.

Alinsky believes "ethics is doing what is best for the most." An analogy may be the police labor leader who possesses a photograph of the mayor with a prostitute. If the association and the city were arguing over whether to strictly adhere to a minor provisions in the contract, would the leader drop that photo on the media? Hopefully not.

If the city was laying off large numbers of officers, breaching the contract, and suspending the union president, would the leader use the photo to win? Probably so. The seriousness of the situation and the impact on the most people of losing may warrant a different ethical posture.

RULE #6: *The less important the end to be desired, the more one can afford to engage in ethical evaluations of means.*

The minor skirmishes can be viewed from above. It would be unethical to expose the mayor to public embarrassment and ruin over a minor contract dispute. The union would receive severe public backlash for overkill.

RULE #7: *Generally success or failure is a mighty determinant of ethics.*

As Alinsky states, "There can be no such thing as a successful traitor, for if one succeeds, he becomes a founding father." The judgment of history leans heavily on the outcome of success or failure.

If the police labor leader rolls the dice and wins, his ethics are not at issue. If, on the other hand, he fails, his ethics will be the focal point. Had PATCO won the strike with the real assistance of the AFL-CIO, the ethical question of striking against the federal government would not have been an issue.

President Reagan offered PATCO a contract *after* the strike commenced. The immorality of the strike by federal workers only became an issue after they refused his offer.

RULE #8: *The morality of a means depends upon whether the means is being employed at a time of imminent defeat or imminent victory.*

Simply stated by Alinsky, "ethics are determined by whether one is losing or winning." What may be considered immoral acts by one facing assured victory would be considered moral by those desperately trying to avert defeat.

An often repeated quote among police labor leaders in Texas when facing insurmountable odds is, "We'll just drop the bomb and live in the ashes." If the city leaves the association no other avenues to resolve the issue, then the organization must be willing to use whatever is its ultimate weapon (strike, slow downs, blue flu, referendums, political action, etc.).

RULE #9: *Any effective means is automatically judged by the opposition as being unethical.*

Oftentimes, associations use available laws to put their issues (salaries, civil service, impasse procedure, etc.) before the voters in the form of public referendum. Why then are police associations surprised when the media attacks the organization for being unethical for forcing a public referendum on an issue? Why would it be unethical in a democracy to resolve issues by a vote of the populace?

Because in the judgment of the opposition, the police union is circumventing the city council (i.e., power structure) and taking the issue to the voters. The city will call the association a "powerful police "union" which is ignoring the wishes of the elected council.

RULE #10: *You do what you can with what you have and clothe it with moral garments.*

Again, if the association's most powerful means is a referendum, wrap the issue in the American flag. First, the law allows the issue to be brought to a vote of the public. Second, Americans died for the right to vote. Third, the elected officials are arrogant and out of touch with the voters.

Alinsky's states, "The first question that arises in the determination of means to be employed for particular ends is what means are available." Has the association assessed its strengths or resources present and can they be used? What is your time frame? Who, and how many, will support the action? What are the means and resources of the opposition?

Alinsky points out how society has divided itself—the "Have-Nots," the "Have-a-Little-and-Want-Mores," and the "Haves." The goal of the "Haves" is to keep what they got. They want to maintain the *status quo* and the "Have-Nots" want to change it.

Any effective means of changing the status quo are usually illegal and/or unethical in the eyes of the establishment. Why do we have right-to-work laws? Why do several states have prohibitions against collective bargaining by public employees? Why do we have "Hatch Act" laws prohibiting political activity by public employees?

"Professional police officers do not get involved in politics." "Unions are as close to legalized communism as we can get in America." "This action will embarrass the department." "I thought we were family." These are the standard lines used by the power structure to keep police associations from challenging the system.

Moral rationalization is indispensable at all times of action whether to justify the selection or the use of ends or means. All great leaders have invoked "moral principles" to cover naked self-interest in the clothing of "freedom" "equality," "a higher than man-made law" and so on. Remember that all effective actions require the passport of morality!

RULE #11: Goals must be phrased in general terms like "Liberty, Equality, Fraternity," "Of the Common Welfare," "Pursuit of Happiness," or "Bread and Peace."

Walt Whitman said, "The goal once named cannot be countermanded." Frequently in the course of action of means towards ends, whole new and unexpected ends are among the major results of the action. History is made up of actions in which one end results in other ends.

Wrap yourself in the flag and push forward with your means towards an end. Surprisingly, you may find that you have accomplished a different end than you expected.

Alinsky states, "The mental shadow boxing on the subject of means and ends is typical of those who are the observers and not the actors in the battlefields of life." If you are an activist, police labor leader, you are on the field of battle making tough decisions every day. The "back benchers" who critique every decision will never know the feel of victory because they chose to sit out the game as a spectator.

Chapter 5

UNDERSTANDING WHO HAS THE POWER
IS IN YOUR COMMUNITY

Before a police association can set out to have working relationships with groups and individuals in the community, it is important to know where the power lies in the community. Because wherever the power to influence events exists in the community, that is where the police association wants to be!

The Important Question Is: Why Are We Always Left Out in the Cold?

Police associations often wonder why they get left out during budget considerations, while the city council or commissioners court can seem to find the money for certain special interest groups. Who makes the decision on where tax dollars are allocated in the community? Are the elected officials the decision-makers? Does the city or county executive and their bureaucracy really decide who gets what amount of money? Or are there other forces at work "behind the scenes" at every level of government?

Who really has the "power" in your community? The truth is that while the power to influence government may rest at times in the hands of a few people or organizations, this power base is always changing as new people and organizations enter, and the old power base leaves.

A community may have a strong mayor who dominates the political scene for a period of time. Different community organizations may rise to positions of influence during certain years. One company may be the primary employer and control the community. A large union in a one-industry town can be a force to be reckoned with on issues.

The old adage that the "squeaking wheel gets the grease" is true in dealing with the government. The civil rights movement of the 1960s forced the government to take action on the complaints of minorities. The protests of environmental groups often block polluting industries in many communities.

Every day of every year, competing special-interests battle for the government's money. While many police associations await the final budget report, other organizations have already cut up the pie in a manner more favorable to them.

How You Can Find Out Who Has Power in Your Community

How can a police association find out who is really making the decisions in its community? First, you should obtain a copy of the political action committee reports of the elected officials having the power to vote. Who gave them campaign money?

Does your city, county, or state require reports from people lobbying elected officials? If yes, then get a copy of their reports and see who they are entertaining. Use the Freedom of Information Act (FOIA) or Open Records Act in your state to obtain a copy of the budget, audit, equipment contracts, consulting contracts, outside law firms, construction contracts, and other financial information from the public employer.

When a lobby report shows that a person, company or organization gave an elected official campaign assistance (e.g., money or volunteers), and that same the person, company, or organization received what it wanted from the government with the elected official's vote, then the conclusion is obvious. There is a direct link between campaigns, lobbying, and government disbursements of funds. If every elected official only voted in the best interests of their community, why would people give them campaign money and spend money "lobbying" them?

Where Do You Find the People Who Have Power?

Now that you have cross-referenced one source of identifying the influential power brokers of the community, where do you find them? Here are the best places to start looking: the country club, private health and dining clubs, charitable events, arts and theater organizations, chambers of commerce, boards and commissions, community events, churches, civic clubs, and political fund raisers. Except for the costs of joining some country and health clubs, the other organizations and events are generally free, or open to the public for a nominal fee.

The police association should adhere to the old saying of going where the "elite meet to eat." Almost every day the powerful and the "wannabe" powerful are eating breakfast, lunch, and dinner at some civic, charitable, political or business function. Were members of your association there to eat and meet? If not, then your organization was missing out on another great opportunity to listen to what the power brokers in your community have to say, and for them to hear what issues concern your association.

The Police Association Should Get Involved in the Organizations Where the Power Players Belong

Which civic organizations do the members of the association belong to? Which local charitable functions does the association participate? Does the association belong to the Chamber of Commerce? Are members of the association active in both political parties and the nonpartisan local political events? When major community events are held, does the association take an active part in planning the event?

The positive public image and group involvement of the association translates into positive community support when the association confronts the political power structure over an issue. Can your association reach out and touch the right people or organizations—the ones who hold real power in the community, and solicit their support in times of crisis?

Almost every metropolitan police association overlooks one of the most powerful political blocs in their community—minority leaders and organizations. While outside the traditional "white male" country club set, minority opinion leaders and organizations can and do influence the government and elected officials. There is much to be learned from the years of struggle that African American and Hispanic organizations faced in forcing the government and politicians to react to their concerns.

One way to reach the political power structure (i.e., elected government leaders) is to be able to communicate with the voters who will be electing or unelecting them. The voting electorate in any community is very small in comparison to the number of actual voters. In many smaller communities, the association can literally identify every household that would traditionally vote in a local election.

Does your association participate in local political campaigns? One way to get to know the politicians is when they need your support. Go to their campaign headquarters and witness the power structure at work—the movers and shakers of your community will always be around somewhere. The power structure never waits until after the election to get involved!

If an issue critical to your association comes before the council, can your group effectively communicate your position by telephone, mail, or in person to the elected officials, the voters, business leaders, community activists, and opinion leaders? Does your association maintain an up-to-date database of these people and organizations? If not, then your group is already one step behind in achieving your organizational goals.

Here Are Some Tips for How to Build Community Power

Here are the key points to remember about building power in the community:

1. You are not the only people in the community with problems. The world does not revolve around the police. While you may not see it, forces are at work every day influencing the political process.

2. Analyze which organizations exist in the community. Find out if you have members in those groups. Designate members to join the more influential ones.

3. Investigate who contributes money and people to political campaigns. Find out who lobbies these elected officials. Analyze the budget, audit, and financial links between the city and the community.

4. You have to go fishing where the fish are. Go to the business, charitable, community and political events where powerful people meet. Relationships are power.

5. Do not overlook minority organizations and opinion leaders. You would be surprised at the common bonds you have.

6. Build a database of voters, businesses, community groups, civic clubs, politicians, and opinion leaders. Communicate with them on issues through your publication.

7. Build a powerful public image. When you are involved in the community, there is a perception that your group is powerful. And perception is reality!

Part II

THE BUILDING BLOCKS OF POLICE ASSOCIATION POWER

Chapter 6

SOME OBSERVATIONS ABOUT BUILDING INTERNAL ASSOCIATION POWER

This part of the book is devoted to explaining how police associations can build power. The accumulation of power is an elusive goal, and there is no one easy formula for reaching this goal. Accumulating power is somewhat akin to building a house—there must be a foundation, followed by a series of careful refinements, all of which will add up to a solid structure.

There are two types of power that any successful police association must strive to build—internal and external. This chapter will look at some basic concepts of internal power.

The First Principle Is to Understand the Sources of Internal Power

The most important lesson in building internal union strength is understanding power. Power comes from having money and members. While some association may be limited in the number of eligible members they can obtain, there is no limit on the amount of money you can accumulate.

Remember that accumulating money without purpose is self-defeating. The members will refuse to support dues and PAC increases if the association has large reserves and no track record of accomplishments. Therefore, while you have to spend money to reach your goals, you also have to have accomplishments which deserve the memberships' financial support.

Financing a Police Association

Every association runs on money. The bigger the organization, the more money it consumes. Association leaders are constantly seeking new avenues of raising money. No matter how much money the association accumulates, the members and board will find ways to spend it.

1. **Dues.** The primary source of association finances is dues. Outside of politics, nothing is more controversial than raising dues. Too many associations set artificially low dues to keep the members from complaining, and then they spend all their time seeking alternative means of funding association activities.

The fact is that the members will complain no matter what they pay in dues. True leaders get as much money from the members as the market will bear. If you are making gains on their behalf, do not be afraid to demand a higher per capita.

Poor leadership and lack of direction cause the members to question the value of dues payments, not the amount of the dues. Police officers will join another association at a higher dues rate if they believe that organization will accomplish their goals.

2. **More members through internal organizing.** Many police associations never stop to think about how they can increase their internal power by the simple step of signing up more members. If your association has 95 plus percent of the available pool (e.g., where the association is the exclusive bargaining representative for a 100-officer unit, there are 95 in the group), then the available market has been pretty well saturated. On the other hand, if you only have 50 to 90 percent (or sadly, less than 50 percent), then there is considerable room for internal organizing.

There is an art to internal organizing. It involves approaching police officers one-on-one, overcoming any objections they might have to membership, and having them make a commitment to join. It can be a laborious, time-consuming process, but the reward is more members, more money, and a more united association.

3. **Fundraising.** Most national, state, and local police associations solicit money from the public to supplement their organizations. If you depend upon the telephone solicitor to make ends meet each month, you are building your association on a foundation of sand.

Police solicitations are the cocaine of the police labor movement! Police associations are selling their good names and reputations to raise money. There is no nice side to solicitations.

Since almost every association solicits, the market is overloaded with pitches for widows and orphans. This does not take into account the solicitors who seek money "in the name of law enforcement."

The most effective use of solicitation money is to fund nonrecurring budget items (i.e., one-time purchases). Also, you might use solicitation money to fund death benefits for the members or to fund community projects. High visibility projects help reduce the negative side of raising money from the public.

The association should avoid budgeting payroll and fixed payments on solicitations. The day you have to have the solicitation "fix" to make ends meet, the solicitor owns you.

4. **Insurance plans and incentive programs.** Many associations have started offering insurance programs to their members (e.g., auto, homeowners, life). The association gets an administrative fee, or in some states, the association can own the agency. This can be lucrative if the association has a large enough membership base.

Investigate the company and the agents. The association may assume liability if the insurance company is careless in offering a policy to the membership with the association's stamp of approval. Your attorney should review any contracts with insurance companies.

Many associations offer credit cards, travel advantages, and other incentive programs. While these programs can offer some financial assistance, they are seldom real money makers. Use them to provide additional services to the members, and not as fundraisers.

5. **Self-funded trust plans.** If you have a large membership base, the association can self-fund some programs (e.g., dental, vision, and prepaid legal). Smaller associations can still use the self-funded trust to fund retiree health care premiums and other programs.

Remember that when you set up a trust, you are assuming huge liabilities. The Internal Revenue Service (IRS) strictly regulates all trusts, and there are never-ending rules that must be followed in administering these trusts. Also, union trust plans have sent many a union leader to prison, so strict accountability is a must!

The rewards are great if you hire professional plan administrators and trust attorneys to advise the trustees. Members who participate in self-funded trusts tend to appreciate the services provided by their association. Trust plans put the association name before the members and their families.

The amount of money that can accumulate in a trust will generally exceed anything the association collects in dues. Since money means power, association trust funds can get you respect in the business community.

An additional benefit of trust plans is that the association is now providing the services previously provided by the city or county. The association can better protect the interests of the members in obtaining benefits.

Trust plans can provide the association with real financial security. The administrative fees can generate money to run the association. Dues money and trust money provide a rock foundation to a police association (for more on trusts, see Chapter 9).

6. **Political Action Committees (PACs).** Power comes from money, and political power comes from PAC money. No association should be without a PAC (see Part III for more information on PACs). You should use every legal means to raise PAC money. If you can get payroll deduction for PAC, press the members to pay the maximum.

Members will often raise the PAC deduction before they will raise the dues deduction. Educate the members about the advantages of having serious PAC money. Politicians respect any organization that can help its friends and punish its enemies.

Whether Your Association Is Big or Small, the Key Is to Keep Members Committed

Associations, like people, go through stages of development. The members will occasionally lose interest in the association when nothing is going on in the community. While lack of interest is always of concern, it should be accepted as a fact of life.

The leadership of the association must work hard to keep the members working toward the goals of the organization. The ebb and flow of the community will cause something to happen in due course.

It is not necessary, nor is it healthy, to keep the association on a war footing at all times. People tire of constant turmoil and conflict. Do not pick a fight just to get the members aroused. When the real necessity for combat emerges, the members will think you are crying wolf.

All real leaders provide a *vision of the future.* Association leaders should strive to communicate a vision of the future for the membership. Establish short-term and long-term goals. Communicate these goals to the members, and motivate them to work toward these goals. Keep the members excited about the future.

Other Keys to Building Internal and External Strength

If money and a committed membership were the only keys to building a powerful police association, it wouldn't be too long before your organization became the Biggest Show in Town. Unfortunately, power doesn't come so easily.

You must develop a long-term **strategic plan** as to where your organization is today versus where you want it to be down the road, and what it's going to take to get reach your new goals. Attention must be paid to the quality of membership services, particularly **legal services** which police officers so frequently need. And there must also be a stronger commitment to developing **external strength** through such programs as **image-building**, development of **community coalitions**, and production of a first-class **newsletter**. We will now look at these concepts.

Chapter 7

STRATEGIC PLANNING FOR POLICE ASSOCIATIONS

Today, the police labor movement operates in a rapidly changing, often hostile environment. The public is mistrustful of labor unions, and skeptical of government employee productivity. Taxpayers are more insistent on getting value for their tax dollars, so there is a constant battle between competing interests over how to divvy up money that police officers want and need for pay and benefits.

There has been a serious decline in the American labor movement in recent years, especially in the private sector. While the public sector is holding its own by being unionized at a respectable 37 percent (with police and fire unions unionized at a substantially higher rate), the private sector work force is only unionized at 11 percent, and dropping.

Union militancy is virtually dead. Strikes are seldom used in the private sector because corporations can easily break the unions with replacement workers. Police associations, which frequently used the strike as a tactic in the seventies, know that in today's environment there is no public support for such a tactic.

Because of these factors, there is a strong necessity for doing business differently in today's environment. That is why strategic planning becomes such an important part of managing the police association.

What Is Strategic Planning?

In order for a police association to survive and succeed in today's high-tech, antiunion environment, more attention must be paid to thinking and planning on behalf of the organization. This process is called **strategic planning**. For the purposes of this chapter, strategic planning is defined as "... a systematic method for setting policy in an organization. It involves analyzing key aspects of the world in which an organization operates (the `environment'), gaining clarity on the objectives the leadership hopes to achieve, assessing the money and people the organization has to achieve those objectives (its `resources'), and reviewing how well its existing methods of operation do in achieving chosen objectives (its `organization').

The major components of strategic plans for police associations are:
1. Analyzing the **environment**.
2. Setting association **priorities**.
3. Assessing present association **resource allocation**.
4. Evaluating the ability of present association **organizational structures** to achieve new priorities."

Analyzing the Environment

Successful police associations recognized five to ten years ago that they had to change with the times and become more political. The battlefield of the future is in the political arena. Of course, it always has been, but police associations failed to understand or appreciate the need to be a political player. To many police officers, their "professional" image and apolitical attitudes have oftentimes prevented them from participating in the political process.

The environment in which police officers work is political—always has been, and always will be! Every single issue impacting police work is decided in the political arena by politicians. A police officer's wages, benefits, hours, equipment, vehicle, district, and assignment are dictated by politicians or political considerations. Who is appointed police chief, and in many cities who is promoted to the top ranks of the police department, are always political decisions.

Why is it that all politicians seek public office on a "law and order" platform, but there never seems to be enough officers, patrol cars, and equipment to accomplish the task of maintaining law and order? No one ever ran for elective office who is "for" crime, but elected officials always seem indifferent to police concerns once elected.

Many police associations are as apolitical as their members. Most police associations do not understand the political environment in their community. Either the police association does not participate at all politically, or the association does not participate at the level necessary to effectively control its destiny.

It is utterly amazing each year to watch police associations make angry comments about the city council not approving much needed budget items *after* the adoption of budget. Once the budget is adopted, it is too late to whine about being left out. It is obvious that the police association did not understand how the budget process works.

The budget is a pie being divided *politically*. If you believe the city staff and elected officials make budgetary decisions based upon what's good for the citizens, then you are naive. Hundreds and thousands of individuals and organizations are at work seeking each and every tax dollar.

Who gets what percentage of the tax dollars in your city or county? Who really makes the decisions behind the scenes? Who funds the campaigns of the candidates? Who gets the municipal or county bond business, consulting contracts, construction projects, and other contracts for tax dollars?

Rank your association on a scale of 1 to 10 as to whether the association has a strategic plan for analyzing its environment.

1. Has your association analyzed the environment and determined "who's who" as an individual and organizational power broker in the community?

2. Does your association even know "how things get done" in your community?

3. Does your association command respect as a "force to be reckoned with" in the community, or is it merely a "force to be placated" during budget considerations?

4. Can your group effectively communicate your message to the politicians and the power brokers in the community and have them act on your concerns?

5. Can your association "make or break" a politician?

6. How many elected officials will pull the lever "FOR" the group if it means denying the money to another special interest?

7. Has your association made coalitions with other powerful individuals and organizations who can influence the actions and decisions of the power brokers?

Setting Priorities

When developing a strategic plan, every police association must determine what its priorities are. At the turn of the century, when AFL president Samuel Gompers was asked what labor unions wanted, he replied, "More." Today, a police association leader cannot simply set his priorities as "more."

What is it that the leadership of the association wants to achieve? Does the membership understand and agree with those priorities? Are the priorities achievable? Can the priorities be achieved within a reasonable length of time? Is the association setting its priorities high enough?

Several years ago, the president of a large Southwest deputy sheriff's association recently had to define the priorities of his organization. The contract was expiring and the county wanted major concessions on certain benefits. A consensus was reached among the leaders and members that the association could not concede benefits beyond a certain point.

If the association could not politically force the county commissioners to break the deadlock and sign a new agreement before the deadline, the group would probably collapse. The number one priority was gaining a new contract that made financial gains while making only minor benefit concessions. Once the members were unified on the objectives, the association successfully pushed its members to bring enough political pressure on the elected officials to settle the contract.

Too many police associations either do not have identifiable priorities or objectives, or the ones they have are so low no one notices one way or the other if they are achieved. The association leadership simply attempts to survive contract to contract without breaking any new ground. Organizations should constantly reevaluate their priorities in light of the changing environment in which they work.

Rank your association on a scale of 1 to 10 on whether the group has a strategic plan for setting priorities.

1. List the top five priorities the group has set for the next five years.

2. If none have been set, what should be the top five priorities?

3. Do the members clearly understand these priorities, and are the members committed to carrying out these priorities?

4. Do any of these priorities "break new ground" in the way the group has been doing business over the past few years?

5. Is your association constantly reevaluating its priorities?

Assessing Association Finances and Resource Allocations

The airline pilots union does not have a large number of members, but has a very large treasury. The Teamsters has both money and members. The United Farm Workers Union has neither a large membership nor any money. Which of these unions would you suspect has the greatest amount of power?

Organizational power is simply money and/or members. Most police associations have an exact number of members (i.e., the approximate size of the department or bargaining unit). However, there is no finite amount of money that an association can accumulate. When preparing a strategic plan, many police groups do not assess their finances or amount of time their member's are willing to donate to a cause.

If you remember nothing else about strategic planning, remember— **YOU CAN NEVER HAVE ENOUGH MONEY!** It is incredible that police associations can complete tough negotiations on a new contract knowing full well that the city intends to be tougher the next time, and the association waits until the next negotiations to start examining its resources for a fight.

The failure to plan for tough times often leads to tougher times. When the city knows that the association has limited resources to wage an extended fight, the city can "plan" to be tougher at the bargaining table. Financially weak associations shall not inherit the kingdom of peaceful negotiations.

A large Texas police association successfully negotiated a four year contract several years ago. Shortly afterwards, the media "exposed" the financial impact of the contract. During the next four years, the mayor supporting the contract was defeated, and a taxpayers group circulated petitions to repeal the bargaining law (local bargaining repeal elections being something unique to the Republic of Texas).

The police association could have rested upon its laurels and waited for four years. However, the association convinced the membership to assess itself $250,000 as a special "war chest" in the event the bargaining law was challenged. The association's political action committee (PAC) doubled its contributions to municipal candidates during the interim, and elected favorable council members.

During negotiations four years later, the taxpayers group turned in the petitions requesting a bargaining repeal election. The mayor and council refused to call the election on a technicality and publicly supported the police association and collective bargaining. By assessing its financial position and raising money in advance of the confrontation, the association prevented a costly election and possible loss of bargaining rights.

If your group is spending money on nonpriority items at the expense of its priorities, then maybe the association needs to prioritize its spending. Some associations have a reputation of "living high on the hog" while skimping on membership services. Is your group caught in the trap of having expensive board meeting at exotic locations because this is the "only benefit" many board members receive?

Here's a final comment about finances. Too many associations depend upon telephone solicitations and other forms of public solicitations to balance their books. If your organization is not on a sound financial footing based solely upon dues income, then perhaps there needs to be a self-examination about financial planning.

In assessing the association's resource allocation, do not forget to evaluate the membership. How many volunteers could you get in a fight? Which civic or social organizations do the members belong to, and could your members influence those groups to support the association? In preparation for a confrontation, have you asked the members to sign a pledge card committing certain amounts of time to the campaign?

Rank your group on a scale of 1 to 10 as to whether the it has a strategic plan for assessing its finances and resource allocations.

1. What is the yearly income versus expenses of the association?
2. What percentage of that income is dues versus other forms of income?
3. What are the reserves of the association?
4. Has the group evaluated the membership to determine which civic and social organizations they belong to?
5. Has the group obtained signed pledge cards from the members committing a certain amount of money and or time in the case of a confrontation?
6. Has the association examined its spending habits to determine whether its spending matches its "alleged" priorities (i.e., costs for board travel and entertainment versus expenditures for membership services?

Evaluating Organizational Structures

When is the last time the association constitution or organizational structure was changed? Is "we have always done it this way" interfering with the organization's ability to carry out its objectives? Is your group living in the past or future?

Too many police associations have organizational structures so cumbersome that they are paralyzed to act in an efficient manner, much less respond to an emergency. If your group has a bargaining team that looks like the one used by the United Auto Workers to bargain against Chrysler, or your board of directors encompasses almost the entire membership, then perhaps you need to restructure the organization.

How many employees and\or board members does it take to manage the association effectively and efficiently? How do the employees spend their time? Do you have too many board members or too many committees? Does your association seem to be meeting around the clock? Does your group suffer from "membership apathy" as the same five members attend every meeting?

When you develop a strategic plan for your association, closely examine the organizational structure to determine whether that structure helps or hinders the group in achieving its priorities. If organizing new members is the association's priority, does it have employees spending their time "organizing" new members or merely servicing existing members? If the priority is getting a "break through" contract, is the bargaining team structure designed to give the team new ideas, or instead to weight it down with representatives from every special interest in the police department?

While the history and culture of an association is important, it should not be the determining factor in how it is managed into the future. Associations that do not bend will eventually break. As the environment changes within the community, the association must be prepared to change with it.

Rank your association on a scale of 1 to 10 as to whether it has a strategic plan for evaluating its organizational structure.

1. When was the last time your group reorganized its structure or amended its constitution?

2. How many members are in your association? How many employees work for the group (include release time of leaders)? Do a brief job description on each employee.

3. Make an organizational chart of the association.
4. How many members serve on the bargaining team?
5. How many committees does the association have?
6. How many members on average attend a meeting?
7. Compare the association's priorities with the organizational structure and answer whether it is efficient or not.

Summary

These four elements make up the basic components of strategic planning. Unfortunately, most associations are not acting on issues, they are reacting to situations. When an association is unprepared for a crisis, the employer wins every time. To prepare for future confrontations, the organization must evaluate its environment, set priorities, assess its resources, and streamline its organizational structure to carry out its priorities.

Successful police associations develop strategies and constantly reevaluate the organization. These groups move to the edge of the envelope and push the organization to new heights. The leaders of these associations are never satisfied with the status quo.

If you want your association to survive for years to come, then you must start planning *now*. You must consider not what is happening today, but what you anticipate will be challenges in the year 2000 and beyond. The visionary leader sees the future and "leads" the association in making the changes it will need to meet those challenges.

Chapter 8

POLICE ASSOCIATION SERVICES–
LEGAL REPRESENTATION

The nature of law enforcement work guarantees that police officers are going to need an attorney at some or several points in their careers, whether it be for administrative discipline, a civil action, or criminal matters arising out of the official performance of duty. Police associations either provide some form of legal representation program to their memberships, or join larger organizations (e.g., statewide police group) for legal defense services.

The entry of police associations into the legal defense marketplace has meant a number of lawsuits by members for failure to represent under a legal defense program, such as a breach of the duty of fair representation under a collective bargaining agreement or a deceptive trade practice claim. It is therefore essential to understand how to best structure a legal defense program and avoid litigation by a member against the organization.

A top-quality, well-managed legal representation plan projects an image of competence and commands respect from the membership. A failed legal plan can lead to disastrous consequences, including the financial ruin of the association.

Police association legal defense services cover a whole range of subjects, even including private matters such as wills and divorces. We will concentrate first on legal defense in job-related cases such as administrative discipline and criminal/civil matters arising out of the performance of duty.

Whatever Legal Defense Plan Your Association Has in Place–Put It in Writing

Many police associations have legal defense plans with all the bells and whistles, including every conceivable form of representation. Unfortunately, members often don't know that these services are available because the association doesn't publish the plan anywhere! It is not unusual for police association leaders to frantically go looking through the minutes of old board or membership meetings to find out what the organization's policy is on a particular legal service.

Rule number one for any police association legal defense program always is: **PUT THE PROGRAM IN WRITING!** There are two very sound reasons for committing your legal service plan to written form.

First, a written legal defense plan will usually avoid any subsequent litigation against the police association by a disgruntled member who has been denied legal services. While the member may disagree with the decision to not represent him or her in a particular case, at least the door is shut on a claim that the association didn't follow its rules, because the rules are there for the whole world to see.

Second, a written legal defense plan makes good internal political sense. Police association members want to know that their dues money is being spent for worthwhile purposes. The written legal defense plan gives a reassurance to members that the association is doing something to protect their job interests.

The best place to advise members about the legal defense plan is in the police association publication. It wouldn't even hurt to put a copy of the plan in *every* edition. And the inclusion of articles describing actual cases where the police association has successfully defended members in discipline, criminal, or civil cases would also be a good idea because the articles reinforce the association's commitment to providing legal services.

Now we will examine the two basic kinds of legal defense plans—automatic and discretionary, and the implications for police associations to provide one or the other.

The Pros and Cons of Automatic Representation Plans

Many police association plans state that whenever a member is disciplined, or is indicted or sued as a result of a performance-of-duty conduct, that the member will be automatically represented by an attorney. While there can be certain exclusions and/or levels of discretion in these plans (e.g., no representation for suspensions under three days, or the board of directors must determine whether an act constitutes "performance of duty"), these plans all take away most discretion from association decision-makers in deciding whether or not to a provide legal defense.

There are some definite pluses to these kinds of programs. First, the limitation on discretion among association leadership removes the element of personalities. We have all seen the "rogue cop" who is fired and many fellow officers say, "he deserved what he got." What these officers tend to forget is that any one of them could be on the firing line some day, and the point of view when faced with unemployment looks considerably different!

For police association memberships in certain parts of the country, the automatic plan is not only wanted, it is demanded. Therefore, the automatic plan makes good internal political sense in places where there is a history of or demand for providing this kind of legal service.

Finally, the limitation on leadership discretion in deciding services cuts down on the possibility of litigation. Remember that the more absolute, nondiscretionary services are provided, the less likely your group will wind up in the courthouse against a disgruntled member.

The down side to automatic plans is twofold. First, whenever the association provides greater coverage, the legal costs will be driven up —you can't expect to represent every officer disciplined, and every officer indicted for job-related actions, and not pay a heavy price in financial resources.

Second, the police association defense of police officers in high profile cases can exact a heavy political price in the community. For example, the Los Angeles Police Professional League's legal defense of its members in the Rodney King incident brought a certain measure of public censure. Many people in the general public simply do not understand the decision-making pressures that police officers face, and the heavy discipline system that second guesses every one of these decisions.

The Pros and Cons of Discretionary Legal Defense Plans

Discretionary legal defense plans are normally one of two kinds. There is the program that will represent members when it is "in the best interests of the police association" to do so, and the board of directors will decide what constitutes "best interests." The second discretionary plan arises out of a collective bargaining relationship, where the police association must respond to a "just cause" disciplinary action taken by the employer, and decide whether the discipline constitutes a grievance by the member under the collective bargaining agreement

The pros of the discretionary plan are the flip side of the automatic plan. The legal representation costs are considerably reduced because there will be fewer cases. Second, there will be less public backlash for the association's involvement in controversial discipline and criminal cases, because many leaders will take the path of least resistance and stay out of the line of fire in a high profile, Rodney King-like situation.

The problem with discretionary plans is the greater likelihood of the police association winding up in the courthouse against a member. Any plan which permits a decision to be made "in the best interests" or allows a board to decide whether a member was terminated "for cause" is facing the likelihood of litigation by a member who feels that the denial of representation was improper.

Most lawsuits against police associations arise out of the organization's failure to represent in contract disciplinary grievances–the alleged breach of the duty of fair representation. In order to avoid this potential liability, some police associations in collective bargaining environments apply the automatic representation method in "just cause" situations, thereby avoiding the decision as to grievability.

Other Tips–Review Your Plan Periodically and Work to Keep Costs Down

A police association legal defense plan should not lay stagnant for years and years. The passage of time brings new conditions that could require modifications in the plan. For example, a rival group which threatens your group's status as exclusive bargaining agent and offers representation for all disciplinary actions might require your police association to reevaluate its "in the best interests of the association" or "just cause" criteria for providing legal services.

The police association should look at every way possible to keep legal costs under control. In many groups, legal defense is the single biggest budget item taking a bite out of dues revenue. There are several ways to control legal costs:

1. If outside counsel is retained, insist on a per-case compensation system and negotiate the per-case fee in advance. Law firms would prefer an hourly billing system, but it is amazing the amount of unnecessary "legal research" that can go into preparation of simple administrative cases! It's your dues money and you should always call the shots on how it's spent.

2. Look at the cost effectiveness of employing qualified staff attorneys as opposed to outside counsel. At the point where your association is doing high-volume legal work, a staff lawyer makes greater sense.

3. Look for ways that nonlawyers such as business agents and paralegals can perform certain parts of your legal defense program. Private sector unions have long used business agents with great success to represent members. But take heed if this path is followed: check with your State Bar Association to make sure that the use of nonlawyers does not run afoul of any Bar rules, and make certain that your members can willingly accept nonlawyers to do this work—police officers often perceive attorneys as the only solution to their legal dilemmas!

Prepaid Police Legal Plans

A more recent development in police association legal services has been **prepaid legal plans**. These plans provide that police officers will have access to an attorney, or may seek an attorney of their own, to represent them with respect to certain specific personal legal matters. These plans normally cover nonduty related situations only—duty-related legal problems traditionally fall within the scope of police association legal plans that are funded out of dues. There are IRS restrictions to prepaid legal coverage under certain conditions.

There are three basic types of prepaid legal plans. Since many prepaid legal plans are regulated by the Bar Associations of the various states, by state insurance boards, and/or various federal agencies, it is *absolutely essential* that competent legal counsel analyze the plan concept and documents. The three types of plans include:

1. **Closed Panel.** With this plan, only a designated attorney(s) or law firm (s) is used to provide services.

2. **Open Panel.** The participating member may select any attorney for the services described in the plan document.

3. **Modified Plan.** An attorney(s) or firm (s) is designated to handle legal claims; however, participating members may select another attorney of their own choosing, but often with restricted coverage.

While there are prepaid legal plans available on the marketplace today from various insurance companies and entrepreneurial groups, it is recommended that the police association create its own a prepaid legal plan. An association-operated **trust** plan gives your organization more control over the plan, provides a tangible benefit to the members, and represents a financial asset to the police association. The labor organization trust is a predominant method used in the private sector for the delivery of personal legal services.

For reasons related to financial stability stated in #4, below, it is much easier to implement a prepaid legal trust where the police association has the right to collectively bargain. Here are some tips for setting up a successful prepaid legal plan for the police association:

1. A trust should be created by a written document that will establish certain responsible leaders of the police association who will serve as trustees for the plan (quite often the police association's board of directors). The trustees will be responsible for supervision of the plan and arrangement of all legal services.

2. Depending on the size of the group and complexity of claims filed (i.e., claims under an "open panel" plan would be more complex), it might be necessary for the trustees to appoint a professional administrator. The administrator will make decisions on claims filed by members as to the extent they are covered by provisions of the plan.

3. Depending on the type of plan, an actuarial analysis would have to be performed to determine the per-member cost of the plan. Costs on a closed panel plan are obviously easier to fix than on an open plan.

4. The key to a successful police prepaid legal trust is **financing** of the plan. The best method by far to finance a legal trust is through the collective bargaining process. The police association should make a bargaining proposal that is similar to a health insurance premium proposal, by asking the public employer to pay a contribution for the benefit. A proposal for employer contribution always raises the issue of an **employee** contribution as well, but the per member cost for prepaid legal is relatively small in contrast to other employee benefits. Depending on the size and type of plan (i.e., open or closed), the per member cost might range from $15 to $30 per month.

5. The trust must establish **eligibility** standards for benefits. When the police association bargains, eligibility for benefits will be determined by the composition of the bargaining unit.

6. There must be some provision in the trust for procedures that members follow to make claims, and for review and appeal of all claims. The trustees or professional plan administrator should be responsible for review of claims, and for hearing claims appeals.

7. The trustees must consider the tax consequences of a legal trust to individual members. At this time, the Internal Revenue Service will exempt a legal trust benefit from being classified as income if the trust is a "recognized" plan under IRS rules. The IRS should be contacted in advance of establishing the trust to determine recognition requirements and procedures. Experts on legal trusts advise that IRS rules on this point are very fluid at this time.

The trust and an accompanying plan document must state the legal benefits that will be covered. The provision for benefits must be related to the actuarial study discussed above, including the types of legal claims that will be covered, and any limitation on the number of attorney hours that can be spent on a covered legal claim. Many legal trusts will have specific hour limitations on each claim in order to avoid excessive plan usage.

Some of the typical benefits of a legal trust include:

• Personal nonbusiness bankruptcy.

• Prosecution or defense of incompetency-related proceedings.

• Juvenile court proceedings involving a child of the household of the officer.

• Family-related matters, including divorce, annulment, child and spouse support, adoption, paternity, custody, and contempt.

• Criminal-related matters, including felonies and misdemeanors of the officer and household member. [NOTE: This benefit can include juveniles; often excludes traffic violations; and will have certain restrictions such as excluding "duty-related" claims that are already covered by a police association defense plan.]

• Defense of civil matters (exclusive of duty-related claims).

• Probate and probate related matters.

• Telephone consultation service.

• Preventive legal services (e.g, wills, contract negotiations, will preparation and estate consultation, real estate transactions, contract disputes, small claims, and letter writing in reference to family legal problems).

The creation and administration of a prepaid legal trust is a complex and highly technical subject. A police association should implement a prepaid legal trust *only* with the assistance of competent trust attorneys and professional administrators.

Chapter 9

POLICE ASSOCIATION SERVICES–
MEMBERSHIP TRUSTS

If you haven't gotten the message yet, we'll say it again–power is members and money! If this statement were not true, then the Ladies Garden Club and the Teamsters Union would have equal standing in influencing the political system. While an organization may be limited in the number of persons eligible to be members, no organization is limited by the amount of money it can accumulate.

One of the most overlooked areas for accumulating economic power for an association is the creation of trust funds. In addition to controlling their pension funds, private sector unions have traditionally used the trust fund concept to amass large sums of money. These funds are generally called "union welfare or benefit funds."

The problem with having large sums of money is that it can corrupt some people who have been entrusted with a fiduciary duty to use the money for the benefit of the organization. Do not let the fact that some union officers have violated their trust–just like some bank tellers and corporate presidents, discourage an association from creating and administering a trust fund.

Police Association Trusts Haven't Been Used as Much as They Should

In the public sector, most employee unions and police associations have lagged behind in taking advantage of self-funded trusts. Some of the reasons are employer resistance, ignorance of available trust options, lack of confidence in managing a trust, or a perception that unions are not in the business of managing benefits.

Why do public employers often oppose the creation of association-controlled trusts? For one, an employer wants the employees to see all benefits as coming from the employer, and not from the association. Second, employers understand that money, even held in trust, means power.

As a police association leader, do you believe that your city, county, or state government exercises due diligence in finding the best benefit programs for each employee? If your employer is self-funding benefits, are the plans being managed for the benefit of the employee or employer? Is the contract bidding process for millions of dollars in insurance and other benefits influenced by who knows whom at city hall?

These disturbing questions point to the necessity for the police association gaining control of membership benefits. Otherwise, the employer will likely do what is in its best interests, and not the best interests of association members.

The Trust Options Available to a Police Association

What trust options are available to police associations? While there may be an exception, self-funded health insurance is extremely risky and should be avoided at all costs. Many police associations are self-funding "supplemental" medical insurance plans, where the trust fund pays a designated amount for certain supplemental health options.

Providing dental benefits through a union-controlled trust carries the same risks as other self-funded health plans. However, larger associations with the financial wherewithal to administer such plans have found them to be a valuable membership service.

Associations can create funds to provide a supplement to pensions, or a supplement to retiree health insurance premiums. Some police associations have convinced the employer to allow retirees to remain in the employer's health insurance plan at a group rate, provided that the union trust fund guarantees or assists with the premium payments.

Funds to provide prescription discounts have been used by many unions; however, caution is advised due to spiraling costs. Vision care plans are easily self-funded as are blood plans. Cash payments to families of members as a death benefit can be self-funded, but remember that such payments may be considered taxable since they are not from an insurance company. It might be more advisable to purchase life insurance from a reputable company, or buy reinsurance to protect the plan.

Disability funds are excellent for assisting members who lose income from extra jobs while sick or injured. Since officers normally have greater benefits for line-of-duty injuries, payment for off-duty incidents only should be considered.

Prepaid legal plans (discussed at greater length in the previous chapter) can also be self-funded. This type of plan can be proposed at the bargaining table, with an objective of employer contributions. A check with the state bar should always be made for possible conflicts.

When Setting Up a Trust, Get Qualified Help, and Be Realistic!

Do not allow lack of confidence about administering a trust cause you to overlook trusts as an option for your association. Police officers serve as fiduciaries of pensions and trust funds throughout the country. The critical issue is recognizing that you are a police officer or union officer, and not a plan administrator or trust attorney.

Start with a professional plan administrator who can design your plan document. Get a CPA to advise you on the financial planning. Hire an attorney with trust experience to file the necessary state and federal papers. Remember that trusts are carefully monitored by the IRS and other authorities. The fiduciary duties of trustees and the liability for the association and its officers must be considered as a risk of doing business.

Be realistic! Providing benefits requires a pool of money and an understanding of the demands on that pool by the type of benefit you are self-funding. You cannot spend more money than the amount of money allocated. Underfunding a benefit is the quickest way to face bankruptcy. Ask yourself if your police association is large enough to have the financial ability and time to assume the liabilities of managing a trust.

Third-Party Administrators for Association Trust Funds

If your police association has a trust fund, or is thinking about the creation of such a fund, then it is *essential* that you consider the employment of a third-party administrator. The term "Third-Party Administrator" ("TPA") is used liberally in the insurance/benefits field to describe everything from insurance agents who help their clients fill out applications and claim forms...to large or small firms which provide comprehensive benefits administration and management services to client plans...to insurance companies which only offer administrative services to benefit plans which wish to self-insure, but want another company to do the paperwork. There is no single definition in federal statutes or regulations for the term "Third-Party Administrator."

What a TPA Can Do for a Police Association

For the purposes of this chapter, a "TPA" means a firm which provides comprehensive benefits administration and management services to client plans. Some TPAs specialize in employee benefits such as pensions, disability, and health coverage. Since a large part of police association trusts focuses on health and related benefits, these types of benefits will be the reference point for discussing TPAs.

TPAs, like their companion professionals–CPAs and lawyers, have an ongoing, long-term relationship with their clients in advising and carrying out decisions, but they do not make decisions themselves. The client (i.e., the police association) retains the legal responsibility for any decisions having to do with the trust. The center of authority for a benefit plan is always the board of trustees of the plan (which is controlled by the police association).

Benefits of a TPA

The use of TPAs has boomed in recent years. Approximately one-third of all workers in the United States are covered by plans administered by TPAs. If your police association has, or is considering the creation of a trust for dental care, optical benefits, supplemental health, or prepaid legal, you should consider the following advantages to hiring a TPA for the administration of the trust:

1. **Cost savings**. An independent TPA can help your police association in several ways. First, your association will not have to pay 100 percent of the costs for in-house administration (i.e., salaries and benefits); instead, you pay a fraction of that cost for a wider range of

expertise. Second, TPAs are focused not on just planning, but also on looking at effective **cost containment** for client plans. These cost containment programs will be customized for the needs of each individual client.

2. **Government compliance.** The federal ERISA statute requires a fiduciary duty and arms-length transactions on the part of the board of trustees, and there is increasing enforcement, litigation, and imposition of fines under ERISA for breaches of fiduciary duties and "self-dealing." The use of an independent TPA is convincing evidence of arm's-length dealings in any plan's fiduciary duties. A TPA can also keep track of and advise a client on the estimated 1,500 laws, regulations, interpretations, and major court decisions which constantly affect trust plans. The TPA can also play a special role in helping a client shape its trust around the quagmire of government regulations, which will protect the plan (and police association) from huge unsecured claims and liability.

3. **Experience.** The TPA normally handles many clients, and has an active "grapevine" with other TPA firms. The TPA therefore has the practical insight from thousand of plans which have faced any number of problems.

4. **Personalized service/flexibility.** When dealing with a TPA, the client is always the number one priority. The TPA will know the plan benefits, covered employees, and providers. It can monitor expensive trends and billing irregularities, which can then save the client large sums of money. Also, personalized service allows the TPA to work closely with the client to further design or modify a trust when the need arises.

Some Concluding Observations

In conclusion, investigate the possibility of a self-funded trust as a method of delivering certain benefits to your members. If you are satisfied with the employer spoon-feeding your members' benefits, and believe that police associations should not be in the business of providing benefits, then you are behind the curve. Your association has little to lose, and everything to gain, by accepting responsibility for providing your members with certain trust benefits.

Chapter 10

HOW ASSOCIATIONS CAN BUILD COMMUNITY COALITIONS

The average police association is elitist. Its members are elitists too. Seldom does a police association see the need to build any alliances with other community and special-interest groups. The usual responses are that police are "different," and that the police have "special needs."

Police associations feel uncomfortable specifically asking other organizations for assistance. They will issue a general hue and cry to the public to "help us" but then do not wish to dirty their hands seeking a solution in a coalition with other groups.

Members of police associations raise hell if they hear about the association leadership meeting and discussing strategy with "suspect" activist organizations. What, horror of horrors, would the chief or mayor think when they learned that the association was talking to these people?

When on occasion the association does build an alliance with one or more community groups on an issue, the issue is almost always a *police* issue. Rarely does the association seek out community groups and offer to help them on their nonpolice issues. Police associations see coalitions as one-way streets—they *ask* for help, but never *give* help.

There seems to be a mental isolation among police associations and their members. Their attitude is that the police are the "be all and end all" of the community. This isolationist attitude causes the association to avoid interactions with the community.

Coalitions Are Two-Way Streets

In every community, coalitions are being formed in and around various issues of importance to the community, and in fact, issues important to the association as a part of that community. Groups representing women, minorities, abused children, victims, teachers, parents, homosexuals, homeless people, the elderly, churches, veterans, the disabled, political parties, taxpayers, homeowners, apartment owners, and environmentalists are meeting and building bridges on issues on concern to them.

Police associations have a common interest with these groups at various times and on various issues. Coalitions between the association and these organizations are in the **self-interest** of both groups. These alliances send powerful messages to the political structure that the association is a player.

However, community coalitions are a **two-way** street! There must be continuous interaction and assistance between the members of the coalition. Whether informal or formal coalitions, the coalition members on a particular issue must work together to communicate a common strategy to the power structure.

Purposes of Coalitions

Alliances between police associations and other community groups can be used for:

1. **Special purpose issues of interest to the police association.** The need to add more police officers or the threat to reduce the number of police officers generally is of interest to groups representing victim's rights and neighborhoods. The association must build a coalition with any organization interested in having adequate numbers of police officers on the street.

Even pay and benefit issues are of importance to organizations interested in seeing that the department is able to hire and retain qualified officers. For example, minority organizations may assist the association on this issue in order to attract minority officers.

Job security issues like bargaining and civil service are understood by unions, teachers, and other civil servants. Groups representing the elderly are keenly aware of health care issues and would support the association in improving health care and retirement benefits.

2. **Specific purpose issues of interest to other community groups.** Unions and businesses will often join together to stop a plant closing or to attract a major company. The association has a self-interest in keeping the tax base stable or growing. Working with these groups gives the association a positive public image of caring about the community.

Depending upon the circumstances, associations may want to aid or defeat efforts to create single-member districts. The power structure likes at-large districts. The minority community wants single-member districts. Remember that it is easier to defeat your enemies and elect your friends from single-member districts.

Bond issues are always controversial, and the association is often asked to join one side or the other. A bond issue to build new parks or a community center attracts a powerful following of community activists. The association may want to join forces with these groups. However, a bond issue on a theater and arts district may warrant a negative campaign especially if the city is not providing adequate funding to the police department.

3. **General purpose political action of common interest.** This issue means joining forces to elect your friends and unelect your enemies. Civic groups may be upset with a certain council member over an issue. Does the association need to eliminate this person also? If so, the basis for a coalition exists.

The business power structure may have hand-picked the next conservative mayor. Should the association build a coalition of community groups and unions to defeat this person?

Education of the Membership

There will be a backlash if the association publicly endorses a controversial issue without the proper membership education. Remember, the membership has individual interests that are often different from the association's organizational goals.

For example, a taxpayers' association files a petition for a tax roll-back. The business community wants the association to join with them in defeating the referendum. Individual members may want their personal taxes roll-backed; however, it is in the self-interest of both the business community and association not to lose tax revenue, which could result in budget cuts and layoffs.

The association must in this instance communicate the organization's goals of continuing employment and better wages over short-term tax relief. The business community generally acts as a cheerleader for the local power structure, and the association can build powerful bridges by coming to its aid.

Identify Areas of Common Self-Interest

What does the association have in common with each community organization? There is usually at least one common concern. Establish communication with the leadership of the community organization. Try to understand how decisions are made in the organization, and work within the framework of the organization's rules to seek assistance.

Attend the events sponsored by different community groups. Make as liberal a donation as the association can afford to their fund-raising efforts. Do not miss an opportunity to appear in their publications, or make an appearance in the local media assisting a particular group. Publish your contributions in their own newsletters (or vice-versa).

Invite the leaders of other community groups to your functions. Give awards to community activists. Take the time to visit with them over breakfast or lunch. Listen to their concerns about the community. Try to determine how the association can help them achieve their organizational goals.

Establish a pattern of on-going mutual assistance. The association **gives** help—the association **gets** help.

Establish Communications

The association should establish a consistent pattern of communication with community organizations. Are the various community groups on your association mailing list? Do you receive the publications produced by the community groups? Does the association attend organization meetings of other community groups? Does the association volunteer to help these groups?

Delegate responsibility among association leaders. There is something going on day and night in every community. One person cannot attend meetings twenty-four hours a day. Find members who have an interest in a particular organization and ask them to report on anything of interest to the association.

Make coalition-building a permanent part of your association's activities. Establish a committee that reports on community events at association meetings. Take a high visibility position in many community activities.

Power is networking. Networking is building relationships. You cannot ask a person or organization to fight for you unless you have that network, and they can trust you to stand up for them later.

Identifying Potential Coalitions

There is a myriad of organizations in any community which offer coalition-building opportunities. A cursory look through the Yellow Pages in any city opens up a world of such opportunities.

Generally, there are two types of groups which offer the best possibility for the formation of coalitions. One type consists of **labor organizations**, which have the same fundamental concerns as police associations (i.e., collective bargaining and employee rights). It is helpful that a police association seeking to build a coalition with labor groups belong to the AFL-CIO and the local Central Labor Council. The cost for membership in these organizations is comparatively low.

Surprisingly, the other type is **minority group organizations** such as the NAACP, LULAC, and other groups which have an ethnic orientation. These organizations frequently push for social and political change, and are supportive of "underdog" issues. Also, the law-abiding people in minority areas of cities generally like the police, since these areas generally have more crime than other parts of town.

Here is a listing of the organizations which would be the most suitable for coalition-building:

- **LABOR ORGANIZATIONS**
  Public Sector
  Fire fighters (IAFF local, state & national unions)
  Teachers (NEA, AFT & Independents)
  Colleges & Universities (professional & blue collar)
  General City & County Workers (AFSCME, SEIU et al.)
  Federal Workers (AFGE, NTEU, NFFE, NAGE et al.)
  State Workers (AFSCME, CWA, SEIU, Independents et al.)

Transit Workers (ATU, UTU, Teamsters et al.)
Private Sector
Construction (carpenters, bricklayers, painters, plumbers, sheet metal)
Ports (Longshoremen, Teamsters)
Railroads (engineers, BRAC, maintenance of way)
Airports (ALPA, TWU, Teamsters)
Hospitals (nurses, maintenance)
Transportation (Teamsters)
Tourism/Hotels (HERE)
Office Workers (OPEIU)
State AFL-CIO
Central Labor Councils
Farms (Farm Workers Union)
Retail Workers (UFCW)
Communications (CWA, IBEW)

- **ETHNIC ORGANIZATIONS**
  African-Americans (NAACP, Urban League)
  Hispanics (LULAC, GI Forum)
  Asians (Pacific-Americans)
  Native Americans

- **CHURCHES/RELIGIOUS ORGANIZATIONS**
  Catholic   Black Protestant
  Jewish   Protestant

- **BUSINESS/FRATERNAL ORGANIZATIONS**
  Chamber of Commerce   Young Men's Business League
  Professional Women's Club   YMCA/YWCA
  Civic (Jaycees, Rotary, Lions, Sertoma, Kiwanis, etc.)

- **PROFESSIONAL ORGANIZATIONS**
  Medical (doctors & nurses)
  Legal (Bar Associations)

- **POLITICAL**
  Party Organizations (both state, county & precinct)
  City & County (council, commissioners, sheriff, etc.)

Special Districts (airports, ports, parks)
State (senators/representatives, judges, etc.)
Federal (senators & congressmen)
Lobbyists (city, county, state & federal)

• SOCIAL/COMMUNITY

Junior League   League of Women Voters
Charitable (United Way, etc.)   Big Brothers/Big Sisters
Boy/Girl Scouts   Women (Rape Crisis, etc.)
100 Clubs   Victim's Rights
Library Groups   Arts/Theater Groups
Country Clubs   Crime Stoppers
Neighborhood Watches   PTA's

• MISCELLANEOUS

Environmental Groups   Homeowners Associations
Veteran's Groups   Civil Liberties
Taxpayers' Associations   Peace Groups
Apartment Owners   Trade Groups
Disabled Support Groups

• INDIVIDUAL COMMUNITY OPINION LEADERS

"Movers & Shakers"   Political Activists
Politically Ambitious   Church Leaders
College Professors   Retired Government
                          Officials

Chapter 11

HOW YOUR POLICE ASSOCIATION CAN PRODUCE A FIRST-CLASS PUBLICATION

Police association publications come in all forms and sizes. There are magazines, newspapers, and newsletters. There are publications full of many articles, and others with very little material. There are slick-looking journals, and others that are more crude in appearance.

Many associations see the publication as a revenue-generating source (sometimes a substantial source of the organization's revenues). Other groups use little or no advertising.

There is one feature common to all such publications. They are produced in an effort to communicate something about what the police association represents as an organization.

And this "something" is where many police associations consistently take the wrong path. There are too many groups which say the wrong things, to the wrong people, and in the wrong way. The end result is that the association's message becomes garbled, ineffective, and irrelevant.

It is important to remember that the police association is a **business**, and a part of that business is selling the organization to your membership and, as you will discover below, to the community as well. Your publication sells the police association best by sending a message to the reader, and the ultimate message that you want to leave is **what the police association represents as an organization**.

Who the Police Association Should Talk To–Members and Potential Members

Before we can discuss what your message should be, it is essential to understand **who** your association publication is talking to, and why these groups of people should be targeted to read the publication. Once the labor leader understands who he or she is talking to, it is much easier to frame the message.

Members should always be the primary focus, and there is a very good reason. You want your members to understand what is the mission of the organization, and to take pride in what the association is doing.

Effective communication will result in better **membership retention** (i.e., keeping your membership base at its peak level), which is a critical financial goal for any organization that survives in large part on members' dues. Also, it will produce a higher degree of **organizational loyalty**, which becomes particularly important, for example, to a bargaining agent/police association facing a rival organization in a decertification election or involved in a major collective bargaining dispute with the employer.

Here is a good illustration of how a publication can affect a police association's membership success. Several years ago, a midwestern, statewide, police association's bargaining agent status among its many city and county chapters was being seriously threatened by an aggressive rival group, and its leadership was frantic. Many of the organization's locals had already left to affiliate with the rival group, and others were threatening to do the same thing.

One look at the association's quarterly magazine highlighted at least one immediate reason why the group was in trouble–there was plenty of material about bowling, gun and fishing tournaments, wives' association information, the upcoming fun-time convention, and the standard article on police "professionalism," but nothing could be found anywhere in the publication about its many successes in negotiating contracts, handling grievances, victories before the state labor board, and work in the state legislature. **When the organization got into trouble, there was no perception among the members that the association was doing what it should have been doing (in fact, it had been doing all the right things!).**

Potential members should be a target audience as well. In the business world, this notion is sometimes referred to as "expanding your market." Even in a fair share state where an association can get a non-member contribution for collective bargaining services, it's better to get the full member dues and commitment, rather than partial payment and no loyalty!

Other Targets of Police Association Publications– Community Groups, Politicians, and Movers/Shakers

Too many police associations forget that their world does not begin and end at the doors of the association hall. It is fundamental that a police association's success in achieving goals is directly related to the group's involvement in building political alliances with organizations and people in the community (see the previous chapter).

The association's publication is *the most* efficient and effective way to talk to groups that you're trying to influence; to send messages to groups, business leaders or politicians; or to simply inform the public about your activities. For example, if your local Chamber of Commerce has gotten in the habit of opposing every association contract, referendum, or other initiative, a strongly-worded article that the association is looking into an economic boycott of Chamber leaders who are behind the opposition might get Chamber leaders to think twice about their stance in future campaigns.

The association must identify which groups and people represent the audience you are targeting. Generally, the organizations you want to talk to are the Chamber and other civic/business organizations, labor organizations, minority and other activist groups, and political parties. The people whom you especially want to target might include major movers and shakers (e.g., newspaper publisher or editor, CEO of the community's biggest corporation, developer, philanthropist); government officials; and political leaders.

One important thing to remember is that you can't let your publication community mailing list become stagnate. Your community, like the conditions in the police department and local government, are constantly changing. Make sure to constantly update your mailing list with new people and organizations that become important receptors of your message.

What Message Is the Police Association Going to Send?

Once the target audience has been identified, the framing of the police association's message is an easy task. These messages can be found in news-oriented articles, editorials, pictures, polls or even advertisements for the association.

There are five themes that should be consistently found somewhere in the association publication:

1. **Organizational successes**. Anytime that the group bargains a contract, wins a grievance, prevails in a lawsuit, or passes a bill in the state legislature, that victory should be trumpeted in bold headlines! This news reinforces the members' perception that they have made the right choice by joining the organization, and makes them proud to be a member.

2. **The "Issue of the Day."** At any moment in the association's history, there is a major issue which predominates the attention of the leadership and members. It can be the upcoming contract negotiations, a hot political endorsement, a fight over a civilian review board, layoffs, and so on. It is important that the publication define the issue in an understandable way to the membership and communicate the association's position on the issue. For example, if a major battle is foreseen over the upcoming contract, then several issues of the publication should be devoted to the association's position in bargaining, responses to a hardened employer bargaining table position, and what will be expected from the members in the event of a conflict.

3. **"The Thin Blue Line."** Any material which emphasizes the importance of law enforcement to the community is vital: stories of officer heroism, injury, officer deaths, and police memorial ceremonies. The biggest thing the police association has going for it is the service performed by the members on behalf of citizens. Don't be shy about promoting this theme because it will resonate with people and organizations in the community.

4. **"We're politically involved."** There should be an abundance of information on the police association's involvement in the political process: forums, endorsements, campaign contributions, membership involvement in campaigns, and political victories. This kind of information sends very strong messages to political players in your community that your group has every intention of affecting the outcome of races that impact your members' lives.

An even more sophisticated approach to the "we're politically involved" approach is to draw correlations between your political successes and perceived results from that success. For example, when you support the mayor (or governor), and thereafter receive a favorable contract (or commission/board appointment), the relationship between the two should be clearly mentioned in your publication. It reinforces the connection between political victory and results to the membership, and it also tells the political world that your program is succeeding.

5. **"We care about you."** Many police associations have adopted one or more charitable programs as a part of their general business: Special Olympics, diabetes or arthritis foundation, drug education, children's camp, etc. The police association's involvement in these programs should be visibly projected in the publication. This theme softens the association's labor orientation, and the community will see that wages and benefits are not the only concern of their law enforcement officers.

The converse to what is going to be placed in the publication is the materials that should be avoided, or at least down-played. The social and fraternal activities of the association should be de-emphasized (unless the governor comes to the annual summer picnic to make a speech, in which case the social event suddenly becomes front page political hoopla!). It is painful to see some of the police labor movement's largest organizations devoting literally pages of space to the Big Softball Tournament, when there are unreported political currents swirling around the group that scream for attention.

Some Common Pitfalls of Association Publications

There are several common mistakes that police associations make in their publications. Each of these mistakes detracts from the message that the association is attempting to send.

One mistake is that association publications too frequently include what are referred to as " mad dog" editorials or articles. These pieces include constant complaints and attacks on the police department or government management. The "mad dog" piece should be distinguished from a good stern shot at management for a real abuse, or from some good old-fashioned Saul Alinsky personal ridicule against a public official who has done a serious wrong against your group.

However, a continual "the-sky-is-falling" theme will not work—it will be perceived by most readers as whining, belly-aching, and an unproductive waste of time.

There is one police association that is infamous for its "mad dog" pieces. The group uses its monthly newspaper to abuse any and all comers—the police chief, the mayor, rival groups and their leaders, the list goes on and on. The articles are mean-spirited, vindictive, and in the end, so pointless that people stop reading them. It is sad that this organization, while having many leaders who are sincerely committed to the labor movement, is known both in its local community and across the country as well primarily for kamikaze newspaper articles, and not for its accomplishments.

Another common mistake is when the police association airs its dirty laundry for all to see. This approach can include an article attacking the association's affiliation with a state or national group, a letter condemning the group's endorsement of a particular candidate, or worse, an article from the association treasurer that goes on and on about the organization's dire financial position.

Remember that your publication is creating an image that the association is strong, politically active, and a concerned community citizen. Anything that detracts from this image is a powerful negative. It creates doubts in members' minds, and concerns in the public, that your organization isn't all that its cracked up to be!

Put aside any notions about democracy in the association journal! Democracy is fine for the monthly police association meeting, where members can come to vent their spleen about what the current leadership is doing, but it has no place where it detracts from that all important impression that you are projecting to your members and the public. Bitter internal police association debates should be confined to membership meetings and "members-only" communications.

Who's Going to Write This Thing, Anyway?

Many police associations start out on their publications with the greatest of intentions. Then the reality of monthly or bi-monthly deadlines begins to set in and suddenly the desire to keep hammering out a publication drops off quickly.

It's great to get a volunteer from the membership to perform the duties of editor and/or writer. But remember first that this person must be *qualified* in the broadest sense of the word: knows how to write, edit, meet deadlines, and follow the editorial policies of the association; and be willing to devote the time necessary to do a first-class job. Many police associations pay the editor/writer for his or her time in the same manner that the association president draws compensation. The theory is that this position is equally important to the president's office.

If your association has the resources, you might want to consider hiring a professional editor/writer who understands the entire publication process. Then the pressure is off of your group to meet deadlines—your only requirement will be to provide material for articles, give editorial direction, and maybe write the editorial column. If the right person can be found, the result can be an exciting, top-flight journal.

What Kind of Publication Is Best for My Police Association?

The kinds of association publications were identified at the start of this chapter—newspapers, magazines, and newsletters. What type of journal your association produces has to do with a number of factors; for example, the need for a revenue-producing publication eliminates newsletters, and compels use of a newspaper or magazine. The personal taste of the leadership and historical customs and practices play a big role as well.

For the ideal police association publication, a four, six or eight page **newsletter** is recommended, published on a monthly or bimonthly basis with no advertisements. Here are the reasons why this recommendation is made:

1. By virtue of the number of pages, the newsletter is self-limiting in what you can say. America is in the middle of an information revolution, and people must wade through overwhelming amounts of visual and written information to stay informed. Most members and community leaders have neither the time nor patience to slog through page after page of paper/magazine advertisements and superfluous articles to find out what the association is really trying to say. The newsletter format makes you say what has to be said quickly; in other words, **to get to the point of your message right away**!

2. The cost to produce a visually attractive, two-color newsletter is surprisingly low, particularly with the advent of computer programs

that allow the editor to lay out the entire newsletter and avoid the need for a typesetter. This one economical step will cut the per-issue cost considerably from what it would cost if laid out by a professional printer.

3. The bulkiness of magazines and newspapers, and the ink stains from newspapers should be avoided. These are little things, but they do detract from your message.

Chapter 12

HOW POLICE ASSOCIATIONS CAN BUILD A STRONG IMAGE

For the purpose of this chapter, "image building" is defined as activity that is designed to influence and shape opinion regarding an institution. In relation to a police association, image building is a planned campaign to reinforce positive attitudes toward law enforcement among voters and elected officials.

Image building, sometimes referred to as "image maintenance," is a part of police association duties that is most often neglected. The association membership, and even often the leadership, is of the opinion that image is for "them"–the politicians and news anchors. The common belief is that any image problems the police have will be taken care of simply by doing the job.

Unfortunately, that is not the case, because what the police do is so often open to interpretation. Without a reservoir of goodwill in the community, routine events can become controversial, and controversies can damage the effectiveness of the individual officer and the department.

The best way to avoid problems and build a base of support for law enforcement is to keep the community informed of what the association and individual officers are doing. The more the public knows about the police job, the less chance that voters will be led astray by misinformation and rumor.

Also, the great need for the public to know more about the police is why we can all be thankful officers didn't decide to become bookkeepers! Generating public interest in pencil-pushing and spreadsheet gymnastics would be a hard row to hoe. On the other hand, getting the public interested in police work is easy. That's why cops have groupies and accountants do not. Even routine activities, with possible exception of paperwork, are often news to the public.

A Good Example of How Image Building Can Help

A few years ago, the Dallas Police Department installed cellular phones in squad cars. Big deal some would say; it's just another tool. But that response wastes a perfect image-building opportunity and leaves the department open to uninformed attack.

On the surface, the cellular phone is just one more expense item added to an already overburdened city budget. It's easy for critics to contend that if cops want to make a phone call, they can use a phone booth like everybody else, or they can make the call from the donut shop where they do all the rest of their business.

Once that criticism gains currency in the community, the police department (and as you will see very soon, the police association) is placed in the position of responding. And that is never as effective as controlling the debate in the first place.

So where is the wasted opportunity in this news item? A reporter riding in the car with a cellular phone in action would see officers answering a call by contacting residents without leaving their car. The reporter could do a story about this new crime fighting tool that allows officers to save time, and in some instances, lets people talk to the police without fear of being identified by having an officer come to their residence.

Once the story appears, then the phones are no longer a perk for the police, but instead, are a new way to save time and encourage citizens to help the police department. People who have been afraid to call in the past may change their mind and do so in the future. Citizens feel less helpless; the department gains an ally; and no one complains about one more cost item in the city budget.

Isn't Image-Building the Police Department's Job?

At this point, a frequent argument is: that's the police department's job. We're the police association, not a public relations firm. But if the department's not doing its job, or the chief simply uses public relations to cover for an otherwise bad job, or **the police association wants**

to get the same message out as a matter of public goodwill, then the association has to pick up the ball. And it's really not that hard.

The rising crime rate, television's interest in cop entertainment programming, and news coverage of urban unrest combine to make today's climate an ideal time to tell the association's story locally, and to find a receptive audience. The preparation can be as simple as tying into whatever is broadcast on that evening's reality television, or conducting a news audit of the preceding year to determine what stories are being covered, and in what instances the association voice needs to be heard.

It is important to remember that the police association's image building program must be viewed as an integral part of any broad-based, political action program. An institution, or collection of individuals, with a bad image cannot realistically expect support from elected officials or voters. And bad image is why many police associations can't win single issue referendums, or don't pursue them at all, or can't get public support for other issues important to the association.

Why It Is Important to Appoint a Permanent Press Liaison

Let's say that instead of your association having a good or bad image, it has no image at all. When you start with a blank slate, the first decision is who will wield the chalk in the future. Someone must be appointed to be the **permanent press liaison** for the group. It is easier to track down one rather than a handful of potential spokespersons.

A single spokesperson also allows the association to control and coordinate its message. A multitude of people dealing with the press often means a muddled and confusing stance on the part of the police association.

Many times it is natural to let the association president also serve as the group's press contact. When the president speaks for the association, he or she becomes the association in the mind of the public and the membership. This situation will give the president a great deal more internal power, and no doubt make his or her administration a lengthy one. It also puts a premium on having a president who is articulate and able to project a good image for the institution.

Sometimes an officer other than the president will be selected who can better project the association's image. Since the media liaison job can prove to be a stepping stone for power within the organization, it is important to determine *before* this person begins that he or she is a team player.

You Must Cultivate the Press If You're Going to Put Forth a Good Image

Once the association has determined who will meet the media, the job of cultivating the press begins. To succeed, the association must discard any vestiges of us-versus-them thinking. No one wants to arm wrestle with a porcupine; and a media liaison who is too prickly will definitely be building an image, but it won't be a positive one!

The police association and media actually have a commonality of interest. You have a point of view to communicate, and the reporter needs a story to tell. It is a mutually beneficial relationship which should work for both institutions.

Also, the association has an advantage because the press thrives on conflict stories, and the police and police associations are surrounded by conflict. Anything having to do with the police versus bad guys, the brass, the city manager, or the council is a story that will definitely get covered!

What's more, it is certain that even if the association doesn't tell its side of the story, the other side won't be reluctant to give its version. The mayor's office, the community activists, the ACLU, or the chief's office will do their best to see that the press has one side of the story, even if association's is completely left out.

For example, police brutality stories are always hot news all across the country. Why not beat the ACLU to the punch by getting the local press to do a series about officers injured in the line of duty? Talk to the press about domestic disturbances, demonstrate nonlethal methods of subduing perpetrators, or tell them how dangerous the job is day-in-and-day-out.

Then when the inevitable brutality story comes up, the foundation has already been laid for some public sympathy. The press has already been made aware of what the police officer's job is like, and with any luck, the media will be less inclined to do a knee-jerk Big Bad Cop expose.

Here's an Example of a Police Association That Dropped the Image-Building Ball

Here's a story of an East Coast police association which is instructive of how critical image building can be. During summer budget deliberations in "City X," the city council recognized that spending cuts would have to be made to cover a revenue shortfall. The police department was already under fire in the local media and among the council for spending money on helicopters.

So the city bean-counters were already taking a close look at the police department, and one of the items they focused on as waste was the yearly cleaning allowance for police officers. The majority of council members felt that the cleaning allowance was an obvious example of government waste. One councilman even commented to the press, "My boss doesn't pay me to have my clothes cleaned."

The police association in this city chose to not participate in this debate! There might have been some sound reasons the group stood on the sidelines of the debate–the outside world was not privy to the group's internal discussions. But what the average voter saw was ignorant and superficial statements like the councilman's above going completely unchallenged.

It would have been easy enough to hold a press conference and ask the city council members these kinds of questions: When was the last time that a drunk threw up on them at their workplace? Or when was the last time they tackled a suspect in their job? Or when was the last time they had to run through a muddy field chasing a suspect? And to really pull out all the stops, the police association could have displayed a uniform with a bullet hole and ask if the city council would mind buying the thread to repair the tear?

As a result of the association's failure to get the message out, the mayor was able to make the following unchallenged statement: "Some people believe that government is nothing more than...pressed pants and government centers." The clothing allowance in "City X" is gone today, which most definitely constitutes a pay cut for the police. And at least some of the public feels that, when it comes to spending, this police department is just a smaller version of the Pentagon.

The Police Association Must Conduct a Media Coverage Audit

It is important to remember that image building does not exist in a vacuum. For the police association image building program to be successful, it must be viewed as an integral part of any broad-based political action program. An institution or collection of individuals with a bad image cannot realistically expect support from elected officials or voters. So it is important to analyze image building opportunities and setting goals for the program.

It is therefore worthwhile to spend some time setting goals for the association's image-building campaign. When there is a target in mind, it becomes easier for the association to measure progress and prevent efforts from going off on a tangent that detracts from the central goal.

Once a goal is agreed upon, then the association can look for potential news stories which advance its interests. After a short time, it will become second nature to include image building opportunities into police association activities.

But before the police labor leader can make realistic plans for where the association should be image-wise in the future, it's necessary to find out where he or she is today. And since there is no "you are here" arrow in the image world, the first step will be to conduct a **media coverage audit**. This process involves some good, old-fashioned detective work.

The first stop is the library, where *every* issue of the local newspaper or papers for the past year must be reviewed. Each time that a story is found with a law enforcement angle, take notes. List the exact headline, a brief summary of the content, who was contacted for quotes, and whether anyone from the association was quoted in the story. A copy of the story should be made as well.

This project is obviously going to take some time, and the police association might want to farm out the work to an outside firm. But without this foundation, informed decisions can't be made about the direction of the association image-building campaign; and even more important, there is no way to gauge its effectiveness.

The Next Step Is to Research and Categorize the Stories

Once the research is complete, it is time to divide the raw materials into categories. The first two divisions are stories which the police association should be a part of, either as the voice of experienced law enforcement or as an advocate for its members. The other category is stories which the association is neutral about, or where participation would harm its image.

Don't worry about where television and radio coverage fits into the mix. The newspaper normally sets the coverage agenda for news in most areas, so if a story is covered in the paper, it has also been covered in the electronic media.

Now take the stories where it is desirable to raise the police association's profile and subdivide them again into four groups. These groups will be: **perennial** stories, **predictable** stories, **unpredictable** stories, and **proactive** stories.

News coverage of any issue or public institution is like the tide–there are predictable highs and lows. There are a certain number of stories which are written every year, and these are called **perennials**: stories about the city budget, FBI or local statistics, and contract negotiations. These stories happen every year about the same time, so getting coverage in the story is a little like waiting for the bus–check the calendar for the schedule, and be standing at the stop when the story rolls by. The coverage audit will also uncover other perennial stories which may have been overlooked.

Predictable stories are items that are always going to come during the year, but you just don't know when. This type includes an officer killed or injured, brutality allegations, internal scandals, and other all-too-regular law enforcement flare-ups.

Unpredictable stories are genuine news which no one could have predicated, or realistically anticipated. Many of these items are crime and victim stories that have a law enforcement angle, but may not lend themselves to participation by an association spokesperson.

Finally, **proactive** stories are ones that the police association generates as part of the overall communications strategy. This type might be a very short stack right now, since there hasn't been a strategy in the past. Stories in this category concern press conferences and other staged events. Chapter 41 on the Ice-T "Cop Killer" controversy is an excellent example of proactive coverage where police associations had a story they wanted to tell to the public. There are other examples as well: a good stab at unresponsive city bureaucrats, officer of the year awards, heroism citations, honoring citizens for contributions to law enforcement, and other community involvement stories.

Once the Stories Have Been Categorized, It's Time to Do Some Planning

Now go back over the perennial stories, count the number, and note the date of each story where the police association could have made a contribution that would have advanced its point of view. Then go to a calendar and mark the weeks where these missed opportunities for coverage are likely to appear in the coming year. The *minimum* coverage goal for the coming year should then be to get quoted in all the perennial stories that deal with law enforcement.

Then complete a time line and begin plans on preparing the association's activities for each story. Will a press conference be held to dramatize how police department budget cuts are hurting law enforcement? Will a reporter be called for a meeting to give the police association's slant on the beginning of budget hearings? Or will you simply call each reporter and ask them to give you a chance to comment whenever they call city officials in regard to a related story?

Then go to the predictable stories and decide if a statement or strategy should be prepared in advance so the association will be ready for the officer injured or brutality case. Being primed beforehand can save a lot of stress later, and even more important, prevent making a public relations blunder in the heat of a controversy.

For the unpredictable stories, just stay loose. Ideas will develop on a story-by-story basis, based on the type of situation and information available during a particular event.

The work really begins on the proactive stories. How much effort is the police association willing to put in to hold press conferences, issue press releases, and think about events when coverage is important?

Now the Association Should Set Some Goals

When the research and planning is done, it now becomes important to set some goals. A minimum is getting a quote in perennial stories.

A more ambitious goal is trying to set the news agenda for the city's budget coverage, or using the release of crime statistics to show how cuts in the police department budget over the past five years have resulted in more crime and less security for the city. The most ambitious thing is doing all of the above, *and* generating fifteen additional human interest stories that showcase the positive side of the police department.

Whatever the police association image-building goal is for the upcoming year, it is important that **you do not attempt to do too much**! It's pretty depressing to start an image building campaign and fail to reach the first goal.

How the Police Association Can Impact the Budget Process Through Image Building–the Philadelphia FOP Experience

Now that your police association has done the audit, it's time to see how it can be put to good use in terms of accomplishing organizational objectives. Association image building can be a key factor in the group becoming a key player in issues that affect the membership.

Let's assume that the association goal is to have an impact on this year's city/county budget negotiations, which is one of the perennial stories we have already identified. The principles discussed here can be applied irrespective of whether the organization bargains or not; and whether it has leverage such as arbitration.

Remember that the association can always use its image building program to influence an unresponsive government bureaucracy. When budget stories begin appearing in the newspaper, it's time to go into action! The minimum goal would be to prevent cuts in the police department budget. And appearing before the city council or county commission to demand "money, money, money" will normally get the group nowhere.

Here's how the Philadelphia Fraternal Order of Police made good use of an image-building tactic. In 1992, the FOP used an equipment issue to put pressure on the City of Philadelphia–the issue was bullet-proof vests.

In a budget-cutting move, bureaucrats at City Hall had decided that following an officer's retirement, the bullet-proof vest would be reissued to a rookie. Philadelphia Police Department rules for the care of vests specified that they were not to be washed, because of the problem of internal deterioration, which in turn could result in sudden internal deterioration for an officer wearing a washed vest if he was hit.

The FOP held a press on the vest issue. FOP leaders pointed out the hygiene problem, the uncertainty as to what kind of care the previous owner gave the vest, and the fact that the City of Philadelphia did not have a useful life index for this equipment. As far as the general public was concerned, this issue concerned equipment and safety only. But for the FOP, the issue allowed the group to remind the public of the risks police officers take, and to raise the FOP's community profile. And most important, it helped to deter cuts in the budget related to bullet-proof vests!

In and of themselves, these kinds of press hits can be immensely satisfying. But always remember that for these kinds of initiatives to be really effective, the story must be a part of the police association's overall communications effort and goals.

What a Low-Profile Police Association Can Do to Build Its Image

For a low-profile police association, it is important for the institution to establish its place in the news coverage hierarchy. The goal here is to become an independent, reliable source of information about the city and law enforcement issues–stories about crime statistics, police budgets, or response time that has a line which reads: "Officer Do-Right of the Police Association said..."

The goal in this case is for reporters to be in the habit of calling an association spokesperson to confirm or undermine city hall or county commission statistics, or to comment on a story. Or even better, the association knows it's doing a good image-building job when you its leaders are called upon to interpret an event for the media.

Other Things That Police Associations Can Do to Build Image

The Fairfax County, Virginia Police Association is a good example of what a group can do in terms of institutional outreach. In 1992, the association established an Officer of the Year award program for both internal morale and public recognition.

You can be really creative in your own area by honoring citizens for heroism or general support for law enforcement. These awards generate positive press coverage and goodwill in the community as a part of your external communications program. Local businesses can be approached about picking up the cost for the event and monthly awards. At the end of the year, you can choose one of the monthly winners as the citizen of the year.

Another idea is to start a college scholarship program for students who want to go to college and agree to become police officers after graduation. The police association can also sponsor an Explorer troop under the direction of the Boy Scouts of America. If the police department isn't doing it already, have association members go to elementary, junior, and high schools to lecture on stranger danger, safety, and related topics. Volunteer to meet with school principals to help improve safety inside the school building.

None of these ideas are particularly new, but they can all work as part of an image-building program. The important thing is to be looking for opportunities to build your image, and make sure that its fits into the association's overall image building plan.

Chapter 13

TEN SIGNS OF A DYSFUNCTIONAL POLICE ASSOCIATION, AND WHAT TO DO ABOUT IT

The authors could not decide whether this chapter should be placed at the beginning or end of this part of the book. A police labor leader should know what elements are necessary to build power; at the same time, the leader must also know the impediments to building power so these pitfalls can be avoided at all costs. We opted to put the positive first, and to leave these negative observations for the end of this part. While some of the problems and solutions in this chapter repeat ideas from other preceding and following chapters, the issue of associational dysfunction allows the leader to see when his group is really in trouble and what might be done about it.

Ten Signs That Your Association May Be Dysfunctional

The traditional American family is not the only institution considered dysfunctional today. The traditional police association is in serious trouble as a representative of the rank and file police officer, deputy sheriff, or state trooper. Years ago, the police association was a major part of the life of an officer and the department. No one ever thought about airing the association's dirty laundry in public or publicly criticizing the association. The situation is different today, and there are various signs of internal instability, unrest, and even chaos showing in many police associations.

How healthy is your police organization? Are the warning signs evident or looming on the horizon? Following are some of the warning signs of a dysfunctional police association—see if your organization

87

faces any of these problems, or members/leaders have these kind of attitudes:

1. **We are not apathetic, we just don't care**. The members are so apathetic that the only thing that might get them to a meeting would be a notice announcing a seminar on "opening a Cayman's bank account and hiding your extra job money from your ex-wives." The same 5 members have attended every meeting all year and can now brag about a complete wardrobe of association t-shirts won as door prizes.

2. **The members eat their young.** After one or two years as president of the association or serving on the board, the leaders quit from frustration and depression. Every meeting ends with some member at the back of the crowd who is attending his first meeting in a year, and who angrily proceeds to tell the president everything that the association is doing wrong because the association has not done anything for *him* this month.

3. **The members are so apolitical they do not even register to vote.** The last time the association endorsed political candidates based on their positions on better wages and benefits without considering how they would vote on gun control, the Trilateral Commission, arms reduction, and foreign aid, scores of members immediately wrote hate letters and dropped their membership in the "commie, pinko, liberal" police association.

4. **Professionalism is more important than money.** The members are proud to have new patrol cars with the latest light bars and truly understand that the city cannot pay decent wages and benefits *and* provide the officers with nice equipment. It is not really a concern to the association and members that the wages are low because coffee shops and 7-11 stores do give the officers a "professional" discount.

5. **Special interest groups do not care about the police.** The police association and members believe that they are elite in the community, and that everyone else is a special interest group of little importance to them. Members become angry when community groups, civic organizations, businesses, homeowners, tenants, developers, and every other power broker in the community takes so much of the budget pie that there is nothing left for pay raises. Doesn't the Bible say the police are God's chosen people?

6. **Let's appoint a committee and hold another meeting.** The association has only three members who are not on the board or serv-

ing on a committee. The association has a bargaining team bigger than the night shift. If the members serving on the board or committees did not get free beer and meals, 90 percent of them would not attend.

7. **Vision? I'm too busy to think about the future.** The association's president and board have no strategic plan for the future. The association *reacts* to one emergency or controversy after another. The association acts surprised that "this year" the city is too broke for pay raises. The members recognize that the association has been nowhere and that they are probably going nowhere in the future.

8. **The association does not speak for me.** Every time the association speaks out on a controversial issue, individual members write letters to the chief and media criticizing the association or its president. Even worse, elected officers of the association attack the association and its president at roll calls over issues when their point of view was not in the majority. Fraternal, ethnic, racial and sex-orientated organizations within the police department claim to represent *their* members on issues normally under the purview of the association.

9. **I have to think about my career.** The association and the chief are at odds over a controversial issue, and the president or board members start resigning in order to "save" their careers. The decision to take the offensive against the chief is delayed or set aside because of fear of reprisals by the chief. The association is often paralyzed with fear if they have to confront the mayor or chief.

10. **The association is respected by the mayor.** The association mistakenly believes that the mayor *respects* them because he says nice things about "the police." The entire council ran for office on a law and order platform, but at budget time they cannot find money "this year" for pay raises. The association continues to endorse the same incumbents each year despite numerous votes by these "friends of the police" that hurt the officers' pocketbooks.

Ten Ways to Avoid Becoming a Dysfunctional Police Association

Any police association facing these kinds of problems and/or attitudes is clearly in a dysfunctional mode, and in dire straits. These dysfunctional habits can, however, be overcome with a little effort and perseverance. Even associations on life support can be saved if anyone cares enough to administer CPR.

The police association business is dog-eat-dog. The association must decide whether it wants to be one of the biggest and meanest dogs in the kennel or whether it wants to be submissive to more aggressive dogs. The fight for power is not for the weak of heart. A police association must be both internally and externally strong. Is your police association so dysfunctional that it cannot overcome all the internal bickering and external pressures that have been described in this chapter? Following are some tips for building a powerful and functional police association that will overcome the problems and attitudes described in the preceding section of this chapter.

1. **Overcome apathy.** We live in a very hectic and fast-paced society. Too many associations waste the members' time with do-nothing meetings. Reduce the number of meetings and increase written and/or one-on-one communications. Get down to business quickly at association meetings, don't allow the meetings to stray from the agenda, and reserve the bitch session for the after-the-meeting, beer drinking crowd.

2. **Ignore the whiners and naysayers.** Police officers simply love to whine and complain. Remember, most elected association leaders will be defeated after one or two terms no matter what they do. There are no rewards on this earth for association presidents, so quit worrying about the complainers, bellyachers, and others who contribute absolutely nothing to the good of the association. Do what you can during the time you have, and accept the fact that every member thought they could have done it better.

3. **Endorse only candidates favorable to the association.** Define the organizational goals of the association (better wages and benefits). Educate the members as to those goals (avoid individual misdirection—personal voting preferences). Endorse only those candidates supporting those goals (why endorse someone who will screw you on wages and benefits). Then let the members know that an endorsement means the candidate supports the association's goals and does not indicate how individual members will vote—they are going to vote for whoever they want anyway. Remember—there is a direct correlation between the importance of the endorsement and the degree of whining afterwards. (AUTHORS' NOTE: Police association political activity is explored in greater detail in Part III of this book.)

4. **Do not trade equipment for better wages.** Too many associations agree to defer wage and benefit increases in order to get new

patrol cars or equipment. It is the city's job to provide the equipment needed to do the job efficiently and safely. The number one focus of the association should be on improving wages and benefits—period. Extra jobs, free apartments, and discount fast food is not a substitute for a fair and equitable wage.

5. **Be a community police association.** The association and its members must be an active part of the community. The fight for better wages, benefits, and budget resources is fought in the court of public opinion. An aloof, elitist attitude by the association or members will alienate the very people paying your wages. The Bible may speak highly of the police profession; however, if association leaders and members want their rewards in this life, they must get a "down-to-earth" attitude.

6. **Revise your constitution.** When was the last time the association constitution was amended? Most associations have too many committees, too many meetings, and take too long to accomplish business. If "we have always done it this way" is your motto, then we know why there is such a lack of interest in the association. Update procedures, modernize your operations, and act like a business.

7. **Develop a strategic plan now.** If the leadership of the association does not know where the organization is heading in the future, how can the average member be expected to know? Every association must have a multiyear plan; otherwise, the association will simply be reacting to the employer's game plan every year. Start preparing for the next contract battle the day you sign this agreement. A leaner, meaner, more financially-secure association is the answer to the employer's tactical maneuvers.

8. **Do not ignore "other" departmental organizations.** It is a sad fact of life that almost every department has ethnic, fraternal, social, and religious organizations that are acting like police labor associations. Unless association leaders develop communication and cooperation with these organizations, these groups will undermine the association's ability to represent the members on matters of wages, benefits, and working conditions. There must be dialogue with and inclusion of such groups, including periodic meetings and exchange of representatives at board or membership meetings, and joint participation and cooperation on projects of mutual interest.

9. **Balancing career and association goals.** Many association leaders go on to become high ranking police officers in their depart-

ments. Other association leaders have had their careers stagnate after serving in an association office. If you are afraid to damage your position or career in the department, then avoid elected association office. There is nothing worse than having the association president "freeze up" during a crisis because he or she is worried about career advancement. The only association leaders who have truly succeeded in accomplishing major goals of the organization are those who have set aside their dreams of upward mobility in the department or their desire to liked by everyone in order to do *only* what is in the best interests of the police association.

10. **Demand respect.** It is immaterial if the city manager, mayor, or chief "likes" the association. It is only important that they "respect" the association. Disrespect requires the association to "punish" those failing to show them respect. Endorsing incumbents who continually act against the association does not earn you respect. If you hammer a disrespectful politicians periodically, the remaining politicians get the message.

Part III

POLITICS–THE LIFEBLOOD OF A SUCCESSFUL POLICE ASSOCIATION

Chapter 14

A KNACK FOR PACs - PRELIMINARY REMARKS ABOUT POLICE ASSOCIATION POLITICAL ACTION

Political action is the lifeblood of any police organization. Successful state and local police association must be masters at passing legislation and killing unfavorable bills at the state level by staying politically active. Political involvement makes these associations powerful enough to stop the evil State Municipal Leagues from destroying a lifetime of benefits accumulated by the police. Successful political action at the local level means getting the wages and benefits that members so richly deserve.

Political action cannot be achieved or maintained without two things—members and money. Successful state and local police associations must donate time to candidates' campaigns. Each member must be asked to put out signs, make phone calls, work the polls, and get out the vote.

Every successful police association should have a General Purpose Political Action Committee (i.e., "PAC") that collects and spends money on candidates. Elections are expensive, and every candidate needs all the money he or she can receive. Use the bargaining process to get PAC deductions in your contract, or use the credit union. If all else fails, raise funds by whatever lawful means are available.

How much money is enough? As an example, if each of the 55,000 Texas law enforcement officers donated only $1.00 per week to a Police PAC, the resulting $1,430,000 per year could probably protect any benefit, and pass any bill in the Texas Legislature! Since that is normally unrealistic on a statewide basis, local police associations must set a goal of $1.00 per week to their local PAC. Many local police

95

associations can then form coalitions to support and oppose candidates in local and state political races.

Remember, the ultimate principle of American politics: all politicians worry about getting elected, and then staying elected! Before a November election or a local city council race, call your state legislators or council members about discussing the issues of concern to your membership. Politicians seem to have more time to discuss issues with police associations at election time.

Each local should host a political forum for all the candidates. The firefighters, other public employees, the public, and the media should all be invited. Exposure to political reality awakens the sleeping membership. Also, it makes aspiring politicians and incumbents make their promises in public.

Don't worry about picking a loser. There is a 50 percent chance of doing that in every election. Work hard for your candidate, and if he or she loses, approach the winner about what he or she plans to do for the police now that the election is over. A candidate's support at the state capitol or city council can always translate into police association support at the next election.

The key word in police association political action is **involvement**. Getting involved means building friendships and relationships. This activity clearly translates into support for passing bills or approving good collective bargaining agreements. But police associations cannot win for the membership if the members do not work for the elected officials. The police association should be a unified group, working to build a better police profession for the members.

Former Texas Agriculture Commissioner Jim Hightower once said, "The only two things in the middle of the road are yellow stripes and dead armadillos." That statement paints the best picture of what the police associations' options are when it comes to political involvement: sit on the sidelines and let others play the game, and reap the benefits, or instead, jump into the political arena with both feet and become a major player in your community.

Endorse a candidate, and once endorsed, give the candidate your strongest support. One of the greatest sources of power that a police association has is in the political arena. It is the only place where the playing field is level between the police association and its usual opponents, that is, the public employers and state Municipal Leagues.

The old adage, "No guts, no glory," really applies to the police association and political action. If you never participate in the political process, you can never experience the rewards of victory. The political process requires that you participate–you cannot expect to pass legislation at the state level or win benefits at the local level if you do not endorse candidates and help them win election.

The political process is the American Way. Police associations are like every other organization that becomes immersed in the politic system–they cannot achieve their goals without taking political risks.

Chapter 15

SOME GENERAL COMMENTS ON THE INTERNAL STRUGGLE OVER ASSOCIATION POLITICS

Almost every police association endorses a candidate or measure on the ballot at some point in its history. Police association leaders who are active in the political arena understand that any endorsement carries with it a potential backlash. Every political endorsement is a two-edged sword.

With each endorsement comes the doomsayers predictions that the association will be "punished" by the unendorsed winner. Some association leaders are defeated for reelection based on the perceived damage done by failed endorsements. Proponents and opponents of political endorsements lash out at each other in association publications.

Political endorsements cause internal dissent and disrupt the normal activities of an association. Members drop out over endorsements and attack the association leadership in the local media for being out of touch with the membership. Police management often speaks out against political involvement by police officers as being damaging to professionalism.

Then why do police associations endorse candidates and measures? Because politics is the essence of power, and power controls the political system that controls the police profession. Associations that do not endorse candidates or participate in the political process are merely observers in the system that determines their livelihood.

The Effect of Endorsements

Opinion polls in many states repeatedly indicate that the endorsement of a candidate or measure by a police association has a 60 to 75 percent approval rating. Translated, that means 60 to 75 percent of the voters are more likely than not to support a candidate or measure endorsed by the police association. Compare the same polls regarding lawyers and labor unions, which generally have a 50 to 75 percent disapproval rating.

Political candidates seek out police associations for endorsements, a good example being the 1988 Presidential race. Bush and Dukakis both competed to obtain police endorsements. The news media was filled with each candidate receiving the endorsement of some police organization.

The conservative candidate wants the endorsement to certify that he is in fact a law and order politician. The liberal candidate wants the endorsement in order to bring his position over to the center. With few exceptions, no politician is opposed to law and order. Both the conservatives and liberals want the support of the police.

Education of the Membership

Too many association leaders attempt to persuade the board or membership to endorse political candidates without an education process. Unless the association has been politically active for some period of time, endorsements are volatile situations.

The association should start the educational process by publicizing the endorsement process. Members get upset if they perceive that the association leadership is trying to push through an unpopular endorsement. Police officers are suspicious by nature, so do not add to the controversy by using heavyhanded methods (see more on the education process in the following chapter).

The Endorsement Process

While every association does not have the time or resources to conduct each suggested step, it is recommended that you attempt as many as possible. The best endorsement process involves having the candidates answer written questionnaires about issues of concern to the members. Second, ask the candidates to attend an association screening committee to answer questions in an informal setting. Third, invite the candidates to a forum where the members can ask questions. Finally, make a decision to endorse a candidate.

1. **Written Questionnaires.** While candidates often avoid difficult questions with evasive answers, a questionnaire does force a candidate to put his answers in writing. This can be useful later when approaching him for delivery on his promises. Make the questions short and insightful.

2. **Screening Candidates.** This vehicle can be a very useful method in sorting out candidates. The informal setting will allow you to focus in on areas of concern. While some associations record or video tape the screening, you might want to weigh the impact that it has on getting real, and not just political, answers.

Use politically astute members on the screening committee to avoid sour grapes later by the candidate. Avoid confrontations with candidates. Remember that your objective is to educate the candidate about your concerns, and to develop a relationship with the candidate if he or she wins.

3. **Political Forums.** Inviting candidates to debate before the membership is an educational process of its own. Unless you have a very large membership, consider inviting the public and/or special interest groups (i.e., fire fighters, city employees, other union members in the city or county). It is strongly suggested that you invite the media–the purpose of endorsing candidates is to gain political exposure for your association.

4. **Deciding on Candidates.** Who should make decisions on endorsements? While the methods vary, most associations endorse based on votes of the board of directors, a political action committee, or a screening committee. While a few associations have membership ballots, it is strongly recommended that the membership **NOT** vote on candidate endorsements–members tend to vote on candidates based upon their **personal** interests, and not on **organizational** goals.

Organizational Goals Versus Personal Interests.

Few issues are more controversial than political endorsements. The association is an organization composed of individuals. The organization's goals and the each member's personal interests are not always necessarily the same. The number one priority of the association leadership is to propel the organization toward its goals.

Too many leaders allow personal interests to misdirect the association from achieving organizational goals. The goals of the organization should **ONLY** be improving the living and working conditions of the membership. The individual member may have interests as diverse as gun control, abortion, national security, crime, or the death penalty.

Once the association starts making endorsements based on the personal interests of the majority, the goals of the organization will become skewed. The differences may be slight at times, but they may be critical in determining whether the organization reaches its political peak.

Endorsements say that the candidate supports the goals of the organization. Individual members can vote anyway they want. If you clearly identify the organization's goals to the candidate, members, and the public, it should lessen controversy.

The Never-Ending Conservative Versus Liberal Controversy

Police officers seem to be, for the most part, politically conservative. They tend to rant and rave about liberal politicians. However, liberals traditionally support the organization and the majority of its goals (i.e., pay, due process, collective bargaining). Conservatives tend to vote against economic and labor issues, while supporting law and order issues.

Police associations should endorse candidates based on the candidate's position on the organization's goals. Whether the candidate is a Democrat or Republican should not be an issue. Associations affiliated with the AFL-CIO may have to follow the endorsements of their national, state or central labor council, all of which tend to support Democratic candidates.

More on Yellow Stripes and Dead Armadillos

Let's revisit for a moment the quote by Jim Hightower that "the only two things in the middle of the road are yellow stripes and dead armadillos." Endorsements require a decision. No action on an endorsement is a decision, and is one that usually leaves the police association in the position of a spectator rather than a player in the political game.

Unless special circumstances exist, the association should *always* endorse in key races. While nothing requires that the association endorse in every race, local races do require action.

Making Tough Decisions

Association leaders must stand tough in making endorsements. You cannot satisfy every member. Forget about whiners and naysayers. They always want the association to take the path of least resistance. Remember that leaders make the tough decisions for the organization because that's what they were elected to do. It seems that members are always worried about endorsing a candidate who may lose. But the fact is that the losers will appreciate your support, and the winning candidate that you did not endorse may want your support next time. Unless the candidate is an absolute idiot, he or she will think twice about "punishing" the association.

Some General Remarks About Assisting the Candidate

The remainder of this part of the book will explore in depth how police associations can become effective in the political process. Following are a few general observations which will lead into our more comprehensive discussion in the following chapters.

Some police associations do nothing more in a campaign than issue a letter of endorsement to a candidate. If your association just issues an endorsement letter, you have really not done very much for the candidate's campaign. The only time where this tactic might be acceptable is a race where your group only has a passing interest; and therefore, the association may not want to invest any time or money in the election.

Here is the most basic and important fact about politics in America– campaigns are propelled by three things: money, money, and more money! If your association has political action committee money, then you have potential power. More than anything else, every candidate needs money to get his or her message out to the voters.

There is an old maxim that goes, "Money talks, and bullshit walks." Applying this statement to politics, it is clear that one form of association power is money. Your organization should therefore raise PAC money any legal way that it can get it. Do not let the nonpolitical members, the naysayers and whiners mentioned before, prevent the association from raising and spending PAC money.

There are many strategic uses of PAC money available to the police association. It can be used for **direct expenses**, such as contributions to candidates, yard signs, direct mail pieces, phone banks, and or the purchase of radio/television spots for the candidate. Or it an be used for **indirect expenses**, such as letting the candidate use the association hall for phone banks or other purposes in the campaign; or holding a fundraiser and buying the food and drinks. (Note: state campaign laws about reporting direct and indirect expenses should be checked and followed very closely; there are serious civil and criminal penalties attached to violating these laws!).

The hardest part of assisting a candidate is getting the association members to contribute their time, and unfortunately, there is no easy way to do it. Police officers hate to go door-to-door or work the phone banks. As you will discover in the chapters following, these tasks are important, so it is essential that members be encouraged and persuaded to commit time to a campaign, even if it is a task of limited duration, such as sign-building, poll watching, or office work.

Chapter 16

POLICE ASSOCIATION POLITICS
FROM A TO Z–WHY ASSOCIATIONS
SHOULD ENDORSE

The ever-recurring cycle of federal, state, and local elections means that every United States Congressman, one-third of the U.S. Senators, many statewide political figures, and too many local officials to count are up for election at one time or another. And as long as crime remains an issue in politics, the endorsement of police associations will continue to be highly valued.

Before any police association makes, or considers making, a political endorsement, there are *five* questions that must be answered by the leadership:

1. Why is it important for our association to enter the political arena?
2. What do we have to offer?
3. Whom do we target?
4. When do we endorse?
5. How do we endorse?

The police association must have well-thought-out answers to all of these questions before the leadership can expect members to support the decision to endorse, and then in turn for the members to support the endorsement with their time, dollars, and/or vote.

Question #1 : Why Should the Police Association
Endorse Candidates?

Answering the "why" question is first, because it is the most important one of all. If your members aren't convinced of the need for them to take an active role during an election year, then the endorsement will be empty, and the police association will be viewed by political officials, and the general public, as a paper tiger.

In fact, it is better to give no endorsement than to give an endorsement that is meaningless, because an empty endorsement is the worst of all possible worlds. The candidate who got the endorsement will feel cheated when the police association fails to come through during the campaign. In turn, if the endorsed candidate is elected, he or she will know that they did it without the association's help. The candidate will not feel any debt of gratitude, and may actually feel hostile.

Should a candidate who did not get the endorsement win, that individual will know that there is no penalty for going against your wishes, and that politician will not hesitate to do so in the future. If there are no consequences to taking a position contrary to the police association's interests, then there is no risk in offending law enforcement.

The result of an empty endorsement is that the police association will become a political laughingstock. Your organization will have absolutely no leverage with the office holders you were trying to influence today, and you may not have any in the future as well.

You've Got to Sell Your Members on the Endorsement Process

The police labor leader must first sell the membership on the importance of the endorsement process. Many law enforcement officers feel that they should be above politics and politicians. They view the entire process with disdain, and are not eager to play any part in a campaign.

Yet this "garrison" mentality is very counterproductive, because it is those same politicians who pass laws or levy taxes that affect salaries, pensions, fringe benefits, and working conditions. Your members must be convinced that if their police association purposely removes itself from having any influence on the process, then law enforcement professionals have no room to complain when politicians fail to give them adequate support and ignore their input.

Therefore, it is the police labor leader's job to **educate** the membership as to what is at stake in the endorsement process. This education process should take place both at membership meetings and through association publications.

The illustration of the political process on members' economic interests is very simple. Use a wallet as an example, and explain that the wallet's thickness or thinness depends in large part upon what politicians do and say. A Social Security card is another good example: ask your members if that is what they want to depend upon for retirement. Health insurance is always a hot topic, and can also be used as an example of why participation in the political process is important. The police labor leader can also use on-the-job issues as examples, for example, equipment, staffing, and assignments. Every one of these issues is part and parcel of the political process.

In explaining the importance of endorsements, the police labor leader might consider using a circus juggling act as a good example of why endorsements are significant. Elected officials have to juggle a number of competing interests. They tend to catch the ones they are familiar with, or the ones who have supported them energetically in the past. The inactive or ineffective groups tend to get dropped when the juggling stops.

Distinguishing Between Members' Organizational and Personal Interests

Another aspect of the preliminary education process is explaining to members why the police association's **organizational** political interests are not necessarily the same as individual members' **personal** voting interests. This dilemma can be best illustrated by the classic example of whether or not the police association should endorse a candidate running for a state senatorial district who is a strong advocate of police collective bargaining and due process rights, and at the same time, a strong proponent of gay rights and unrestricted abortion. The candidate's bargaining and due process positions concern **organizational** political interests, and should be the *only* focus of the police association. The gay rights and abortion issues have to do with **personal** interests, and should *only* be the concern of individual members when they walk in the voting booth and exercise their right to vote.

It is *absolutely vital* that the police labor leader explain the distinction between organizational and personal interests as a part of the preliminary education process, and *before* any endorsements take place. Otherwise, there will be a vocal outcry from any number of individual members objecting to a particular endorsement because of their personal views alone. Any visible, strong disagreement of this nature can do nothing but undermine the credibility of the police association's endorsement later.

Chapter 17

POLITICS FROM A TO Z–WHAT DOES THE ASSOCIATION HAVE TO OFFER?

Now we ask the question: What does the police association have to offer? Typically, law enforcement groups have five potential things that they can offer candidates:

1. money
2. media support
3. personnel
4. information, and
5. auto-pilot endorsement

Few groups will be able to give all five, but there is enough variety among the items on the list that any group, regardless of how feeble and apathetic the membership, can offer one or two items as part of its endorsement package. Here are some of the specifics so you can tailor your endorsement to the abilities of your membership.

Money

At the top of any candidate's list is **money**. If your group has an ample political action committee that can send a campaign contribution of a few thousand dollars along with an endorsement, then you will have an impact with that campaign.

But if you don't have a treasury that can afford to send thousands of dollars, your police association can still offer something to the campaign. A $500 contribution that would disappear in a United States Senate or state gubernatorial war chest can have a significant impact on a city council or state legislative campaign. The most important consideration is to assign priorities and direct your limited financial resources into races where it will have the most impact.

You might also decide that instead of giving money directly to the campaign, you would rather make an independent expenditure, where your police association spends its money in support of a candidate. As a part of an independent expenditure, you may elect to produce and broadcast radio or television ads, or send direct mail in support of your candidate.

The independent expenditure has two advantages. First, it can give your police association endorsement real leverage with the person you are endorsing, because the candidate can see the direct link between your support and assistance to the campaign. Second, this method allows the police association to control the content and context of your endorsement message.

Media Support

There are a number of other things that police associations can offer to a candidate that are as valuable as money, and just as memorable after the election. **Media support** is at the top of the list. But don't confuse media support with allowing the police association's name to be used in an ad. This passive approach to candidate support won't earn you any points with the candidate after the election!

Media support means that the police association leadership will be out front and visible during the entire course of the campaign. The leadership must be willing to appear in endorsement press conferences, issue press releases and even conduct opponent attack press events. And these aren't necessarily one-shot affairs—in a statewide race, police association representatives may have to travel on a press caravan to get the message out, hitting a number of media markets in a single day. This kind of support can mean much more to a candidate in a well-funded race than a $500 check that the candidate may never personally see.

Personnel

For some reason, many police associations and their members don't like to get involved in the day-to-day work of a campaign, but this aloofness will be costly after election day. Remember: after the election, candidates recall who helped them get where they are, and those groups that provided **personnel** to the campaign will be rewarded later.

The reason that firefighters have had so much influence at city halls and state capitols throughout the country is that they own the yard sign franchise in many localities. Every year, candidates are getting yard signs printed, and in many cases installed, by firefighters.

Police associations can do the same thing. Obvious areas where volunteers can make a difference are door-to-door canvassing, working telephone banks, or helping out at campaign headquarters. If association members aren't keen on these activities, then they can volunteer, make an in-kind contribution, and stay in uniform by providing free security at campaign events. This volunteer effort can include guarding the proceeds at the ticket office, crowd control, and/or directing traffic.

The use of police association members to serve in a security capacity will save the campaign a significant amount of money. Also, the police association can have a visible role in the election, and your members will be doing something that is familiar to them.

Information

Knowledge is power, and lack of knowledge can be a weakness in any campaign. Along with an endorsement, the police association can function as an independent source of **information** concerning law enforcement in your city, county, or state. Police association leaders can often give candidates information that they cannot get from the city manager, the mayor, the city bureaucracy, or the police chief.

Police labor leaders know where the bureaucratic skeletons are buried. This kind of inside information is priceless to a campaign when crime is an issue. Challengers are particularly grateful for this knowledge, but incumbents who are on the outs with the establishment and candidates who are being mislead by government bureaucracy are also likely targets.

The best thing about information is that it is free, and can have a big impact on the issue side of a campaign. If your membership is too apathetic to get involved, then information can often take their place as the association's contribution to a campaign.

The Auto-Pilot Endorsement

The **auto-pilot endorsement** is mentioned last because it has the least impact of any police association contributions to a campaign. A mere endorsement is better than nothing, but not by much.

An endorsement with no other association contribution has little impact, because the candidate's campaign has to do all the work. If your association can do no more than issue a press release, it is indicative of a weak group, and the political insiders know it. The candidate will accept and use your endorsement, but the campaign will also remember how little effort you put in to support it.

In deciding what to do for a candidate beyond an endorsement, the police labor leader must first decide what the membership can and will do. The crucial thing to remember is don't overpromise. The police association's failure to live up to its assurances can equal betrayal in the fevered environment of a campaign.

Chapter 18

POLITICS FROM A TO Z–WHOM DO WE TARGET?

The third question is: Whom do we target? The answer to that question largely depends on determining where the endorsement can do the most good for your organizational interests.

In the long run, does your police association benefit more from helping your friends or hurting your enemies? These questions must be asked and answered before making any decision to step into the political arena. Otherwise, you will make ill-advised endorsements which could have disastrous consequences for your police association.

Helping Your Friends

Any police association has two categories of friends: current and future. Your current friends are incumbents. These officeholders have been supporters in the past, and you want to continue to have their support in the future. What's more, protecting incumbents may involve so much work that your efforts are limited to them alone.

Fortunately, incumbent endorsements are the safest for the police association to make because year in and year out, most incumbents are reelected. Unfortunately, the incumbents are well aware of this fact. Consequently, the impact of your support is reduced.

The endorsements that produce the most influence for your association are those that have the most impact. For example, an early endorsement of a candidate in a multicandidate field can give him or her credibility with the fund-raising community and the press. This kind of endorsement has great impact and can be a building block for the campaign.

Helping Future Friends

The early, credibility-building endorsement is most often found in a race for an open seat where there is no incumbent running. A successful endorsement in a race for an open seat can produce future friends, and can get you in on the ground floor of their political career. As the officeholders's power and influence grows, law enforcement's voice becomes even stronger.

But you must remember to choose wisely in races for open seats, because if your candidate loses, you have a problem. At the very least, you will be viewed with suspicion by the winner for the first term of office, and at worse, you'll have made an enemy for the course of a political career.

An endorsement in an open race can also be an attempt to take charge of the future. In your situation, it may not be so much that there is a great candidate that you want to support, but rather one candidate is so bad that your association can't afford to have this person win. In this instance, the police association's efforts are devoted more at one candidate's defeat than the other's victory, which is simply choosing between the evil of two lessers.

Endorsements as Western Union

Your police association can use an endorsement to send a message to an incumbent by supporting the opponent. And you don't have to win the election for your message to be received loud and clear.

By supporting the opponent, you show an unfriendly incumbent that there are unpleasant consequences to being on the bad side of law enforcement. If your association is smart, the leaders and members will work very hard for the opponent, and make this election a living hell for the incumbent, assuming he or she wins. If the incumbent loses, so much the better!

After the experience of a tough campaign against your police association, a reasonable incumbent may decide that voting against your interests is more trouble than it's worth. This former enemy may be more open to your interest in the future, because he or she has seen firsthand what can otherwise happen.

If your association chooses the Western Union approach, you must avoid becoming irrelevant. If you send a message, make certain that it arrives. The police association must marshall all of its resources for the campaign, and must be enthusiastically supported by the membership. Otherwise, your follow-through will be weak; your association will be embarrassed; and this enemy will write you off forever.

Endorsements as Absolution

There are candidates that need your police association much more than you need them. These candidates have a problem. They can be incumbents, challengers, or running for an open seat, but all of them have a blotch on their political record that a law enforcement endorsement will do a great deal to cover. Examples include a former ACLU attorney running for district attorney, an incumbent with a driving under the influence conviction, or a former Operation Rescue member running for anything.

When your police association endorses this type of candidate, you are more or less absolving the candidate of his or her political "sins." The police association endorsement tells the voters that in spite of this transgression, law enforcement thinks that this candidate is qualified, worthy of support, and deserving of forgiveness.

It is not essential that the association endorse a candidate for absolution. But if your group does make this kind of endorsement, extract a price. This candidate needs you much more than you need him or her. Get this candidate's binding promise to support the pay raise, new collective bargaining agreement, or whatever else is your top issue *before* you make the endorsement. Then remember to collect after the election.

Challengers: Another Way to Build for the Future

Incumbents don't often lose, but when they do, it gets everyone's attention. A visible effort by the police association on behalf of a successful challenger sends the entire political community, challengers and incumbents alike, a message. Your power and leverage will increase geometrically as a result of this one victory.

If a loss is closer than expected, flying in the face of the so-called conventional wisdom, it will have much the same effect. Supporting a credible challenger with potential may not pay off the first time, but the second race, oftentimes a victory, will bear dividends. A good challenger may not win the first position he or she attempts, but may surface somewhere in the future.

Chapter 19

POLITICS FROM A TO Z–WHEN DO WE ENDORSE?

As far as the question of–When do we endorse?–it's a matter of timing that has to balance when the endorsement will do the most good for the candidate, with when it best serves the purposes of your police association. Remember that your goal is not simply to elect people; if it was, you'd be a political consultant. The goal is to maximize your group's influence on the political process by influencing voters, and by electing or defeating candidates.

There are basically four times that your police association can endorse: early, late, both, or at the candidate's discretion. In order for the endorsement to have the most potential influence, your association must have an internal endorsement mechanism in place to begin interviewing candidates and determining how to distribute your support *before* the campaign season begins.

If there are primaries in the races your association is concerned with, the group must start identifying potential candidates weeks before filing deadlines. This process might mean that the leadership will start looking at these campaigns the year before the election is held. What's more, your association may make primary endorsements and then endorse again in the general election.

This entire process takes time and organization that must be in place, and agreed upon, weeks before it's time to decide a particular endorsement. It doesn't do a challenger, who needed an early endorsement in May, much good to finally get your blessing in September. A police association that can't properly time its endorsements isn't going to have a great deal of impact on the political process.

116

Early Endorsements

Early endorsements are most valuable to challengers, candidates in a crowded field, and first-time candidates. For challengers and first-time candidates, your endorsement provides credibility. These candidates can use your seal of approval to begin the process of persuading others to join their effort.

The early endorsement tells editorial boards, political activists, and contributors that this candidate is credible. It also puts your association in at the beginning of this candidate's career. You automatically become one of the core supporters, a member of the inner circle, and someone the candidate turns to for advice and listens to when it comes time to vote.

An early endorsement helps a candidate in a crowded field to stand out from the rest. It gives him or her a point of distinction and something that can be used as an issue or advantage when contacting voters and contributors.

In an election year when crime or law enforcement-related issues are paramount, this early endorsement gives your candidate a great advantage over the opposition. Other candidates have to scramble to get endorsements from other law enforcement groups in order to negate your candidate's early advantage, or they risk losing this important issue.

When your association chooses to make an early endorsement, it is best if that event isn't the last contact with the campaign. Stay in close contact, be an advisor, offer some of the other facets of an endorsement that have been discussed previously, and in short, be a presence for the duration of the campaign.

The Late Endorsement

Done properly, a late endorsement can tip the scale and put a candidate over the top. It puts your group in the position of being a king (or queen) maker as you provide this last bit of organizational and public help for a campaign. Unfortunately, it is hard to make late endorsements properly.

For a late endorsement to work, the association has to carefully judge the available options in the race. You are choosing late, so you must choose well. This race should be carefully handicapped, and that means you have to do your homework. A late endorsement will usually be a very public event, so backing the wrong candidate can result in a very visible failure.

But in an evenly matched race, a strong endorsement package can determine the outcome. This scenario won't happen too often in a congressional race, because too many variables are at work. But in a city council or mayor's race, and particularly in a judicial race, a late law enforcement nod can be crucial.

Early and Late Endorsements

These types of endorsements are for highly organized law enforcement groups. This combination means that you do the early endorsement events with accompanying press conferences and public appearances. Then the campaign takes the ball and runs with it.

At the close of the campaign, your association appears again, this time with some form of paid endorsement support–a television spot, radio commercial, direct mail piece, block-walking, or placing members at the polls with slate cards to remind the public who your chosen candidates are.

This kind of effort also serves to remind the candidate of just how crucial your support was to his or her victory. It also will pay big dividends later when your issue comes before that officeholder.

Candidate's Discretion

In this situation, the candidate decides when and where your endorsement will do the most good. Your group can earn plenty of points for being cooperative, but there is a danger in letting your association be taken for granted.

This "candidate's discretion" arrangement works best with candidates that your group knows, and whose judgment you trust. This option is not recommended as the choice for first-timers, or candidates with whom you have not had a relationship in the past.

Chapter 20

POLITICS FROM A TO Z–HOW SHOULD
THE ASSOCIATION ENDORSE?

Now we'll attempt to answer the final question: how does the police association make the public aware of its endorsement? If it's an auto-pilot endorsement, the candidate's campaign will take care of notifying the voters. But if you have decided to determine your own fate, the methods by which your association makes voters aware will depend in large part on the size of your budget.

There are several ways of getting the word out to the community: television, radio, direct mail, and print ads. Let's look at each of these methods.

Television: Large Impact–Large Expense

Television is expensive for two reasons. First, it costs more to produce the advertisement. Production of a fairly basic television spot can cost $2,000. A more creative effort can run more than $10,000. Second, television is a mass medium, which accounts for its impact, and buying time can be expensive.

Given the reality of considerable expense, it is important to consider ways to make television ads less expensive. On a cost-per- thousand-voting-age-population basis, television can cost a half of what a direct mail piece does. In congressional races where there is a great deal of wasted coverage, a candidate can broadcast three television spots for a cost per thousand of less than $200, compared to a mail cost per thousand of $350 to $400.

So why don't all candidates use television instead of mail? Because broadcast television has only one list (i.e., the entire television market), so you have to buy everyone on the list; that is, you're buying the entire voting (and non-voting) community that watches television.

For a community of 200,000 voters at $200 per thousand, the cost is $40,000. With mail, you can choose any number of lists that vary by size; so instead of trying to reach 200,000 voters, your association might mail to only 10,000 voting households for a total cost of $3,500.

Cable TV: Using the Television Alternative

Cable television can cut the size of the television list down to a manageable size. Even in a city that's 100 percent wired for cable, a spot will cost much less than one broadcast over the airwaves.

This situation makes cable a good compromise that still gives the impact of television, with less cost than the broadcast version. However, you must remember that the association will be reaching fewer households.

In an area that has less than 50 percent cable market penetration, cable subscribers are usually upper income residents. When cable penetration exceeds 50 percent of the market, the makeup of the cable subscriber universe begins to accurately reflect the demographics of the area.

Radio: Broadcasting Without the Bite

If your police association can't afford television advertising, then radio will become the broadcast medium. Costs in this instance are much less for both production and time. However, it's difficult to reach as many people as you do with television advertising.

A typical radio spot costs under $600 to produce, and the cost of a sixty second commercial is usually half of what the equivalent time would cost on television. What's more, your association can target potential voters fairly precisely and with less waste, since radio stations have different formats and listener profiles.

For example, the police association won't reach many voters when it puts its endorsement on a heavy metal station, but the same ad on a news/talk station will hit many potential voters each time it is broadcast.

If the association is going to use either radio or television, plan on a minimum two-week buy. Any less time will not allow your message to penetrate the market. If your association has the money, three or four weeks is the most effective period of time for your endorsement buy.

Mail: Hitting Them Where They Live

If your association can't afford radio or television, then mail is your last really effective mass contact alternative. When using the mail, it is best to keep your mail message simple and direct. You don't need to do an entire brochure to tell why your association likes candidate X. The candidate should have told his story long ago. All your association should do is tell voters that it supports the candidate and his/her program. An oversized endorsement postcard in the last two weeks of the campaign will accomplish this goal nicely.

Your toughest decision will be who should be targeted for the mail out. The largest possible list is registered voters in your area of both political parties, but this mail out will be expensive and not target efficient. This list can be reduced by mailing only to voters who voted in the last primary, or last municipal election. Ideally, the candidate who's receiving the endorsement can give you the mailing list where the endorsement will do the most good. Then, all the association has to do is buy the postage and print the mail out materials.

If the candidate can't supply the list, then the association will have to purchase it from a list broker. These brokers will charge you based on the size of the list and how much trouble it was to compile the names. Once you obtain the list—usually in the form of labels, the association can deliver the labels, the mail out, and a check to a mail house for delivery to target voters.

Print Ads: The Last Alternative

Print ads are expensive, and they require as much repetition as broadcast advertisements. If your association is going to use print ads, don't do any less than a one-half page ad, and plan on running it three or four times.

To reach the most voters, you should request that the ad be placed in the metro or city section of the paper, or in the sports page. These placements may cost a little more, but will be worth it.

If you do a print ad, get a professional to design it. Don't run "An Open Letter to the People of Metropolis," because these ads are dead letters. The only people that read them are you, the candidate, and the opponent. A clean, well-designed layout will pay off in increased readership and impact at the polls.

Endorsing Candidates on a Shoestring

If your association doesn't have the money for any of the above advertising programs, but you still want to do something visible, then push cards and volunteers are the last alternative. Call the candidate and find out where the most important target precincts are.

Line up enough volunteers to cover those precincts on election day. Print a small card with your endorsement on it and pass these cards out to voters as they approach the polling place.

Uniformed officers will have the most impact at the polls, but in jurisdictions where law or regulation prohibits wearing a uniform for political activity (probably most states), use off-duty or retired officers in your association's jackets, T-shirts, or ball caps. It's a personal touch which can help persuade the undecided and remind the already decided.

Part IV

POLICE ASSOCIATIONS AND CONFRONTATIONS

Chapter 21

ABOUT ETHICS, CONFLICT, AND TACTICS

Conflict has long been the way that people and groups have changed the system. Nineteenth century, black activist Frederick Douglas had this comment about conflict: "If there is no struggle, there is no progress. Those who profess to favor freedom, and yet depreciate agitation, are people who want rain without thunder and lightening. They want the ocean without the roar of its many waters."

In the twentieth century, one of the most famous advocates of conflict as the method for organizations to achieve their goals has been Saul Alinsky. While Alinsky's philosophy was discussed thoroughly in Chapters 3 and 4, a few of his principles should be restated here as a reminder of the inevitability of conflict and confrontation that police labor leaders face:

1. Change comes from power, and power comes from organization.
2. The first step in community organization is community disorganization.
3. The leader must simultaneously breed conflict and build a power structure.
4. No one can negotiate without the power to compel negotiations.

There is no point in rehashing the entire Alinsky philosophy, since that task was completed elsewhere in the book. It should be strongly emphasized, however, that no police labor leader can really succeed in achieving organizational goals without anticipating, and at some point, facing some degree of conflict and confrontation, and no leader will feel comfortable in this role without an understanding of Alinsky's principles.

"Principle-Centered" Negotiations and Impasse Arbitration

A great deal of attention has been paid in recent years by academia and public sector management associations to the concept of "principle-centered" negotiations and leadership. Unfortunately, the real world does not find an abundance of principled management negotiators and public leaders—decisions are more often than not made on the basis of trade-offs, *quid pro quos*, business and political relationships, and other factors totally unrelated to sound public policy.

If decisions were, in fact, made according to some absolute, universal standard of public policy integrity, then there would be no need for lobbyists, political action contributions, and other pressure points to persuade public officials on the "rightness" or "wrongness" of a particular issue. Then the authors would have no need to write this book, or you to read it! It is therefore tragic that many police labor leaders have bought into the notion of "principle-centered" negotiations without giving their acceptance to the idea some thought.

In states where law enforcement collective bargaining is permitted, this path of least resistance results in lukewarm negotiations, mediocre wage and benefit offers by public employers, and oftentimes, mediocre settlements mandated by third-party neutral impasse procedures. These arbitrator-driven settlements are safe, that is, decisions which will not greatly offend employers or the public. Police associations rarely have the opportunity in this process to break out of the pack with a significant wage settlement or a new benefit, because state bargaining laws normally require arbitrators to adhere to a strict wage and benefit "comparability" standard.

Any police association leader who feels smug that his or her state bargaining law is all that is necessary to achieve the interests of the membership is sadly mistaken. There are untold number of police association leaders throughout the country who have been condemned and driven from office by frustrated members who felt that the contract settlement or arbitration award was insufficient to satisfy their economic needs.

If the police association is going to break through the maze of backroom power brokering, ivory-tower decision-making, and lackluster contract settlements that often disregard the needs of association members, then conflict becomes *inevitable* for the successful police association. It is the essence of what will bring the association to the center of power.

Using Conflict and Confrontation for the Benefit of the Police Association

There are three things that the successful police association leader must do to achieve short- and long-term goals for the membership. First, conflict must be accepted as an essential component of any success you might achieve. Then, the leader must understand when and how to engage in conflict. Finally, conflict must be used when it becomes necessary.

Conflict does not, however, always have to be severe—a stern, well-publicized letter to the mayor or city manager protesting certain actions of the city can sometimes achieve the desired goal. At the same time, a pitched political battle against an incumbent mayor who has not been the association's friend, or a high-visibility referendum against an antiemployee city manager, might become necessary as well.

The police labor leader must always be aware that conflict for the sake of conflict will wear thin with the members, with the public, and even with political allies and friends, and in the end, will prove to be unproductive. The police association leader must have a strategy that centers on calculated risks which will achieve calculated gains. The organization should pick the fights that are vital for the achievement of short- and long-term goals.

The use of conflict and confrontation is a touchy business—it's an art, and definitely not a science. This part of the book will examine how to go about using conflict and confrontation in the police labor leader's arsenal: how to conduct referendums; how to gather public support for police wage and benefit issues; how to select political consultants who can assist your group in waging high-visibility conflicts; using other pressure points such as challenges against the Chamber of Commerce, attacking public bond issues, and police chief "no confidence" votes; and finally, understanding that in all fights, there inevitably must be a winner, and a loser.

Chapter 22

PUTTING PUBLIC PRESSURE ON FOR POLICE WAGES, BENEFITS, AND WORKING CONDITIONS

There have been at least two northeastern police associations within recent years which became so frustrated with pay and working conditions that they have taken the fight public. Coincidentally, both groups used billboards to make their displeasure known. And just as coincidentally, nothing has been heard from either group after the first billboard.

The general view on billboards among political consultants in any type of public and political campaign is very simple. There are only two really effective locations for a billboard: one is outside your candidate's bedroom window; the other is outside the opponent's bedroom window.

But the goal here is not to make it harder for the billboard salespeople to make their house payment, or to pick on those two police associations, both of whom should be commended for trying to do something. Instead, what should be emphasized is that if your police association is planning a public pressure campaign over wages, benefits, or working conditions, then it must be fully planned *before* you go public.

This chapter will look at how to effectively bring public pressure to bear on the politicians in order to improve police compensation packages and working conditions. And for those readers who bargain and think that they don't need to read about the use of public pressure to get things which you normally negotiate for, think again. Both of the billboarding associations cited above had collective bargaining laws and were located in states with compulsory, binding arbitration laws!

There are three elements which a public pressure campaign must contain if it is to have a chance for success: a clearly defined goal, an evaluation of what tools you can bring to bear in the coming fight, and control over the outward appearance of the campaign.

Defining Public and Private Goals

The decision to go public means that the police association is embarking on a political campaign. Successful campaigns have a central theme or message that drives the entire enterprise. If you're really serious about being successful, then you'll devote a great deal of time to this stage of the process.

The association members may simply want a raise, but let's face it —a campaign based on "give us money" isn't a campaign. It's no more than a ransom note.

Your job is to frame the pay raise argument so that the public is willing to take money out of their pockets, sometimes in the form of higher taxes, and to put that tax money in your pocket. This task is not easy during hard economic times.

The first step in this definition process is to get specific—simply asking for a pay raise is not enough. You must know exactly what you want, and what the members will accept. For example, you might take the position that you want a 6.5 percent pay raise to make up for the erosion in paychecks since the last pay increase, and you want shift differential pay increased by 1 percent to keep pace with what other comparable law enforcement agencies are making.

Once You Know What You Want, Find Out How to Pay for It

The city or county's response will normally be: "We can't afford it." So the next step should be to find the money.

Hire an outside economic expert or get a friendly professor at a nearby college to analyze the budget and find money that can be redirected to the police department. Show how eliminating the city staff's take home cars, cellular phones, and tub club memberships will free up some funds. You're not making a stock offering here, so the numbers don't have to stand up to SEC scrutiny; but it is nice to give your reasoning a little academic camouflage.

If the numbers don't completely add up, add a small tax or fee increase to the package. Earmarking the funds, that is, dedicating them specifically to law enforcement, is a nice touch which shows the taxpayers that the money won't be lost in the general fund.

The Next Step Is to Define Your Public Message

It is crucial to remember that the public's perceptions about the economy and their lives have a great deal of bearing on how they react to your message, and therefore how successful your campaign will be. You must wrap your pay raise in a message that will be accepted by taxpayers who might be worried about keeping their jobs, to say nothing of their concern over a pay raise from their boss.

The downside to Misery Loves Company is that miserable folks don't like the idea of someone doing better than they are. If you want a raise when John and Jane Q. Public aren't getting one at their office, then there has to be some perceived benefit for the public before they will support you. That new bass boat you've had your eye on won't do it.

That's why you also have to define your public goal, which may differ in emphasis from the private goal your members are seeking. While local conditions vary, here are a few ideas for positioning your pay raise or working conditions request:

1. **Upgrade the force.** To reflect the growth and complexity of modern law enforcement, we need to attract the best and brightest to the force. We can't attract quality with our current bargain basement pay scale. Adjusting the pay scale will attract quality officers.

2. **Stop the exodus of trained officers.** We're losing trained, experienced officers each year to other departments with more realistic pay scales. The result is that the city is wasting hundreds of thousands of dollars in training costs to replace these veterans. Adjusting the pay scale would retain these officers, cut training costs, and give the taxpayer better protection than with a rookie-heavy department.

3. **Put more officers on the street.** Based on national statistics, our force is currently understaffed by X number of officers. If we are to have any hope of stopping the rising tide of crime, we must have more police officers. The solution is to add X officers each year *and* adjust the pay scales to attract the kind of applicant we need.

4. **Envy of low self-esteem.** Our police are the lowest paid in the county, state, and probably the world. Why just next door in

Classyville, police officers are paid 25 percent more. If we don't raise our pay scale to parity with Classyville, our crime rates will go up, and Classyville will get all the new business and tourists.

In your city or county, you can mix, match, or come up with an entirely different message. The important thing is to think like a taxpayer. If you're paying taxes in your town, would this argument convince you to dig a little deeper?

You've Got to Plan Your Campaign Well

Any campaign that has a chance of succeeding must be well planned, because you will be using intangibles to attempt to force someone with real power to do what you want. City hall already has the votes; otherwise you wouldn't be unhappy in the first place. To get the city council or commissioner's court to change votes will require a carefully orchestrated plan of action.

Here are some basic principles: spur-of-the-moment protests and one-shot displays simply won't work, because the opposition can wait you out. The police association must have more than one arrow in its quiver, or it goals will become irrelevant. Governments can adapt to pain or insult, just as the body can.

Let's take the billboard example we discussed previously as an example of these principles. The morning the billboard appeared attacking city hall on pay or working conditions, it was a slap in the face. The mayor talked about it, the newspaper covered it, radio talk shows discussed it, and your members wanted to act as if it was your fault. The next day an editorial ran in the newspaper wringing its hands, and urging the police to work within the system. The third morning, the billboard was discussed in a city council meeting where members of the council said they were deeply hurt by this attack, and that they had always been strong supporters of law enforcement.

The next week, the powers-that-be looked at the billboard and said, "Is it still there?" Then they went on about their business.

When You Get in a Fight with City Hall, Escalation Is the Key

Your association must have a plan with options for escalating the intensity and/or direction of your pressure. Here's an example of public escalation from the political campaign in a mayor's race. The female candidate was a woman who was trying to force her opponent to debate during a two-week runoff election for a vacant mayor's seat. The opponent was currently the sheriff, and had been running a macho, law enforcement campaign against the woman.

The first step in the female candidate's attack was to run a full-page newspaper ad with a headline reading: "SHERIFF ANDY TATE: COME OUT AND FIGHT LIKE A MAN." The press thought that the idea of a petite little woman challenging a gun-toting sheriff was great! She got coverage on every news media vehicle known to man.

Step two was interrupting Andy Tate's press conferences. She drove up outside his campaign headquarters in a motor home, got out and erected a table with a large sign that said, "DEBATES ARRANGED WHILE YOU WAIT." At the same time, her representatives sat in the waiting rooms of his campaign headquarters and asked for the members of his steering committee. Each of her representatives had full authority to negotiate debate terms. Her people sat there all day and tied up his organization. Again, she received massive news coverage.

Step three was never taken. It would have been another full-page ad that read: "FOR A GOOD DEBATE, CALL 555-1026" (Andy Tate's campaign headquarters). But the ad never ran because the other candidate caved in and agreed to debate.

Why did he agree? Because the woman candidate continued to escalate the pressure, and the other side finally had no choice. The opposition's campaign simply couldn't function and that's what your police association must do in a public campaign.

Your goal must be to set up such a flood of events and distractions that the pressure becomes unbearable. You want for city hall to become so frustrated that the political leaders will give in or agree to negotiate just to have some peace.

Here's a Practical Example of How to Use Escalating Tactics

Now let's go back to where we started, with our billboard that caused the one-day sensation. Billboards do have some advantages for a public campaign, assuming that you get the right location. This site can be near city hall, near the mayor's house or business, near the city manager's house, near the newspaper editor's home or business, or any other location which provides a daily irritant to those you wish to influence and affords some public visibility. Billboards can be especially useful if you can get them donated to your cause for a few weeks by the owner.

So here's the situation. Your association has two donated billboards, one in a location that's across the square from city hall and one on the main road into town. Your budget is so low that you won't be running full newspaper ads, and your membership is apathetic and only good for one rally. Is there any way you can have a sustained, escalating campaign?

In this situation, the answer is yes if you just keep changing the billboard message. You could start with a message that says: "__ murders and __ assaults while the city council fiddles over police manpower/training package." The second week, you can update the figures using a ceremony that provides visuals for media coverage. At the council meetings on the third week, you can bring in cardboard tombstones signifying each murder in the city this year.

To the public, it's a public safety issue; to your members, it's a pay increase; and to the association, it's a way to go public that increases pressure, doesn't use much money, and doesn't require 100 percent participation from the membership. And it all started with a billboard and some planning.

Remember That When You Begin to Apply Pressure, You're Going to Get a Dose of Your Own Medicine

When your police association runs a successful pressure campaign, the plans will include a number of events calculated to increase pressure on city hall, and to keep the opposition off balance. But always keep in mind that pressure works both ways, so you must prepare the membership for a little squeezing too.

While your association applies pressure to the mayor for a pay raise, the police chief is going to be leaning on you and the rank-and-file to stop the campaign before you've achieved your goal. And the chief won't be alone—he'll be joined by other pillars of the establishment and status quo who will tell you, your board of directors, and your members that this campaign is hurting the whole city, and will backfire on you with the voters.

The pressure will be intense. And since police forces are hierarchical organizations, the members are accustomed to taking orders from the establishment. Many of your members will be uncomfortable with defying authority.

You will also encounter this pressure when you meet with the editorial board of your newspaper, or the board of directors of the local chamber of commerce. These people are the movers and shakers with influence in the community, and you must meet with them. So while you are at the meeting, never lose sight of the fact that these guys and gals are cheerleaders for the establishment.

These self-appointed Judges of What's Right for the Community will wring their hands, shake their heads, and "tsk, tsk" during the entire meeting. With pained expressions, they will urge you to be a team player and work within the system.

But the point is, going public with your desires is part of the system, too. And once the pressure from above starts to build, you have to remind your members that there's nothing wrong with public conflict. The members must be resolute in the face of this pressure, or your campaign will fail miserably.

One Alternative for Confrontations That Doesn't Work Very Well - Job Actions

Now that you have issued Kevlar drawers to the members and are prepared for the fight, what can be done to draw attention to the issue? One of the first suggestions might be a job action, but this approach is problematic for cops because it's so easy to be accused of abusing your authority.

Take traffic tickets for example. If officers write citations for *every* violation of the speed limit, then the public is going to be hot, and that's who you want to support your position. If you announce that you won't be writing any tickets, then the public is happy, but at least as far as the public is concerned, there is zero pressure. In fact, the public may want police officers to stay unhappy so you won't go back to doing your job.

So let's say that you don't write tickets, but you don't announce it either. Instead, you wait for the administration to see the drop in revenue and respond. This process takes much longer and exposes your organization and members to a number of variables: state laws that call for firing public employees and union officials involved in a job action, and ticket quota systems that can be applied in performance review or disciplinary settings.

For a job action campaign to succeed, there must be absolute membership solidarity, which is at best a questionable pursuit in the police labor movement. If management pressures officers to start writing traffic tickets and makes life impossible for traffic unit officers, then there must be some other response, like refusing voluntary overtime assignments.

As you can readily see, the police association's options are limited because you can't appear to do anything which makes the city less safe for the taxpayers. This scenario means that the administration can play dirty and your side cannot.

That's why job actions are a difficult road to success. However, if any readers have had a successful job action, the authors would like to hear about it. What's more, we'll write an entirely new book devoted to your clear thinking and strategic insight!

Three Types of Public Pressure with a High Likelihood of Success—#1: Embarrassment

Once you have excluded job actions from your arsenal, there are three types of public pressure left. These forms include **embarrassment**, **political**, and **drama**.

Embarrassment is just that: the police association discloses information about your enemy that is embarrassing to them when made public. Contrasting the city council's refusal to implement a manpower program with the $125,000 they spent on a trip to Aruba for a planning retreat is a powerful public comeuppance.

Examining the city manager's car phone records and listing the private calls he made at taxpayer expense are good ideas. Then release the manager's car phone number, and ask the public to call him on that number and tell him to quit wasting money. That tactic will get some attention at city hall.

Go over all the opposition's expense accounts and office accounts for suspicious spending. These items are public records and available for your amusement and edification. Have a certified public accountant go over the budget with a fine-tooth comb and point out any waste. Make the council justify spending money on the chamber of commerce or convention center, and not on law enforcement.

The term "blowing the whistle" didn't come from basketball—it came from English Bobbies who used to blow whistles instead of sounding sirens. Make your goal to blow the whistle on waste and recruit whistleblowers in government who will help your cause.

Examine all the records and see what looks fishy, or what the public would question. Decide your timetable for release, and how to do it in the most effective and embarrassing manner; and then get to work.

More About Successful Pressure–#2: Political Pressure

Political pressure is probably the most powerful tool. In response to a proposal for a police civilian review board in Dallas, the Dallas Police Association (DPA) gathered petitions for a referendum on a measure they drafted banning civilian review boards. The DPA used the threat of these petitions to force an uncooperative Dallas City Council to make changes in the proposed board.

If local ordinances permit, and you are organized enough to gather names, these petitions are a very useful lever. Some petition options include a referendum, recall, or just for the purpose of registering a protest over an issue.

Your first move is to gather names. This step shows power and public support. The next move is threatening to file the petition. You may win here, but since city hall might not respond to your threat, **don't make the threat unless you are prepared to carry it out**!

The third move is to actually file the petition, and it is here that things start to get complicated. Once you go to the mat, you either have to win, or come within a whisker of victory. A big loss is fatal at the time, and even worse, the hangover can linger for years.

That's why your best bet is to get what you want without the election. Even if the city thinks it can win, elections do cost money and staff time, and the outcome is uncertain. Such an election can be a distraction the city may not want, so the police association could get a useful compromise at this point.

Going for an election when the police association has not done its electoral homework can be a disaster. If the city wins big, your goals will disappear for a decade. If the city wins by a whisker, you're in better shape to get petitions again. The second time, you may get a compromise without an election. (NOTE: See more about referendums in the following chapter.)

And Even More About Successful Pressure–#3: Drama

Going the drama route, you will soon discover that public pressure equates to press pressure. Obtaining press pressure means that what the police association does has to be interesting enough to merit media coverage. Any activity that lends itself to a photo or dramatic television event has an even better chance of making the news.

You should plan press conferences and activities with an eye toward producing an interesting picture. Some of these activities include distributing leaflets at shopping malls in your town, warning of crime dangers for holiday shoppers, and/or dressing your officers as Santa Claus warning about crime.

Even better, you can announce that the police association will be passing out flyers at malls in other towns next week, warning shoppers not to come to your city. This idea is an escalation that builds even more pressure.

You can also take out newspaper ads in other cities complaining about crime. Off-duty officers can distribute flyers at the airport warning tourists and business people of crime dangers in the city or downtown area.

Support for your cause can be generated through appearances at city council meetings where the wives and families of officers killed in the line of duty ask why the council is abandoning law enforcement. The police association can hold a press conference with a bullet-riddled vest as the centerpiece.

You can recruit other organizations to speak out or hold press conferences on your behalf. These groups might include neighborhood organizations wanting police coverage, the downtown merchant's association, veterans groups, the National Rifle Association, or any organized group with some clout who will join your effort.

Hold a media event where you make chalk outlines representing every murder in the city during a certain period of time (week, month, year, etc.). If it suits your purpose, make it look like a crime scene, and have the outline represent injured or killed officers.

If you have the budget, use radio ads for real impact, or even cable television. Association leaders can write op-ed pieces for the newspaper. Have officers write letters to the editor. Put presentable officers on radio, television, or cable talk shows.

But keep in mind that you always have to control the message. So any time you are dealing with the media, be prepared for trick questions, and stay on the themes and points that are central to your campaign. *Always* be professional and well organized when dealing with the media.

Chapter 23

VOTER REFERENDUMS AS A CONFRONTATION TACTIC

The use of initiative and referendum is often overlooked as a political tactic by many police associations. Police labor leaders often do not realize that by forcing a public vote on an issue, they are using the ultimate tactic of confrontation—they are taking power away from the public employer to control events, and placing it in the hands of the police association to control its own destiny.

The use of the initiative and referendum does not have to be limited just to police labor issues. It can be employed as well for other issues, and the police association's participation then sends a "message" to the employer that the organization is not pleased with some aspect of the labor-management relationship.

Voter referendums have a long history among activist groups in this country. Very simply, initiative and referendum is the process of petitioning voters to require public officials to place a particular issue on the ballot for a single-issue election. The terms "initiative and referendum," "voter referendum," and "single-issue election" will be used interchangeably throughout this chapter.

The Legal Framework

The first question that any police association must always ask is whether or not initiative and referendum is permissible in your jurisdiction. Each state and/or local law empowers the initiative and referendum process in a different way. Here are some of the methods found throughout the country:

139

1. **State laws on charters.** Many states provide for a specific method by which voters in home rule cities may petition for amendments to city charters.

2. **State laws on specific police issues.** A few states permit initiative and referendums on very narrowly-defined labor issues, such as civil service, pay raises, or the right to collectively bargain. These often apply to municipal and county law enforcement employees.

3. **City (or county) charters–charter change.** The charters of many home rule cities (and some counties) provide for a system where voters can petition for amendments to the charters. Such provisions will sometimes have specific restrictions on the type of amendments that may be brought (e.g., no amendment may be initiated that requires an appropriation of money).

4. **City (or county) charters–adoption of ordinances.** Some charters provide that petitions may be initiated for adoption of city (or county) ordinances. This approach can be very limiting, because there is usually a time period–often one year, after which the ordinance may be modified in any way by the governing body.

Remember that the question of how a voter referendum may be set into motion is complex. Competent legal counsel should *always* be consulted when evaluating your options to use initiative and referendum.

Preparing for an Initiative and Referendum

Any issue that is brought to the voters will be controversial to some interest groups in your community - the local governing body (i.e., city council, county commissioners); minority groups; taxpayers associations; senior citizens; etc. The decision to carry through with a voter referendum will, by the very nature of this adversarial process, put your association at war with a certain segment of the community. And like any war, **the failure to prepare in advance of the voter referendum virtually guarantees that the police association will be defeated at the polls.**

A police association should *only* use the voter referendum system when the association is sufficiently prepared to go forward. Following are some key preparation tips that will give your association a strong foundation once the commitment is made to proceed.

The two easiest things that the police association can do are (1) vote to seek a referendum and (2) collect the signatures on the petition. For the unprepared association, the referendum starts going downhill from that point, because the police association leaders have failed to understand the political system that they have now entered.

The cardinal rule for all police association referendums is: **Public approval of the "police" does not translate into a vote "for" a police issue on the ballot!** Voters can, and will, vote against pay, civil service, collective bargaining, and other labor issues and still visualize themselves as "pro-police." The burden lies with the association to run a **political** campaign, and not necessarily a **public relations** campaign.

A police association that is considering an initiative and referendum should seek **professional assistance** before it is too late to turn back. It will be too late to turn back when the leaders or members become emotionally charged, and vote to seek a voter referendum that they have given no previous thought to winning. Or, the police association might file a voter petition that is legally inadequate, and the public employer challenges the legal sufficiency of the petition, delaying the election for several years while the attorneys argue over minute points of law.

Professional consultants should be sought out *before* the decision is made to seek a referendum to educate the police labor leader about your options, and to help to develop an effective political strategy. Your chances of victory will be increased.

Therefore, the wise police labor leader seeks two types of professional assistance before deciding to embark upon a voter referendum:

1. **Legal.** As discussed above, competent legal counsel should be consulted as to the proper statute and/or charter provision to follow; and the legal sufficiency of the petition should be carefully analyzed before circulating it among voters.

2. **Political.** A political consultant with polling expertise should be retained to perform a survey poll that will give the police association some feel for the public's attitude toward the police in your community and the issue being considered. A decidedly negative public view as to public attitudes toward the police or the issue itself should make the police association reconsider the timeliness of an initiative and referendum. It would also be good to initially retain a general political consultant who can give some sound advice on preliminary matters. (NOTE: See the following chapter for an in-depth discussion of political consultants.)

The last preparation tip is to realize that all *successful* political confrontations, whether involving candidates or single-issue ballot measures, require four essential elements. These four elements are money, membership participation, membership commitment, and expertise.

Sample Voter Referendums–Labor Issues

The initiative and referendum can be used to raise any number of issues that are directly related to police labor concerns–manpower, wages, civil service, collective bargaining, work week, pensions, etc. The process can also be used for other issues that, while not directly related to labor matters, are of immediate public concern and can bring the police association into coalitions with other community interest groups. Such nonlabor issues might include single-member districts, term limitations, and governmental restrictions on use of tax money. Following are illustrations of labor issues:

1. **Minimum staffing.** A minimum staffing petition is an excellent option for a police association where the law enforcement agency is suffering from a marked personnel shortage that can be easily demonstrated through unacceptably high response times or threats to officer safety. If your population is increasing, it is recommended that the police association petition for a minimum number of police officers per 1,000 population (e.g., 2.0 police officers per 1,000 population). This approach might even include a graduated scale, such as 2.0 in 1997, 2.2 in 1998, and 2.5 in 1999. If your population is stable or decreasing, then it is recommended that the association set a fixed number of police officers for the agency (e.g., a minimum of 100 officers).

One important consideration in staffing petitions is to insure that the petition guarantees that the city or other governing body cannot lower or reduce the hiring standards or qualifications, or reduce the wages and benefits of officers because of the fiscal impact of implementation of the minimum staffing election. Otherwise, your association's sweet victory at the polls will turn sour later by an employer looking for ways to avoid the intent of your proposition.

2. **Pay increases.** In states where a public sector collective bargaining statute exists and a binding impasse procedure is in place, the use of pay increase referendums is of dubious legality and negligible value. However, in any state with no bargaining law, or bargaining with a

nonbinding impasse procedure (e.g., fact-finding), the possibilities for voter referendum pay raises are endless! City charter amendments can be proposed that will seek the following: a one-time across-the-board percentage raise; annual raises tied to the Cost of Living Index (COLA); a wage formula (i.e., future raises tied to percentage raises given to officers in comparable cities); or a restriction on future employee salary reductions.

There are two cautions when analyzing the wisdom of pay raises. First, a wage increase is a pocketbook issue, and voters know that it might cause a tax increase. The local economic conditions are *the most* critical factor in deciding whether to seek a pay raise election. If the voters perceive that times are hard, they will vote against anyone else receiving a pay raise. Careful polling before initiating a voter referendum on pay will let you know the public perception.

Second, there is a down side to seeking a police pay increase, because it impacts other government workers and projects. The city or county will calculate the pay increase based on every other worker receiving an equivalent raise, or the reduction in government services (e.g., "meals on wheels" to the elderly). A perception of greed by the police always lingers in the background of pay elections, and can quickly strike a blow to the campaign.

3. **Civil service or due process.** A voter referendum is an excellent way to deal with civil service or due process rights. This option would not likely be available in states where a statewide civil service system already exists. Initiative and referendum could be used to petition for a comprehensive civil service system (i.e., hiring, promotion, and discipline); strengthening of a weak civil service system (e.g., replace the commission with an independent hearing examiner in discipline cases); a fair grievance procedure, including an independent final resolution of grievances; or creating a job property right for employees in at-will employment systems.

If at all possible, the police association should include all city or county employees in the petition for civil service. The employer will raise the issue of an elitist, police-only election if you do otherwise, and the other employees will be unnecessarily alienated.

4. **Collective bargaining.** In states where there is no statewide collective bargaining law, but collective bargaining is permitted on a local option basis (e.g., Arkansas, Louisiana), there is a wide-open opportunity for the police association to propose a bargaining law through

voter referendum. The beauty of this concept is that you will be able to draft a bargaining law that suits your needs entirely, so long as it can be sold politically to the public. Even in states where a bargaining statute is in place, initiative and referendum is available to petition for any number of impasse options. These options can include compulsory arbitration, fact-finding and/or public referendum. There is even legal authority in some states to tinker with an impasse procedure mandated by state law through local voter referendum.

5. **Pension benefits.** While most pension plans are regulated under state laws, these laws often provide for various options that employers might not choose. The police association may be able to initiate a voter referendum to require the city or county to pay maximum benefits. Another approach is to propose a prohibition against the city or county from using tax money to fund deferred compensation plans for department heads; or where a local pension system is in place, prohibiting the system from loaning money to the public employer (a financing system that has been on the increase in recent times).

6. **Work week/overtime.** If your employer is regulated by the Fair Labor Standards Act (FLSA) only, and there is no bargaining agreement in place, you may want to petition for change of the following matters by initiative and referendum: the work week, the overtime accrual rate, the work cycle, or overtime compensation based upon hours paid for (as opposed to actually worked).

7. **Residency requirements.** If the city or county has a residency requirement by ordinance or charter provision, you can petition to modify or eliminate the requirement. For example, the police association might propose to eliminate residency as a condition of employment, but require that an officer live within a thirty-mile radius of the police department. Here's a cautionary note on a residency proposition: you will be asking the residents of the city or county to allow you to move out and cease paying taxes. This proposition makes for a tricky political argument, so be prepared to campaign on the issues of fairness and the United States Constitution.

Sample Voter Referendums—Nonlabor Issues

There are a variety of nonlabor issues that are susceptible to initiative and referendum proposals. Many of these voter referendums are not directly related to the immediate needs of police officers, but they are matters of public concern that can unite the police association with other political activists in the community. And it obvious that many of the referendums listed below will strike fear in the hearts of public officials. Consider some of the following options:

1. **Term limitations.** It is currently popular to campaign for term limitations on political offices. If your city or county has no such limitations, your police association might want to amend the charter to set limitations. It should be noted that there will be a tremendous political backlash from incumbent politicians if this issue is brought to the voters. You might consider assisting a taxpayer's group, and playing a secondary role.

2. **Single-member districts.** In a city where council members are elected on at-large basis, there is a distinct advantage to the police association seeking a change to single-member districts. It is much easier for the association to reach and influence a smaller constituency than a larger one; and therefore to bring more pressure to bear on local political officials.

3. **Lobbying with tax money.** If your city or county is using tax money to lobby against you at the state capital, your association might consider a petition to prohibit the use of tax money to influence legislation. As a prelude to such a campaign, use the Open Records Act in your state to find out how much the city or county is paying for lobbying activities (e.g., food, drinks, travel, entertainment, professional consultants).

There are also a number of other miscellaneous nonlabor propositions which, under certain conditions, might be wise choices for an initiative and referendum. For example, in a situation where a city council is demanding employee salary reductions, give-back concessions, or layoffs, a charter amendment to reduce the salaries and other perks of council members would find a great deal of public support, particularly in hard economic times. Remember that politicians are generally not trusted or respected by the public; if your association can make a case that police officers are willing to suffer the effects of tough times, but the politicians must do so as well, your proposition will receive a great deal of enthusiastic support!

Another excellent proposal is an initiative and referendum to require the election rather than the appointment of the police chief. This proposition is quite effective whenever a tyrannical police executive is in power, but the most beneficial effect of such a proposition would probably be the public scrutiny of the police executive's conduct caused by the **announcement** of the election rather than the election itself. In other words, this proposal works best as a bargaining chip, as opposed to actually bringing the issue to the voters.

Here is an specific example of how a nonlabor issue can work to the police association's benefit. In 1987, the City of Galveston, Texas and the Galveston Municipal Police Association (GMPA) were in a bitter collective bargaining dispute, with both sides taking hardened positions on wages and benefits. During this same period, the City decided to eliminate its Sanitation Department, and contract out for garbage collection—this decision was going to cost the jobs of more than 100 Galveston sanitation workers, most of whom were black.

The GMPA developed a charter referendum amendment that would prohibit the contracting out of city services to private contractors without a vote of the citizens. This action was taken to send the City a message that there would be a heavy price for the City to pay for its inflexible position at the bargaining table. The GMPA then worked with black community activists to gather petitions and campaign for passage of the initiative.

City of Galveston voters approved this charter amendment! And today, the City of Galveston cannot contract out sanitation or any other city service to private enterprise without first getting voter approval. This victory won over black sanitation workers and community activists that the police association was sympathetic to their interests and concerns, an important factor whenever the GMPA would need political assistance on future issues.

How a Police Association Referendum Can Succeed

By the time that a commitment is made by the police association to proceed with a voter referendum, the police labor leader should already have a complete understanding of the many critical factors that spell the difference between winning and losing an election. These factors might include available referendum options, association resources, membership commitment, the community political and economic climate, possible opposition groups, possibility for compromise, and the potential backlash from losing. Once the police association is ready to proceed, there are a number of factors that go into making a police association referendum a successful venture:

membership education, coalition-building, strategy, campaign tactics, and get-out-the-vote. We will now look at each of these factors.

Membership Education

The association will commit a fatal error by not educating the membership about the referendum issue. While pay referendums are self-explanatory, other issues are much more complex. Many members do not always support the referendum issue the police association leadership is proposing, and some members have false information about the issue.

A divided membership is the kiss of death to an association political campaign! Many police associations have split over an election, and killed any chance of its passage.

It takes time, money and energy to educate your members. A workshop or training session is crucial to educating members and winning their support. At these programs, association leaders should attempt to win over members to the proposition, or to at least neutralize any opposition. The association newsletter can also be used to provide factual information.

Finally, a voter registration drive among your membership and their families should be a part of the association education process. It is amazing how many association members are not registered to vote!

Coalition-Building

We have already discussed the importance of the police association having formed relationships with other special interest groups, and these relationships become critical prior to the election. This activity should be directed toward educating these groups about the referendum issue; and either neutralizing them to not oppose the referendum, or convincing the group to endorse the issue.

There are several key groups which should be targeted by the police association:

1. **The political leaders.** Political leaders (e.g., city council, commissioner's court, sheriff) will remain neutral if they understand the association's referendum issue. Neutrality is as good as an endorsement from political leaders!

2. **The media.** The news media in any community sees itself as the protector of Liberty, Truth and the American Way of Life. In fact, many newspapers, radio/TV stations are owned by biased individuals who are opposed to your exercise of power. To the extent that you are able to recruit respected community opinion leaders, the more likely the police association will get fair coverage from the media. An attempt to persuade the editor of the paper or station toward your issue should *always* be made.

3. **The power structure.** Every community has a power structure, which includes elected leaders, business owners, bankers, civic activists, and other "movers and shakers." If this group of people is not neutralized, they will be the ones to fund an Opposition Group against the police association. Seldom, if ever, will the power structure endorse your effort to seize power at the ballot box, but these people *must* be contacted prior to publicizing the referendum in order to keep as many of them neutral as possible.

4. **Labor organizations.** There is a vast resource of support for your voter referendum among various labor organizations in your community. These groups include firefighters, organized labor groups (AFL-CIO), teacher associations, and other general city/county employee organizations. In the case of firefighters, AFL-CIO groups, and teachers associations, they can be a source of political activism, knowledge, and assistance to your campaign that is invaluable. But each group must be courted and convinced that your issue is worthy of their support and commitment. In the instance of general city/county employee organizations, they must be sought out because the city or county government will tell these people that your referendum will cause layoffs or reduced benefits! The majority of the governmental work force must be convinced to be on *your* side, and not in the opposition's camp.

Planning a Strategy

There are a number of long-term strategy questions that must be discussed and planned at the outset of a voter referendum campaign. Following are highlights of the most important considerations:

1. **The petition.** As noted earlier, competent counsel should be consulted to prepare a legally sufficient petition. Otherwise, the campaign is doomed from the outset.

2. **The petition drive.** The best method to gather the required number of signatures is to target an election date as the day the police association circulates its petition–since every person you contact at the polls is a registered voter, you can often obtain all the signatures necessary in one day.

3. **Timing of the election.** There will normally be some requirement in state law or local charter as to the dates upon which a voter referendum may be held. Among the timing issues that must be looked at are: how much time to leave for the petition drive and validation of signatures, when the proposed measure would take effect, and possibility of other ballot measures or candidate elections that might help or hurt the association's campaign.

4. **The pledge.** Before starting any campaign for a specific purpose election, the police association should require each member to sign an individual pledge or petition committing themselves, both financially and time-wise, to the campaign. If the vast majority of members do not pledge to support the referendum with money and/or time, **DO NOT PROCEED!** You will lose the election.

5. **The internal campaign.** There must be internal responsibility conducting the referendum. An association member must be assigned to coordinate the day-to-day activity–this person should be a police officer who can best motivate other members, and handle the pressure generated from an intense campaign. A campaign committee of police association leaders should have the responsibility for planning and supervising the general campaign activities. A separate campaign office and campaign bank account are also recommended.

6. **Money and the budget.** Here is the major key to referendum success: **Money is the driving force of any referendum campaign!** There are three sources of campaign financing: dues (unlike for candidate elections, most states do permit the use of dues money for single-issue campaigns); special assessments of members; and contributions from citizens and businesses. Once the finances are reasonably fixed, a time-line budget should be set establishing when each event or activity will occur, and the amount of money needed to fund it.

7. **The professional consultant.** If the financial resources are available, the police association should hire a **general consultant** to manage the campaign, and hire **special consultants** on an as needed basis for such projects as direct mail, polling, media advertising, and fund raising.

8. **Database computer files.** Regardless of whether a specific purpose campaign is planned, your police association should collect computer files for political activity. The association must be able to communicate with all aspects of the community, and voting lists can normally be purchased from county clerks or the Secretary of State's office.

9. **Specific purpose PAC.** Most states require PAC registration and reporting for single-issue referendums. These requirements normally vary from candidate elections, so consultation with an attorney, political insiders, and appropriate government officials is encouraged.

10. **Citizens' Committee.** Your opposition will form a "Citizens Against the Police Issue," which lends credibility to the opposition's position. In order to counter this tactic, a "Citizens For Committee" should be formed to take a position in support of your issue. This group should be a cross-section of the community, and can issue news releases, attend civic meetings, write letters to the newspapers, and generally defend the issue.

Campaign Tactics

The *entire* purpose of the police association campaign effort is twofold: get-out-the-vote (GOTV) during early or absentee voting (as applicable), and GOTV on election day. Every effort and activity by the police association must be *only* to accomplish these two purposes. If you fail in your GOTV effort, you lose!

Set forth below are some campaign tactics that will assist the association's GOTV activity. Remember that where possible, these activities should be undertaken with the help of a political consultant. Also, all tactics should be geared toward sending a simple, understandable message to voters.

• **Direct mail.** Mail pieces to voters' homes can be helpful, particularly to targeted groups where a "working class" issue will be received well. Also, use the union bug for all direct mail - union members will usually notice the absence of a bug.

• **Newspaper advertising.** The usefulness of newspaper ads in a political campaign is debatable. But in smaller communities where the newspaper owners are generally a part of the business community that will oppose your proposition, a newspaper ad can somewhat neutralize the editorial pages.

• **Radio spots.** Many police associations find radio advertising to be an effective campaign tactic—it is relatively inexpensive and reaches a wide audience, and can target people more likely to vote.

• **Television commercials.** A large police association in a market with television stations might want to consider TV advertising. It is expensive, but reaches a large audience in a visual society. You cannot, however, "buy" an election through television. It should only be one of the tactics in your arsenal.

• **Telephone banks.** Volunteer telephoning is inexpensive and highly effective. Telephoning voters should be taking place from the beginning of early or absentee voting, all the way through election day. Voters who are called and indicate a preference FOR or UNDE-CIDED about your issue should be recontacted prior to election day.

• **Door-to-door.** This tactic is absolutely one of the best campaign tools. The personal touch, **especially by police officers who have a stake in the campaign,** convinces voters that you really need their support. Households where voters live should only be targeted for your door-to-door campaign—this approach requires a great deal of preplanning.

• **Other Campaign Tactics.** Some other activities that might be successful, depending on the number of association workers and its financial resources, include a Speaker's Bureau, press releases (cheap, but often of limited effect), bumper stickers, billboards, yard signs, and bus bench advertising.

Some Final Thoughts

The initiative and referendum is an excellent method to accomplish association goals that can't reached through more conventional means. Remember that most single-issue police referendums are con-troversial, and experience has shown that the election will usually be won or lost by a slim margin. The campaign must be geared toward getting one more "yes" than "no" vote through the application of prin-ciples discussed in this chapter.

Chapter 24

EVERYTHING YOU NEED TO KNOW ABOUT POLITICAL CONSULTANTS

The two previous chapters have looked at how a police association attempts to convince the public that the association's position on a particular issue is valid. It could be a pay referendum, manpower issue, tax rollback, civil service repeal, or collective bargaining vote. Your goal might be winning an election in a city the size of New York, or pressuring two city council members to change their vote. Regardless of the situation, your chances for a successful outcome become stronger if you have the proper political guidance from the beginning.

The need for political advice means hiring one or more political consultants to shape and direct your effort. It is axiomatic that law enforcement professionals tell civilians not to chase thieves, not to confront armed suspects, and not to take the law into their own hands. But all too often, when confronted with a political problem, those same officers will take off in hot pursuit of a potentially deadly issue without the least bit of political backup.

Consultant as a Generalist

The consultant you are most likely to have had some contact with in the past is the campaign manager/general consultant. These individuals are the jack-of-all-trades of the industry. It is a prized position in most campaigns, because a big part of the job description is acting as the gate keeper.

The general consultant assembles the entire campaign team, and suggests who the association should interview in connection with their particular problem. He or she also sets the basic guidelines for what kind of campaign should be run, and what constitutes a realistic fund-raising goal and campaign budget.

In a traditional candidate campaign, the general consultant plans overall strategy, directs message development, allocates resources, and works directly with the candidate. But in an issue campaign like the type that police association leaders will sometimes be running, it is more common for the general consultant to be what is called a **hyphenated consultant**. In other words, the lead consultant will most likely be a media-general consultant or polling-general consultant. Without a candidate to babysit, and a headquarters staff and volunteers to organize and direct, the generalist role in an issue campaign is a good place for one individual to fill two slots.

Media Is Still the Message

Since an issue campaign or referendum is mostly message, it's only natural for the **media consultant** to function in a dual role as general consultant. However, a media consultant's primary duty is to oversee the development of the campaign message.

This message or theme is a part of every communication effort your campaign has. This theme will be the foundation of the paid media, free media, and any speaking engagements that occur in connection with the campaign. It will, in fact, dictate the entire direction of your campaign. Only the budget has an equal impact on what you do to communicate with the voting public.

The media consultant must ruthlessly cull any extraneous ideas or slogans from the communications efforts, because these only distract voters and defeat campaigns. The hands-on portion of his or her part of the communication effort is writing and producing the radio, television, and print advertising. At the same time, the media consultant will direct the association spokesperson in the free press strategy (see below), and recommend other campaign specialists for your association to interview and possibly hire to join the effort.

The media consultant your association selects *absolutely* has to be able to take an issue that is important to your group as law enforcement professionals, and to put that issue in a context that is relevant to voters who may have a very different set of priorities. Otherwise, your campaign is guaranteed to fail.

Voter Contact: Retail Politics

While a media consultant's messages reach large numbers of voters simultaneously—in a wholesale fashion, the **voter contact specialist** touches voters on an individual basis through the use of direct mail, phone banks, or door-to-door canvassing.

A limited budget may dictate that mail is your association's only paid form of contact with the electorate. Or a larger budget can allow your group to use mail in a mix with electronic media to give your message an even greater impact. Either way, your voter contact consultant must be able to express the theme in each of the individual contacts with voters regardless of whether it's a brochure, a phone call, or knocking on a door.

Voter contact firms that operate in what can be best described as a one-stop, shopping operation will provide phone banks, targeted direct mail, recruitment of block captains for walking door-to-door and getting out the vote. In a campaign effort where money is at a premium, this type of operation may be all that your association can afford, and in the end, all your group might need to win the election.

Press: If Only Free Media Was

The newspapers and television stations may not charge you when they cover your press event, but your association must still work very hard to get them there in the first place, and must also make sure that the press leaves with the correct story. What's more, there is a big difference between standard public relations and political press relations. The most obvious difference is that at the end of the public relations campaign, the audience is not asked to vote, but at the end of a political campaign, the audience does vote.

The free press message is therefore very important to any issue campaign. As a matter of fact, it can be the single most important factor in determining the outcome of an issue campaign with a limited budget.

With so much at stake, it is crucial to have someone who knows what they are doing—a person with press contact responsibilities (i.e., called a **press secretary**). Since free press sometimes has to take the place of paid media, it is important for the press person to be capable of thinking visually and creatively, so as to generate maximum coverage. Although the press secretary must be creative, he or she must also be willing to stay in the background and let the designated members of the association be featured in the news coverage.

Finally, the press operation, regardless of the overall campaign budget, must be expressing the same theme that appears in the paid media and other voter contact methods.

Polling: The Pulse of the Electorate

The pollster provides research for the campaign that is vital to message development and election strategy. The **benchmark poll** is where the campaign begins. Here is where your association can determine the existing state of mind among the electorate. What are the voters supporting? What will they vote against? What messages will work to your association's benefit in the campaign? What attacks will you have to prepare to deflect?

The benchmark poll becomes the knowledge base upon which your group builds the rest of its issue campaign. The numbers here are used as a baseline to judge if your campaign is progressing according to plan, or falling behind.

Polls taken later on the campaign are called **tracking polls**. These are brief snapshots of the electorate that tell you about the association's message. Is the message working? Does it need to be adjusted? Does your association need to spend more money to gain greater voter penetration?

In addition, a polling firm may recommend that the campaign conduct **focus groups**. These are small groups of six to ten people who are interviewed as a group for one or two hours. In a focus group, the association can learn how voters discuss the issue. What language do they use? How deeply do they hold their issue positions? And can their minds be changed?

How Many Is Enough?

In a small issue campaign, the police association may hire only one or two political consultants, while a large referendum may have one of each type directing campaign efforts. How many, and what kind are determined by your campaign budget, the size of your electorate, and how strong the opposition is.

Hiring a Political Consultant–The Three "E's"

The best advice for hiring a potential political consultant is to follow the three "E's": Experience, Expertise, and Enthusiasm. If you hire one, or a group of consultants who qualify on all counts, your chances of success in your political campaign are greatly improved.

1. **Experience.** Everyone has to get experience somewhere, but the question for you is: Do you want it to be *your* campaign? There is nothing like working in political campaigns to give political experience. Corporate public relations is not political experience; teaching political science at the university isn't political experience; labor organizing isn't political experience; and covering the crime beat for the newspaper isn't political experience. The foregoing backgrounds can be useful when combined with political experience, but by themselves, these activities aren't as useful as political experience.

If your potential consultants all have over ten years as either heads or members of their current political consulting firms, that's great. But this fact should not automatically rule out the person who is just starting a new firm. Although the particular company may not have been in existence long, the principals could be veterans.

Or there could be a situation where a long-time administrative assistant to a congressman or local official decides to go out on his or her own as a general consultant. This person might not have a great deal of experience as a general consultant, but would have a wealth of political knowledge.

2. **Expertise.** There is a big difference between the consultant who has ten years of experience, and the individual who has one year of useful campaign experience that he or she has been using for the past ten years. Your potential consultant with ten years experience would likely have been learning something during each of those years, while the person with one year, ten times would be of less value. Whichever person you are considering, your goal is to discover that individual's skill level, and the ability to apply those skills in different political situations.

The best way to evaluate a consultant's expertise is to look at the person's work. Media consultants and voter contact specialists are prepared, even eager, to have you look at what they've done in the past, and to dazzle you with their footwork.

But keep your budget situation in mind as you examine their work. The fabulous commercials done for Senator So-and So's re-election campaign probably had a bigger production budget than you will be offering. And the spectacular four-color mail pieces may have a lot of impact, but if you can only afford black and white, can the consultant do equally effective work? Consultants accustomed to lavish budgets may suffer from creative constipation when asked to work with a smaller amount.

Another question to ask is: Does all the work look the same? If the consultant's style dominates the work to the extent that it interferes with communication, that's bad. Or if the spots all look or sound so similar that the only difference is the name of the candidate or committee, that's bad, too.

You want to avoid at all costs being caught in your media/mail consultant's rut. You deserve to have work created especially for you, not material already in the can that has been resuscitated for one more campaign.

Polling firms are something of an exception to the "showing samples" rule, and might have a problem when it comes to showing past, and probably confidential, work. When dealing with pollsters, you will have to judge them based on presentation and client references. There is a similar problem with general consultants—they have few work products, so you should ask to see a copy of the campaign plan for former clients and be energetic in following up on references.

With respect to *all* consultants, the police association should do some detective work. Check on the consultant's reputation, and whether it is good or not so good. This research should be done not only in your city, but other areas where the consultant has worked as well. Persons to talk to should include local newspaper reporters, political party officials, other clients, and political experts.

3. **Enthusiasm.** You may think that this term is out of place, and that the authors are reaching desperately for an "e" word that would fit. But in fact, you want a political consulting firm which views your account as important, and not as an "overhead" account, that is, an account which the firm is not excited about, but sees as payment of the monthly light bill.

You want your phone calls returned quickly. You want the work done for you to be original. And you want the advice and strategy suggestions you receive to be thoughtful and timely.

That's why you want to know how many other campaigns the consultant will be working on during the three to six months that your effort is peaking. If the consultant has ten statewide campaigns, four congressional elections, a big city mayor's race, and your issue, guess who will be at the bottom of the totem pole?

There are only so many hours in the day, and a consultant who is stretched thin doesn't do very good work. You deserve to have a reasonable share of the consultant's time, and shouldn't have to fight to get it! A firm with too many races is too busy for you.

Interviewing the Political Consultant

Your police association will be in the market for a political consultant whenever is it involved in a single issue campaign such as a pay referendum, manpower issue, tax rollback, civil service repeal, or collective bargaining vote. You can narrow the field to a manageable number of possibilities without ever seeing any of the consultants face-to face.

Your decisions can be based upon how professional the firm's proposal is, how interested they seem, and any preinterview research you do with the consultant's former clients. But eventually, it will necessary to schedule an interview, either in your city, or possibly in Washington, D.C. or New York City, where a large number of political consultants are located.

During the interview, all the potential consultants should be judged according to the three "E's" discussed above: Experience, Expertise, and Enthusiasm. With these guidelines in mind, you are ready to begin the interview process. Each firm deserves a reasonable amount of time to make their case. Anything less than one hour cheats them, and turns your meeting into a cattle call.

It helps to have a question list or meeting agenda so you can structure each session as equally as possible. Now you'd think of all possible groups in the United States, police officers would be the least likely to feel uncomfortable asking tough questions during an interview. But it does happen. Like most suspects who won't confess without you first asking a question, the majority of political consultants won't volunteer unfavorable information unless you ask.

So now that you know why asking questions is important, here are a few of the questions that should be asked, and more important, *answered* during an interview.

1. How long have you been working in politics?

2. How long have you been with this firm or had your own consulting business?

3. If the consultant has changed fields (e.g., gone from campaign managing to media consulting), why did he or she make the switch? (The ability to charge 15 percent commission on the media buy is *not* an acceptable answer).

4. If this campaign is the consultant's first political race, why should you be providing on-the-job training and paying for it to boot?

5. What races or campaigns in the past have you had that are similar to the police association's campaign, or would have given you experience that will be valuable in our situation?

6. Did you win that campaign? Or, if you lost, what did you learn?

7. Will you give us the names and telephone numbers of the principals in two winning campaigns and two losing campaigns for recommendations? (If he or she will not provide names, watch out!)

8. What samples of work do you have that are applicable to our campaign?

9. Exactly what was your role in the production of these samples?

10. How well known are you in your industry? Do you participate in professional organizations? Have you been a speaker at industry conferences?

11. How many campaigns will you be participating in during the next three to six months when the association will be the most active? Please include both candidate and noncandidate campaigns.

12. Of these active campaigns, which is the most important, or the largest?

13. Who will be the primary contact person in your firm for our campaign? If they aren't at the interview, why not?

14. Who will be doing the actual creative work on our campaign, if any? If they aren't at the interview, why not?

Coming to a Decision on Who to Hire

Once you get some answers, how do you know that you have the right ones? In many instances, you will have to trust your own instincts. Was the consultant forthcoming, or did he or she appear to be threatened by your questions? Did the consultant seem evasive, arrogant, or condescending during the interview? Is the consultant the type of individual you can trust and rely upon for the next few weeks or months?

These impressions are judgment calls. If you're lucky, someone on the association selection committee, or an advisor, may have had past campaign experience that will help you during the interview/evaluation process. The references that you obtained during the interview might possibly fill in any blanks you might have.

Finally, if you are still in a quandary, talk to other police associations about the candidates, or ask the other associations for references of qualified consultants who might be able to advise you on your choices.

Put It on Paper

Once you get answers that you like, make certain these answers stay to your liking throughout the campaign by having the political consultant put it in writing in a contract. Have the names of the client contact person and the creative person in the contract.

Also, ask the consultant to include anything else that you feel is important in the contract. If they refuse, find out why. If the reason is acceptable, fine. If not, then continue the interview process. It is better to take enough time to do it right the first time, than to try to find the time to do it over later.

Finally, don't make your search criteria too narrow. Hiring consultants who have only done your kind of campaign—pay raise referendums in cities between 100,000 and 250,000 in population occurring in the last quarter of an odd-numbered year, means that you are going to eliminate very good, creative consultants who have had similar, useful experience, but not the exact type of experience as your situation.

Chapter 25

OTHER CONFRONTATION PRESSURE POINTS–CHAMBERS OF COMMERCE

The public pressure tactics and referendums discussed in Chapters 22 and 23 aren't the only ways to go about achieving organizational goals. There are other pressure points in a community which can be pushed, squeezed, prodded, or otherwise brought to the aid of the police association's goals. For example, if the city management and political structure has been consistently inflexible in contract negotiations, and the prospects for improvement don't seem to good anytime in the future, then it's time to get city hall's attention with stout opposition to something important to the city: a sacred cow bond issue, a professional contract proposed to be awarded to one of the mayor's cronies, or serious questions about the amount of money the city throws into the annual "Octoberfest" or other yearly festival that comes to town.

This type of opposition is called **linkage**–after opposing one or a few of the government's pet projects (and hopefully, police association victories), someone at city hall will figure out that loosening the purse strings at the bargaining table might decrease your rabid attention to these seemingly extraneous issues. This and the next two chapters will examine three specific areas of linkage which can bear fruit for the police association–taking on your local Chamber of Commerce, opposing bond issues, and police chief no-confidence votes.

Chambers Often Go All Out Against
Police Association Initiatives

It seems to be standard operating procedure in many parts of the country for local Chambers of Commerce to attack referendum propositions being advanced by police associations. Three campaigns in the early 1990s where a Chamber lashed out against the police association were the Stockton, California police arbitration referendum; the Little Rock police/community groups' single-member district initiative; and the Bexar County, Texas collective bargaining referendum. Not coincidentally, all three propositions failed at the polls.

There's definitely something going on between Chambers of Commerce and public employers in various parts of the country! While Oliver Stone won't have enough material for a conspiracy movie on this subject, there clearly seems to be a collusive relationship between government officials and local Chambers of Commerce to oppose proposals made by local cops and deputies for improvement of rights and benefits.

This trend is alarming, particularly because many of the leaders of local Chambers of Commerce are the real movers and shakers in the community. For example, Executive Committee members on the Little Rock, Arkansas Chamber have in the past included the publisher of the only daily paper in the city, and the general manager of one of the local television stations. Your proposition is in *real* trouble when you've got the folks who control the media against you going into a fight!

What's really alarming about the tactics of some Chambers are the sleazy, low-ball campaign lies used to scare the voters: "taxes will skyrocket," "outsiders will come into our city," *ad nauseam.* And then after the election, a Chamber representative will often come forward with a pious statement like, "It's nothing personal, and we'd still like to be your friends."

It's ironic to watch how eager Chambers are for police associations to jump on the bandwagon whenever there is a major bond or tax referendum proposal that helps local businesses. But when the police association initiates a political campaign which helps its membership, the general Chamber reaction is often to spearhead the opposition.

Police Associations Must Take a New Approach

Police associations need to start turning up the heat on the fat cat business people who oppose their most important programs. If you don't start neutralizing the Chamber, your association will be behind the eight ball anytime you go into any public issue where there's stiff opposition from your employer. Government officials have deep roots in the business community, and a few well-placed telephone calls from the mayor, city manager, or a county commissioner can put your campaign into deep freeze quickly!

Here are a few things to remember about the people who make up the Chamber of Commerce. First, most Chamber members need the business patronage of your police officers and other citizens. And the Chamber leadership vigorously seeks your police association support when the business community wants those bond issues passed that are going to pump more money into the community through land deals, construction, special districts, etc. There are definitely vulnerable points in the Chamber of Commerce armor that can be exploited.

Here's Some Tips on How to Deal with Your Local Chamber

Your police association must take a more aggressive posture when dealing with the Chamber of Commerce; otherwise, your group and members will be the losers. Here's some tactics that police associations might consider to neutralize their local Chambers:

1. First and foremost, **JOIN THE CHAMBER!** This one act has several advantages. First, it allows you to communicate with movers and shakers who mold community opinions. It is much easier to go ask a group to support your position, or not oppose your position, when you are already a member of the group–**it's harder for people to oppose you when the issue is personalized!**

2. Another advantage to your Chamber membership is that the police association can then demand accountability from the Chamber leadership for who makes the decisions on Chamber public positions, and on whether the organization follows its internal rules on taking positions that affect the police. If the Chamber opposes a police association initiative on the basis of a telephone call from the mayor to the chamber president, you are entitled as a Chamber member to chal-

lenge both the Chamber president's conduct and the chamber's position. If you're on the outside looking in, you can't effectively challenge how the Chamber made its decision.

3. Look for financial relationships between the government and the Chamber. Use the Open Records Act to find out how much tax money is being funneled to the Chamber, and use your Chamber membership to find out how tax money is being spent once the Chamber gets a hold of it. If the financial relationship looks too cozy or out of line, make the relationship a public issue. Remember that the basic purpose of government is to provide essential public services—when the government becomes too involved in helping the business community make money, the relationship has become skewed.

4. Whenever the Chamber begins one of its let's-vote-for-that-deal-of-the-century-bond-issue campaign, take a look at who benefits from a "yes" vote. There's a better than fifty-fifty chance that there's all kinds of financial goodies in the bond package for the local movers and shakers: land sales; construction contracts; and sale of the bonds themselves. Make sure that the public knows about who's getting their pockets lined (more on this subject in the next chapter!)

5. *Before* you start a referendum campaign or other campaign that benefits your membership, go to the Chamber and line up support for your issue. If you wait until after your campaign begins, it's most likely too late! The government politicians will have already drummed up opposition in the business community. You should make a well-reasoned, accurately prepared presentation, and you should make it clear to Chamber members that as the protectors of the community, you *expect* the support of business people. Even if you can't line up the Chamber's support, you might at the very least be able to neutralize the organization and keep it from opposing you, which is almost as good an outcome.

6. When the Chamber conducts a lie-driven, political campaign against your police association proposition, then it is time to pull out all the stops. Always remember that some person or persons made the final decision to oppose you! First, you should find out who made the decision (Warning: Those who made the decision will try their hardest to evade responsibility—they don't want to be identified as the bad guys.) Then, you might select one or two of these people and consider an economic campaign against them. This campaign would involve identifying these business people as **antipolice**, and calling for a con-

sumer boycott of their business through billboards, flyers, and demonstrations in front of their businesses. While it might be too late for this campaign, the people opposing you won't be so eager to jump on the antipolice bandwagon in the next fight your association has with the city or county!

Chapter 26

OTHER CONFRONTATION PRESSURE POINTS - BOND ISSUES

When city hall or the county courthouse hires a battalion of bond lawyers, bond consultants, accountants, financial advisors, and economic development specialists, your police association had better get prepared. It is likely that these early signals point to a decision which will be clouded by more propaganda than fact—the city (or county) bond issue with a price tag in the tens or hundreds of millions of dollars.

The government decision to proceed with a bond issue will affect not only the interests of your police association, but all voters and tax-payers as well. That is why it is essential that you understand how bond issues work, and what the implications are for your organization.

What Are Bond Issues, and Why Should Police Associations Be Wary of Them?

Bond issues are nothing more than a community deciding whether or not to go into debt for something that it needs. This proposed debt could be for new streets, public buildings such as recreation centers or jails, a new museum, library, airport runway, fire fighting equipment, or even a tourist facility such as a convention hall.

Police associations, voters, and taxpayers should always be wary of proposed bond issues. The choice to issue bonds really involves many other choices which are often hidden, and seldom openly discussed with voters:

- Many facilities can be financed on a pay-as-you-go (or pay-as-you acquire) basis. This approach avoids millions of dollars in interest

166

payments which typically flow to out-of-community bond holders (i.e., the people who buy the city bonds). On the other hand, this approach requires "up-front" funds which must be set aside in a savings account to build the project when enough funds are accumulated.

• Facilities such as convention halls, sports stadiums, and other entertainment or tourism-related facilities are often portrayed to the voter as "economic growth" projects which will create jobs and increase incomes. Unfortunately, this scenario is too often not the case because of a flawed perception of how economic growth really occurs, and who pays for it. Watch out for "economic growth" slogans which promote stadiums, arenas, and convention halls.

• The political gurus at city hall will frequently entice the tax-resistant voter with a "sweetener" in a bond issue to capture votes for a marginally-justified bond issue.

Here is an example of the last point. In a 1991 Little Rock, Arkansas bond election, two-thirds of the city's largest bond proposal ever ($187 million over 20 years) was aimed at convention halls, stadiums, and arenas. Only one-third was devoted to police, streets, and housing improvements—the real needs of the citizens. And this bond issue was defeated primarily because the voters knew that they did not have to build an arena costing $42 million to get more cops in their neighborhood.

Be Skeptical of City Hall's "Experts"–Demand Independent Sources of Information

It should be recognized that when bond issues are on the table, the discussion immediately will be dominated by experts who suddenly appear at the mayor's side and sound awfully sure of themselves. Bond attorneys, financial consultants, accountants, and marketing experts (many of whom, by the way, do know their business and have sound advice to offer) all stand to pull down substantial fees if the bond issue is approved. These experts normally take a percentage of the bond issue as their fee, and the fees can run into the hundreds of thousands of dollars!

Here is one of the *first* questions an inquiring mind should ask: "How did city hall choose this *particular* bond attorney, bond brokerage house, or accountant?" It is amazing to discover the political ties between government officials pushing the bond issue, and the experts who are hired to give advice!

At this early stage, your police association should stand its ground and *demand* that the city employ a reputable, *independent* financial advisor who is not tied to a particular bond broker or other bond specialist who may have been taking the city staff to dinner, or making campaign contributions to political officials. This approach should be standard procedure for any city, and reputable financial advisors will be happy to compete on a competitive interview basis for the opportunity to assist the city. An interview board (including citizens, police association leaders, business people, labor officials, and others) perhaps ought to help select the financial consultant. This one step would involve a broader base of the community, and increase the credibility of later decisions to be made during the debate on the bond issue.

How Bond Projects Are Funded: General Obligation and Revenue Bonds

The city will most likely have a long list of projects that it wants to finance. An early question which deserves much attention is whether the projects ought to be financed with **general obligation bonds** or with **revenue bonds**. General obligation bonds are repaid with tax dollars, and taxes must normally be approved by voters in a special bond election. General obligation bonds are normally used when the projects have a clear and broad community benefit—new arterial streets or a new jail, for example.

Revenue bonds are better suited when it can be determined beforehand who will be the users of the needed facility. If the users are a narrow group of people and not the general public, then it seems logical that only the users should pay for the construction of the facility. For example, a college might build a new student union and pay off its construction bonds with a student fee. Or in the illustration of a stadium, ticket revenues paid by fans should pay the bonds instead of a city tax.

Revenue bonds are popular because they connect the cost of the project to those people who will use the project. Revenue bonds typically do not require a public vote. In almost all cases, however, revenues for tourism and entertainment projects are almost never enough to pay off the bonds. And this situation is when city hall will turn to the public and ask for additional general obligation bonds to also be approved.

Whenever City Hall Seeks General Obligation Bonds for So-called "Tourism" Projects, Put Your Wallet in a Safe Place!

Almost always, the appeal for the general obligation bond financing for stadiums, arenas, and convention centers will be advertised with "evidence" that new visitors will come to town, spend lots of money, create new jobs, and raise incomes as this "new" money circulates through the local economy. These claims are typically more propaganda than fact, except in those cities which are already identified as legitimate tourist destinations.

If your town wants to issue bonds for tourism, and thereby begin to compete with other established cities for the tourist dollar, valuable tax money is more than likely being wasted. The reason is simple, but bond lawyers and bond brokers usually don't care for voters and taxpayers to know about it: unless the bond promoters can produce solid evidence of visitors coming from outside of your economy area (probably at least beyond one hour drive time, or 50-60 miles away), then the project will not be generating any "new" money or create "new" jobs.

Ticket purchasers at an arena built under a bond program are *already* spending money in the local economy on groceries, clothing, pizza, and the rent. When tourism projects are promoted by bond specialists, they simply want to transfer some of this spending to spending on *their* tickets. The overall level of new money will *not* increase—it will simply be moved from one part of the local economy (e.g., household expenditures) to another part (tickets for entertainment on Friday or Saturday night).

Unless a solid competitive analysis of the tourism market for your town is thoroughly researched and conclusive, it is a mistake to blindly accept the claims about tourism and related projects. In the Little Rock example cited above, the promoters of a new arena costing $42 million, stadium expansion to the tune of $15 million, and convention hall expansion at a cost of $15 million, *never* produced any statistics which demonstrated that sport or music fans outside of 50 miles around Little Rock would be showing up to buy tickets.

The fact is that only the out-of-town money—the "new money," would have actually created new activity for Little Rock and the rest of central Arkansas. Otherwise (and more to the point of reality), the ticket buyers would only be of Little Rock and nearby residents (within 50 miles), whose money was already in the Little Rock economy.

Here's How a City Bond Project Can Really Hurt the Police Association's Interests

Bond projects for tourism can be lethal to city hall's financial structure! Let's go back to the Little Rock example one more time. Although the voters wisely rejected the bond issue in October, 1991, if the bond promoters had triumphed, $16 million per year from an *existing* city sales tax would have been tied up for at least eight years to pay off the bonds. Out of the $128 million devoted to these projects, $44 million would have been devoted to interest payments alone!

So the bottom line is this: if the proposition had passed, $128 million of tax money would have been tied up on projects which were of dubious validity. Think about how this money could otherwise be applied in Little Rock *or in your community* to spending needs of much greater priority: more police on the street, additional funds for fighting drug enforcement and DWI, and of course, additional monies available for much needed wage and benefit improvements!

And when suspect bond issues are rejected, then more needed programs can work their way to the top priorities in city budgets where they should have been in the first place. It is fascinating that during the Little Rock bond campaign, city hall claimed that there could be no increase in police personnel unless the bond issue was approved. And after the defeat of the bond issue in 1991, the city in fact added 30 new police officers to the Little Rock Police Department. How quickly priorities can change!

How Your Police Association Can Defeat a City Bond Issue

If your group is faced with bond issue proposal that lacks merit, you should go all out to defeat the proposition! Here some suggestions for things you can do:

• Remember that the voters are skeptical of any issue that involves tax increases and increased spending. You are going in with a built-in advantage. Most bond issues fail when there is strong opposition.

• Don't oppose the bond issue without building an opposition coalition with other community groups. There are normally many other organizations which will agree with your position against the proposition—taxpayers associations, homeowners groups, minority organizations which feel they are not getting enough out of city services as it is —the list goes on and on.

• Make certain that you are armed with **facts**. Don't make half-baked accusations that won't hold up in the light of day.

• Conduct an aggressive political campaign against the bond issue. Since the police association normally has a high degree of credibility in the community, and there is built-in skepticism toward the bond issue, a high-visibility campaign, **with the Police Association as one of the leaders of the charge**, has a great prospect for victory.

The lesson is clear—when armed with the facts and coupled with determined political action, the voters will speak clearly about what they want, and how they want to pay for it.

Chapter 27

OTHER CONFRONTATION POINTS–
POLICE CHIEF NO CONFIDENCE VOTES

Police associations sometimes use a "no confidence vote" on their police chief as a confrontation tactic. Some of these votes are successful, and others are dismal failures. More often than not, the association announces a no confidence vote, the media covers it for one-day, and the chief survives another day to continue whatever policies or practices caused the vote in the first place.

Like any other tactic in the fight to build power, the no confidence vote should be just one of the tools in your arsenal. Remember that it is always easier to block the hiring of a particularly bad chief than it is to get rid of one after he or she is sitting in the big corner office on the top floor of headquarters. However, it is normally difficult for an association to block the appointment of a chief.

Therefore, if the association has to deal with a chief who consistently acts against the interests of your association and members, and no common ground can be found between the chief and association, then set out below are some pointers on using the no confidence vote to weaken or topple the police chief.

It should be *strongly* emphasized that these steps should only be taken after the association has taken every possible step to reach common ground with the chief. A no confidence vote is controversial among association members, the media, and politicians; all of whom will be feeling and/or expressing discomfort over the association's action. If your group doesn't go about a no confidence vote deliberately and systematically, there will be enormous backlash and the end result will likely be a no confidence vote against the association!

1. **There is no one knockout blow.** If the police association can topple the chief with a simple no confidence vote alone, the chief is already packing his or her bags. The association needs to outline an overall strategy that includes any number of tactics designed to weaken or topple the chief. The no confidence vote should be the icing on the cake and not the grand finale. Remember, the association must have all of its ducks in a row before starting a no confidence vote.

2. **Do your homework on the chief.** In their haste to satisfy an angry membership, too many police associations fail to do their homework. The association should have a file on the chief that includes his or her work history, accomplishments, failures, and publicity. Out-of-town chiefs come and to your department with a clean media slate. Call or visit the chief's prior departments and make copies of his or her press file. Many police chiefs come to your town because they were run off at their prior departments. A past history of confrontation with the officers and/or association should be exposed.

3. **Polling the membership.** There are several ways to determine the degree of unhappiness and the commitment to doing something about it. One of the most effective methods is to hire a local college professor to conduct the poll. This "independent" academic expert gives the poll credibility. The professor can also attend the press conference and/or council meeting and explain the poll's accuracy. If you announce the "conducting" of the poll beforehand, you can get media coverage for several days in advance of the poll results. The poll should ask about the specific concerns officers have about the department and the chief's conduct and leadership capacity, and if each member is willing to commit his or her time and money to the fight. Without a commitment by the members, you may not want to pick a fight with the chief.

4. **Know what public thinks.** It is surprising how many police associations attack the chief without having the slightest idea of what the public thinks about the chief's performance. Whether you drive an old patrol car, miss lunch breaks, have to work rotating shifts, or have poor equipment is of little or no concern to the public. Conduct a legitimate poll using a political consultant to determine what the public thinks about the police department, the chief, and the officers. If the public has a high anxiety about crime and safety issues, whom do they hold responsible? If the association does not have a high favorability rating with the public, the association's negative attacks on the chief

will backfire. The higher the favorability rating of the association, the more negative the association can be in attacking the chief.

5. **Don't publicize the internal reasons for dissent.** All disputes with a chief include both internal and external reasons. The internal reasons include unfair or excessive discipline, biased promotions, lack of support for officers after shootings, or poor management practices. The minute the police association publicizes the real reasons for the anger among the rank and file, the media and the chief will put their spin on the confrontation. The media will tag the association as "whiners," "disgruntled," "good ole boys," "racists," or "obstructionists."

6. **Publicize only the external reasons for dissent.** The key to winning a no confidence vote is to focus the "message" on the reasons the public should be concerned about the chief's performance, not the internal reasons motivating the rank and file. Poor response times, high crime rates, fear of crime, anxiety about the safety of their children, misuse of tax dollars, political favoritism, out-of-town trips, and lack of commitment to the community are all issues the public cares about and will be responsive to the association's no confidence vote. Remember that you will never win this particular fight without getting the public indignant over the chief's conduct.

7. **Use paid media for payoffs.** Deliver the association's message with paid media. On the day of the press conference to announce results of the no confidence vote, run radio spots that track the message. (Example: chief is spending so much time on the road consulting for other departments that his face is on a milk carton as a missing person.) If possible, buy a large advertisement that "briefly" states the external reasons the officers (not the association) have no confidence in the chief. Use a professional to design the ad.

8. **Be prepared for management spin control.** In politics, spin control is what your opponent says to "spin" your message into something less harmful to them. Police chiefs are political animals appointed by more politically-aware animals. The chief or his/her surrogates will put spin control on the no confidence vote. For example, if the chief is a minority, the association leaders will be characterized as a bunch of racists. If the chief is a woman, the association leaders become sexist. If the officers are upset over discipline, the association is protecting bad apples. It is guaranteed that all "New Age" police chiefs (i.e., super politically correct) support community policing, and therefore have some key support throughout the city. A chief under

assault by a no confidence vote will immediately start meeting with the community–citizens and leaders, to build support his or here cause.

9. **Be prepared for backlash from members.** Before the association starts preparing the no confidence vote, the leaders should meet with other groups within the department and determine how they feel about attacking the chief. Female and ethnic organizations may have a different perspective about the chief. Supervisors will often break ranks and support the chief. Remember that nothing undermines a no confidence vote more than to have scores of officers holding a "support the chief" press conference!

10. **Be prepared for a long struggle.** Remember Rule No. 1– "There is no one knockout blow!" Develop a long-term strategy and stay the course. Efforts to oust the chief can drag on for months, and sometimes even years. Keep the pressure on the chief. If you let up, he or she will get their breath and reestablish his/her position with the politicians and the public. Change tactics constantly. A tactic that drags on too long gets boring. Remember the old adage, "if you are going to kill the king, you had better kill the king."

Chapter 28

THE DOWNSIDE OF DEMOCRACY: THE POLICE ASSOCIATION CAN LOSE

Winning is over-emphasized. The only time it is really important is in surgery and war.

–Al McGuire

In the chapters on politics and confrontation, you have been given a wide variety of tools, techniques, and ideas that can be used to increase your police association's impact in the political arena. You can vary the application of your political power, giving one candidate a simple endorsement and permission to use the association name, while another one gets a donation and volunteers. Or you can jump head first into an initiative and referendum campaign to improve wages, increase staffing levels, or achieve some form of employee rights. Or you can take on the Chamber of Commerce, a bond election, of the police chief.

But anytime that there's an election (read: battle), there will be a winner, and unfortunately, a loser. And the odds are 50 percent that your association and you will have grim faces after the final votes are in on election night.

What Happens When the Association Comes Out on the Short End of the Election Stick?

Everything goes along swimmingly until election day approaches, when the possibility of losing starts to give you indigestion. So what happens if a candidate or proposition loses? Is that the end of the police association as you know it?

Probably not, since in many police associations the membership isn't keeping a box score with political winners and losers. Politics is still beneath many police officers, and they think that if you want to mess around with politicians, then you need to wear rubber gloves.

A loss will mean more to an association membership that has never endorsed or been involved in a referendum campaign before, and wasn't entirely sold on the idea in the first place. In one mountain state, an association board of directors endorsed a mayoral candidate without consulting the membership, and when their candidate lost in one of the truly surprising upsets in American politics, the membership voted them out.

The big mistake that the board of directors made was bypassing the members, but even then their jobs might have been saved if they had endorsed a number of council candidates too, and done better in those races. Then they could use statistics to show a certain percentage winning record in council candidate endorsements (*"There are three kinds of lies: lies, damned lies, and statistics."*–Benjamin Disreali).

Now you know why incumbents get all the endorsements! Still, if the police association educates the membership about the risks of endorsing or proceeding with a referendum, and that even a loss can send a message, the chances of weathering defeat are greatly increased.

The Worst Kind of Loss–the Benefits, Rights, or Working Condition Issue

But what if you happen to lose an election that is much closer to home, say for improving pay, increasing staffing levels, or deflecting a civil service repeal. Now that's a fish of an entirely different color. Here the results have a direct bearing on the police association. The message that members often take home from this kind of defeat is that not only have they lost the issue, but that the public is a bunch of ungrateful pissants, and that there won't be a whole lot of warning tickets given out any time soon.

For police association leadership, this kind of reaction means that morale for the foreseeable future is shot. In one association in the Southwest, the loss of a civil service election meant that turnout for political events dropped from 180 volunteers to put up yard signs to 2 volunteers in the next council race. Attendance at the regular association meeting plummeted, and you could cut the depression at the police department with a knife.

How do you avoid this postelection despondency? The easiest way, of course, is to not tackle this kind of election in the first place, but then you'll never be in control of your fate. A better way is to explain to the membership before they enter the election fray is that they can lose, and if that should happen, the members should view the setback the same way the Corrleones did in "The Godfather": "Nothing personal —it's just business."

If the police association leaders have done a good job of handicapping the election and explaining that there might be a loss, the letdown won't be so severe. If your issue came very close to a victory, it may be almost as good as a win, since the city may be eager to compromise and avoid a loss in the future.

If you got your clocked cleaned in the election, the leadership didn't do its job! You embarked on an election you couldn't win, and the membership has a right to be angry.

What Happens After the Police Association Loses A Single-Issue Referendum?

What do you do after you have lost one of those life-or-death election campaigns over a benefit, rights, or working condition issue? The first thing is to explain to the membership what the association intends to do to regain some political power. The members' fear of their group becoming irrelevant will often paralyze them—they go into a kind of collective fetal position.

Also, analyze the election results and decide what kind of argument or organization made the difference. If the Homeowner's Association beat you, then explain to its members the downside of having a crippled police department. If it's the Chamber of Commerce, set out to neutralize the group by having your leaders join. Then you can get into the inner workings of the Chamber and try to hijack the controls of the organization. If you can't do that, then you will at least become real people to the Chamber leaders, and not a faceless lump of police officers who just want more tax dollars.

This kind of community missionary work is extremely slow, and the results often are difficult to measure. But it has the virtue of paying off in the here-and-now, rather than after you're dead!

Finally, if you can't convince the membership to do anything, and they just want to hide under a rock after a loss, then tell them they're a bunch of weenies! Explain to these rough and tough "po-leece" officers that if they had acted this way the first time they got roughed up or lost a street fight, they wouldn't be cops now—they'd be hairdressers.

Getting beat is a part of life. Winning is getting up after you've been knocked down and trying again.

Part V

POLICE ASSOCIATIONS AND THE NEWS MEDIA

Chapter 29

THE IMPORTANCE OF GOOD POLICE ASSOCIATION - MEDIA RELATIONS

Running a police association isn't an easy task. You're responsible for keeping the members happy and the management folks at bay. When someone comes to you with the bright idea about maintaining good media relationships, it just seems like another drain on your time without a tangible payoff.

So when you ask, "Why bother?", here is a very simple answer: the media owns the printing presses and the radio/TV stations, and you don't. If you have a story to tell or a response to deliver, the media is going to do the delivering.

Press Purgatory–A Place Your Police Association Doesn't Want to Be

There is a cardinal rule in association-media relations that stresses the importance of keeping the relationship positive: **Never get in a fight with someone who buys ink by the barrel!** A poisonous relationship results in fatal coverage for your organization. And don't make the mistake of thinking that when a certain reporter leaves, that your problems are over.

News organizations have institutional memories, and like most people, the institution remembers the bad and forgets the good. While a certain reporter is there who is constantly bad-mouthing your organization, this negative perception can infect the media's management structure, and it will linger with whomever is selected to replace the problem reporter who has moved on down the road.

You can become a problem area when reporters are thoughtfully warned about your association before they do the first story. Then all you have to do is give their preconceived notions of your intransigence a little encouragement, and you're back where you were with the old reporter. It's instant, hostile coverage, and it only took a little effort on your part.

What hostile coverage means is that you never get the benefit of the doubt. When reporters are uncertain, they naturally assume that you are lying or engaged in a cover-up. Your statements are never trusted, and they always try to find someone to contradict you. Any time you oppose someone who has better relations–the mayor or police chief, for instance, you are not viewed as a credible source. This situation is press purgatory for you, and for the members you represent.

Let's say that you don't want hostile coverage, or if you've got it, you'd like to change coverage for the better. The first step is to put one individual in charge of your association press effort. Ideally, that person should be the president, but if there are too many demands on your time, then select a board member who reports to you and makes press relations his or her number one job.

Another option is to hire a professional public relations consultant. But to be effective, the consultant needs a contact person within the organization who can say yes or no, and sign off on projects.

The First Step–Find Out Who Is Covering You

The first step in good media relations is to discover who the association deals with in the media, and then make a list. This effort will involve some research, but fortunately, police are trained investigators.

Starting with the newspapers, find out who is assigned to the police beat. If there's a primary reporter, who covers during vacations? Where newspapers don't have a police beat, find out how assignments are made. If they're made on a rotating basis, do you have a relationship with the city editor or assistant editor who will be assigning reporters? You also need to know whether the paper has a local columnist who covers law enforcement issues.

Find out about the newspaper editorial board. Is it generally pro or anti-police? Is there a member of the board who specializes in that kind of editorial? If so, and the member is one who is not necessarily controlled by the Conservative Thought Police, can you develop a relationship with that person? If no one specializes now, can you interest one of them to specialize in police editorials?

There are fewer instances of beat reporters in the electronic media. That's because broadcast outlets come equipped with a revolving door outside the personnel department that turns so rapidly that, if attached to a generator, the stations would no longer need to rely on utilities to supply power. Additionally, most in-depth local law enforcement coverage consists of extreme closeup bloodstained footage, and even then you get potluck in who arrives to cover the story.

Television assignment editors make the calls on what gets covered, and who is sent to cover the story. Developing a relationship with these editors can be very helpful. Some stations have local interview shows or regular longer news segments. Find out who does the booking for the show, and talk to them rather than the show personality.

Radio suffers from a combination of high turnover and low staffing. Here again, look to the assignment editors. Talk radio always has locally-oriented shows, and sometimes has more than one. Find out which shows would best showcase the police association message, and work toward a spot on that program.

What Stories Are the Media Reporting?

Before deciding how to cultivate the media, you have to evaluate the job the police department or city hall are doing. This evaluation will determine if you're going to supplement what is being done, or compete with it. If the police department has a good image and the media coverage is favorable, then your association can concentrate on labor and organizational viewpoint stories to supplement existing coverage.

Your job is much harder if, because the police department isn't doing its job, you have to do general law enforcement public relations as well as labor public relations. In this instance, you must bolster the general media view toward law enforcement before, and then along with, the slant towards your police association.

There's Gold in Them Thar' Hills if You Cultivate a Good Relationship with the Media

There is clearly a payoff for any police association that takes the time to work on a positive media relationship. Some police departments have successfully established a media relations council where representatives of local newspapers and broadcast outlets met with department officials to discuss media coverage, and how both the media and department can do a better job in providing and covering events. This council made the police departments more open in their information, and the media more even-handed in its coverage.

Don't expect to bat a thousand every time that you deal with the media. Unless it's in your association newsletter, you'll never be completely happy with a story. Even a generally favorable story will have a quote or an opinion you don't like. Your goal is an overall positive coverage environment, and in that environment, there will some bad with the good. When the inevitable bad coverage comes, don't take it personally.

Remember that a reporter is a communications tool. You don't hate the telephone after you get a bad phone call, and you can't afford to disconnect the press. It's fine to reward your friends with tips, but don't count on punishing those you view as hostile.

Police associations can have a positive relationship with the media. And the result can only be more positive coverage for the association.

Chapter 30

GIVING GOOD NEWS CONFERENCE–
GET THE MESSAGE RIGHT

In law enforcement, it is pretty much a given that unless you come in as chief, you will have to make an arrest sooner or later in order to be successful. The same thing applies to news conferences and good media relations–it's very difficult to have one without the other.

Holding a successful news conference isn't rocket science, and it shouldn't be limited to large police associations. It is something any association can do without outside help, but only when leaders are willing to devote the considerable time necessary to do the ground work to identify the message, identify the targets for the message, and make adequate preparation to deliver the message.

News conferences are like a communications minuet. The media and your association do this little formalized dance routine, with a lot of insincere bowing and curtsying, and hope that after it's all over, no feet were stepped on, and that your partner won't gossip and say bad things behind your back.

However, you can reduce the chance for a news conference catastrophe with a little preparation. And at the same time, you can greatly increase your chance for generating favorable news coverage.

What Is the Message Going to Be at Your News Conference?

The first thing that must be determined is: what is the message going to be at the police association news conference? What do you want the public and the opposition, if any, to know after the news conference is complete? What do you want reporters to leave the event thinking

187

about? If the police association doesn't have a one paragraph answer to this question, then there is no reason to hold a news event!

Your message needs a clear statement with facts—numbers, graphs, and flip charts to support your main statement. For example: Center City voters need to approve the minimum staffing referendum that will add sixty-four officers to the force because it will reduce response times by three minutes and make the entire city 25 percent safer from crime.

Your message should never, ever be a whine session where the association representatives gripe about how bad the mayor, city council, county commissioners, governor, or Judge Wapner are treating the police. If you go down this path, you'll lose credibility with your audience quickly, and the whole purpose of the news conference will be lost.

The message should be clear and simple, and told from the point of view of the public. It is not an inside-the-force laundry list of wants, goals, and aspirations of the police association. If you're preaching to the choir, then you are wasting the media's and your own time!

Is the Message You're Communicating Important?

Here is the bottom line when it comes to getting covered by the media: if your message doesn't have one of the "Six Cs"—conflict, controversy, change, contrast, confounding preconceived notions, or celebrations, then you just aren't going to get the "Biggest C"—coverage! The reason is that you are competing with many other people and groups over a finite resource—the media's time.

In any major city, there can be up to ten news conferences per day, all competing for the media's attention. In Washington D.C., where hot air is the most important product, there can be over twenty news events daily. So if your message doesn't measure up in importance and impact to what other groups are trying to get covered, then you will be ignored.

That's why any news conference, and the preceding media advisory had better have one the "Six Cs." The press eats up any kind of news that sells well to the public, and that means something which is disturbing, exciting, sensational, or involves groups or people having some kind of friction.

At the Press Conference, Remember to Answer the Most Important Question: Why Are We Here?

Without a clear message, your conference is a muddle, and there is literally no telling what the media may decide to write (assuming that they even show up!). The lack of a clear message makes for a dangerous, uncontrolled situation, and your police association runs the risk of looking like a bunch of unprepared, naive amateurs.

Your message must be succinct, and easily contained in a single paragraph. Here's a great example:

> The City Council's priorities are out of whack! Spending $100 million for a baseball stadium, instead of hiring 250 more police officers to fight the wave of gang violence, is short-sighted. No one is going to a baseball game if they have to shoot their way into the stadium.

Now that's a message. And it should be distinguished from whining. Whining is not a message, and should be avoided at all costs!

Once you have the message, do not deviate from it. In the example above, talk about wasting money on the stadium, gang crime, and what the extra officers will do. Don't discuss residency requirements, the pension dispute, raising taxes to pay for the cops, Rodney King, or the price of rice. **None of these subjects advances your agenda, so don't talk about them!**

Also, a press conference isn't a polygraph test, so you don't have to answer all the questions. It's your party, and you'll dodge if you want to.

Chapter 31

GIVING GOOD NEWS CONFERENCE–
LOGISTICAL CONSIDERATIONS

There are a number of factors which can make the difference between a spectacular success and a dud. These factors include maximizing your coverage, getting the word out, and preparing for the event.

Think of Ways to Maximize Your Coverage

There are scheduling techniques that can be utilized to increase the chances of coverage. Monday and Tuesday are traditionally slower news days with fewer competing events. Saturday is also very slow, and getting coverage then will put the event in the Sunday paper, which is the most read edition of the week. But the trade-off on Saturday-Sunday coverage is that news crews are short-handed on the weekend, and it takes a whole lot of selling to get any media to materialize at the police association event.

Choosing the right location can also make it easier to gain coverage. Many cities have a standard location where all the talking-head news conferences take place. The location is usually convenient for the media and accustomed to catering to reporters.

If you don't know of such a location, make a few calls. Contact the public relations head of a large local company, utility, or charity, and find out where they hold news conferences. In a pinch, and assuming you can get in, hold your event where the chief holds his news conferences.

Imagery can really add to a news conference, so sometimes the location can make a visual statement that supports your message. Going back to our staffing election, you could schedule the event under a large clock to emphasize response times.

Some of the best uses of location to make a point in the news conference were used during the 1992 fight between Time Warner and police associations from around the country over the Ice-T song "Cop Killer." When the Combined Law Enforcement Associations of Texas held the initial press conference that caught the nation's attention, it was held immediately adjacent to Time Warner-owned Six Flags Over Texas in order to emphasize the contrast between Time Warner's public image as a "family values" corporation, and its involvement in a song promoting the death of police officers. A few weeks later, the Arkansas Fraternal Order of Police held a similar news conference with more than thirty police officers standing under a huge movie marquee in Little Rock advertising Time Warner's latest "Batman" film.

These locations made a powerful connection between Time Warner and the rage of America's police officers, and must have made a pretty big impression on one of America's largest corporations. The "Cop Killer" record was withdrawn from production soon after these (and other) press events, and Ice-T's contract with the company was later canceled. (AUTHORS' NOTE: See Chapter 41 for the full story of the Time Warner conflict.)

Getting the Word Out

There used to be a radio station billboard just outside Norman, Oklahoma on I-35 which read: "To sell 'em, tell 'em." And that's good advice for news conference organizers too!

Before reporters will appear at your event, they have to know about it. A few days before the event, you should send a written **media advisory** to assignment editors at broadcast outlets and city or metropolitan editors at newspapers.

The media advisory is a very simple fact sheet regarding the event. It has a list of headlines which should read: Event, Time, Place, Speakers, Organization, and Background. Beneath each headline is a brief summary that gives details. This advisory is not a press release, it is only an invitation.

This advisory should be sent to every news organization in your area, along with the Associated Press and the PR Newswire. Some media experts recommend six days prior notice, which is certainly fine for noncontroversial events, but if you're getting ready to attack the mayor, then you shouldn't give the opposition too much time to anticipate your event.

Once the advisory is sent, make follow-up calls on the day of the event. The call consists of asking if the editor received the event, and if there are any additional questions. Don't annoy the editor by asking if someone will come...that's considered bush league.

One special case is the weekend event. You send the advisory early in the week to get in the media event file, but you should then fax it again on Saturday morning about 8:00 AM and make your follow-up call an hour later. That's because the weekend assignment editor is different from the editor who received the release during the week.

By the way, faxing is a great way to distribute all your advisories. It's more immediate than the mail, and less expensive than Federal Express.

Be Your Own Best Advocate

You must be willing to sell the press conference and sell your message. If you aren't enthusiastic about the subject, why should the media be? If the press calls asking what the press conference is about (after you've already sent them a fax telling just that!), this moment is your chance to make this media event rival the Second Coming in coverage priority.

Make it sound important, make it newsworthy, and tell them that the competition has already called and plans to be there. If you act embarrassed, or hem and haw about the event, you will have single-handedly cut down on media interest and attendance.

There are a lot of folks who want the press at their events. They may be holding a press conference at the same time you are. If the competing event is run by people who are more alert and better sales people, that's where the press will be.

Press Conferences Shouldn't Be Secrets

It is a good idea to include a map of how to get to the event. The organizers of some press conferences have been disappointed about how few members of the press appeared, only to find out later that other stations were there, but couldn't find the location.

The day before the event, you should call and ask the press contacts if they need any more details regarding the event. Put the hard sell on the assignment editor. Create a sense of urgency.

On the day of the event, expect some of the media to be late. They are normally on the run from one event to another, and they often can't make it to your press conference on time. In this instance, be gracious and do the whole event over if necessary. It is important to remember that you need them more than they need you!

And Finally, Remember These Other Logistical Considerations

If you have an indoor event, choose the room to fit the expected crowd. A room that's too small is better than one that is too large. If it's in a hotel or conference facility, post a notice in the lobby giving directions to your event. Locate electrical outlets for broadcast media, phones for newspaper reporters, and have a sign-in sheet for reporters so you'll know who to contact for follow-up.

Make a press kit available for each reporter who attends. The kit will contain a formal press release, a biography and photos of speakers, a fact sheet regarding your message of the day, a background sheet on the news environment surrounding the message, any newspaper clips that are germane, a fact sheet on the police association, and calling cards of association contacts.

Before your police association holds a press event, find out who is covering police and law enforcement issues. Ask yourself about the coverage climate: Is it hot? Cold? Indifferent?

Chapter 32

GIVING GOOD NEWS CONFERENCE–
SELECTING THE RIGHT SPOKESPERSON

Everyone is familiar with the importance of the will to win. But the will to win is nothing without the will to prepare. Every police association wants a successful news conference, but only the associations that prepare will have one.

The most important task is choosing and preparing a good spokesperson. This individual must be able to deal comfortably with hostile questioning, and must be able to think on his or her feet. It is deadly to plant the police association president behind the podium where he reads an announcement verbatim, and then leaves.

It would be wise to spend a few hundred dollars of association money on a media trainer for your spokesperson. This money will be a great investment, because it will pay off in more successful communication.

The spokesperson must always be prepped for the event. Hold a practice news conference where potential questions are asked. Help the spokesperson formulate brief but clear answers to every question you can dream up. If possible, make the answers snappy sound bites.

This exercise is just like an attorney who coaches witnesses, and will definitely pay off on the day of the event. A well-prepared spokesperson is one who will make few mistakes. While reporters don't issue Miranda warnings, it is guaranteed that anything the spokesperson says can and will be used against your police association in the court of public opinion.

The spokesperson should anticipate tough questions, but evade questions which have nothing to do with your message. If your news conference has to do with a minimum staffing referendum, and a reporter wants to know your opinion on a recent police brutality allegation, don't answer. A response to an unrelated matter is called **stepping on your message**, because your answer on the brutality question will become the story.

Instead, the spokesperson should say that the brutality question is outside the scope of what's being discussed today, and that it's not proper to comment on a matter which is currently under investigation by internal affairs. The same response goes for any other questions from reporters that are a distraction from your message of the day.

The perfect example of stepping on your message was provided by President Bill Clinton in the first year of his administration. Earlier in that year, the message was the importance of the economic stimulus package, but all the administration was able to talk about was homosexuals in the military. As a result, the economic stimulus package got lost in all the media clutter.

Program the Spokesperson

Police associations occasionally need someone other than one of their own to be the front man or woman for the event. This person could be the citizen Chairman of the Staffing Level Referendum Committee, or a person with a telegenic smile and smooth speaking style hired specifically to deliver your police association messages. There is nothing wrong with this eventuality, so long as the spokesperson is firmly under your thumb.

Cops can be amazingly passive away from the job. For some reason, they are reluctant to get a commitment or set the ground rules when outside spokespersons are used. This passive approach can be fatal in a press event. Your outside spokesperson must agree to meet with you before the event to hold a mock press conference to prepare answers; he or she must agree to follow your message script exactly; and they must know when to shut up.

If the potential spokesperson won't agree to all of these conditions, then find someone else, or do it yourself. There is nothing worse than having a police association press conference turn into fiasco because of some embarrassing misstatements by your press representative.

The Spokesperson Should Never Wait for the Magic Question

As a part of your news conference, the spokesperson may have important facts to announce that support your message. Ideally, a reporter will ask a question that allows the information to come up naturally. But if that question isn't asked, use another question and make the facts part of the answer.

The Press Conference Graveyard is full of spokespersons who failed to discuss one really important part of the message at a news conference because they weren't asked the question they expected. Don't let this misfortune happen to you! And the converse is that if you're asked a question you can't answer, just say so but promise to get answer before the reporter's deadline; then stick to your promise.

When the formal news conference ends, have enough time available for one-on-one interviews with broadcast reporters if they request one. Have the association photographer make some black and white photos for any weekly newspapers which did not attend. And make sure to call any radio stations which failed to show and ask if they want a telephone interview.

Once the Press Conference Begins, the Spokesperson Should...

Start out by stating the message clearly and concisely. As a general rule, you should begin by gearing your message to the electronic media first–they are generally looking for capsulized versions of the story which can be compressed into a 30-60 second piece on the six o'clock news. Particularly work toward concise, attention-getting sound bites which will more than likely get an attentive ear from the newsroom editor: "In all my years of representing the police association, the firing of this fine police officer is the worst instance of injustice ever committed by the department's command staff!"

You should use examples and facts to elaborate on your message. These examples and facts are particularly helpful to the print media, and you should plan to stay around at the close of the formal press conference for any additional information that the print media might need.

At the end of your statement, *always* allow time for questions from the press. Otherwise, it looks like you're trying to hide something. And the important thing is to keep coming back to your message during the question period. In other words, there's nothing wrong with being a broken record.

Finally, always keep in mind that you don't ever want to needlessly antagonize the media. They can, and will, outlast you.

Chapter 33

HOW TO DEAL WITH CRISIS COMMUNICATIONS

Now we will look at the issue of crisis communications. Every organization that deals with the public needs a plan for crisis communication. And that goes double for any group that issues and uses bullets. And the police association can face any number of crises: an officer charged with excessive force (ala Rodney King), an internal conflict among leaders or members, a rival organization raid, a wildcat slowdown over a contract dispute...any scenario is possible in this business!

There are three main components to any news media crisis plan: who does the talking, when to talk, and what should be said. It goes without saying that it's better to answer these questions weeks before they come up, rather than seconds before a press conference.

Who Does the Talking?

It is strongly suggested that the association president be responsible for press relations during a crisis. The president is the chief executive officer of the association, and the press wants to hear from the top during a crisis.

This approach means that the president, and *only* the president speaks to the press during a crisis. There is absolutely no room for mistakes in this situation; and the press is known for pouncing on any gaffes. The more people who are talking, the greater the chance for confusion, and an increased chance of a public relations disaster.

If the association president isn't comfortable speaking with the press, then send him or her to a media coach. A media coach is a sensible investment—part of the president's job is representing the members, and if the president can't function in front of the media, then the members are being cheated. Even worse, your message won't be effectively communicated.

When dealing with the press in a crisis, remember to be human. You don't have to be perfect—that's what the chief of police is for! Do the best you can and let the media know that you don't view yourself as infallible. Also, display some personality—a lifeless communicator usually means a lifeless message.

You should always make an effort to know whom you're dealing with at a crisis press conference. You should have already done your homework by now—you know who are the saints, and who are the snakes. Be especially cautious in this situation when dealing with a reporter known to be hostile.

When You Should Talk

If you want your views represented in the media, you have to talk. Just because you don't choose to comment, however, doesn't mean that the story won't run. The story will run, but the only consequence will be that it won't have your point of view. So while the American Civil Liberties Union or police chief is putting a harmful interpretation on the day's crisis event, your members will be voiceless. Mum is the word only for people and groups who aren't subject to approval ratings!

In responding to a media crisis, speed is of the essence. If you can't get it together and respond before the deadline, your chance to influence that story just went down the drain. **You can't stall in a crisis.** Realistically, you have until late afternoon to get an answer ready; otherwise, it's too late for the television news and the paper, because the reporters are on deadline and won't be making any changes for the disorganized.

During the crisis, if you can't answer questions directly, or seem to answer directly, avoid television. You'll look slimy if you try to dodge questions from Mike Wallace. Your eyes will dart around, you'll sweat, you'll look like you've just been called into internal affairs and discovered your ex-spouse is conducting the interrogation!

Before you have your first crisis, try to be a source before you are a subject. The time to establish a relationship with reporters is *before* you hit the iceberg. Find out who is a professional, and who is composed entirely of hair spray. If you've taken some time to build some rapport before crunch time, it is entirely possible that the media may give you the benefit of the doubt during the controversy. But if they don't know you, then they won't be receptive to taking your story on faith.

What to Say During a Crisis

Here's the first rule of thumb on crisis message content: **Cork your lawyers!** Lawyers will tell you to be quiet and let them do the talking. Of course, many of them charge by the word. If you're losing in the court of public opinion, winning in a court of law months later isn't going to help. Damage control starts when you have damage.

Don't be afraid to face the facts. If your association has made a mistake, admit it and move on down the road. Explain what happened, and how you intend to avoid having it happen in the future. If it's one of your officers, have an expert explain the pressures of the job, or have a citizen tell about the good things that officers have done. Remind folks that cases shouldn't be tried in the media.

Tell the truth or say nothing! If you lie and are caught, you will never be believed again. Think of the implications for your membership and your career as a police labor leader.

Do try to control what you can. If you release bad news yourself, then you won't be surprised. Set ground rules when you talk: explain the topic, announce that you intend to take a limited number of questions, and refuse questions too far off the subject or purely hypothetical.

Crisis communication is like riding a tiger: it's exhilarating, but it can also be fatal if you make a mistake. Lay the groundwork before you need it, so you can concentrate on solving the immediate problem and not trying to do what should have been done long ago.

Chapter 34

MAKING THE MOST OF NEWS OPPORTUNITIES

The rule of thumb for evaluating the potential coverage on any news event, spontaneous or contrived, is: "Dog Bites Man" isn't news. On the other hand, "Man Bites Dog" is. An event that goes against a stereotype will generate coverage, while something that happens all the time—unless it involves plenty of blood and grieving relatives, is ignored or generates minimal coverage.

That is why police misconduct stories get major play—we're supposed to enforce the law, not break it; so going against type is news. But that's a bad news story, which is not something any law enforcement organization wants to encourage.

The stories that association leaders attempt to generate should be positive, but this goal is a difficult and oftentimes thankless task. You work hours on a press event only to have another news event dominate coverage and news resources (e.g., "Daryll Gates Performs Citizen's Arrest on Michael Jackson"), or worse, you're ignored by lazy reporters and detached editors. In this final chapter on police associations and the news media, let's look at how to make the most of a news opportunity.

Take Advantage of Opportunities When They're Handed to You on a Silver Platter

There is sometimes an occasional pot of gold in the puddle at the end of the rainbow. In rare instances, a positive news story can drop out of the sky. Then the job of the association leadership is to find a way to maximize the impact of the story.

A recent example occurred in a southwestern police department. The police department instituted a stepped-up enforcement program in some of the poorer neighborhoods of the city. Predictably, feathers were ruffled, and as a result, citizens/activists began appearing before the city council complaining about police brutality.

Before too much time had passed, these complaints evolved into a call for a police review board. So far, it's all very predictable, but not very positive. Then good fortune smiled upon the city.

A group of minority businessmen, ministers, and residents of the area offered another viewpoint to the council. In their appearances, they stressed how important the police were to the general safety and well-being of the area, and that without the police presence, the neighborhood would deteriorate past the point of no return.

In terms of minority/police relationships in the news, this is the "Man Bites Dog" story. That doesn't mean that's the way it should be, or will be in 10 years; it just means that minority community leaders calling for a police presence in their area is a very big news story!

What the Police Association Should Do When Presented with This Opportunity

Ideally, the police association should have been involved with the appearance of these individuals. Joining with the minority leaders' testimony would have accomplished two goals: provided rebuttal testimony to the brutality lobby, and helped to deflate the calls for a civilian board. More important, it would have been another step down the road that leads to the conclusion that minority neighborhoods are as anticrime as rich folks' neighborhoods–they just can't afford to hire rent-a-cops.

Instead, let's assume for a moment that the police association did not arrange for a joint appearance. So aside from the association's own testimony before the council, there isn't much maximizing to do here.

Then the bad boys came to our rescue. One of the more prominent ministers received threats on an answering machine as a result of his appearance before the council. The gist of the threats was to destroy his church and harm him personally.

This moment was the perfect opportunity to maximize the law enforcement versus criminal element story, and in particular, highlight how the police association wants to help citizens who have helped the police. What should have happened was the police association calls a press conference on the steps of the minister's church, and announces that off-duty policemen will be volunteering their services to protect both the church and the minister. The theme would be: "he took a stand for us and now we'll stand beside him!"

Interviews with some of the officers volunteering their time could have been done the next day, giving the story another day's play. The association leadership could have met with the editorial boards of local newspapers, and used this incident as a part of an effort to down play the desirability of a review board, generating even more positive coverage.

But Here's What Happens When Your Police Association Let's One of These Golden Moments Pass By

If the scenario outlined above had in fact taken place, the unexpected event (i.e. the threat on the minister) would have turned a one-time-only news report into a week's worth of positive coverage on behalf of the police association. Unhappily, that's not the way this story really turned out.

What did happen in this city was that the police department parked a cruiser in front of the church as a measure of protection for the minister. There was no real news, and no positive public relations for the police association, and even worse, there was a bad message for citizens sitting on the sidelines who might otherwise support the police, but will be intimidated by what happened to the last guy who stuck his neck out for the men and women in blue.

This type of scenario has occurred in many other cities, and many other police associations have let golden opportunities slip through their fingers. These kinds of moments are rare, which is why they make news. So don't let them be rare and wasted by taking a passive approach to shaping law enforcement news coverage. When opportunity knocks, **answer the door**!

Part VI

CASE STUDIES ON POLICE ASSOCIATION POWER, POLITICS, AND CONFRONTATION

Chapter 35

INTRODUCTION TO THE CASE STUDIES

The first five parts of this book have concentrated on the theory of how police associations become successful; that is, how they accumulate and use power to achieve the goals of the organization. However, the skeptical reader cannot (and should not) be truly convinced that the ideas proposed in this book really work without being offered some firsthand experiences of police associations that have applied the ideas contained herein, and become winners in labor-management conflicts in their communities.

The material that follows is a compilation of case studies involving local police association issues from across the width and breadth of this country between 1991 and 1993. These issues involve all kinds of scenarios–collective bargaining disputes, candidate elections, referendum elections, a fight over civilian review, and the famous conflict between the law enforcement community and Time Warner over Ice-T's "Cop Killer" song.

The case studies in this part of the book appeared originally in a monthly newsletter–*The Police Labor Leader*, a monthly journal produced by the authors between 1991 and 1993 which covered issues of police labor power and politics from around the country. While the time period for the studies is limited, their instructive value is enduring. At any given moment in this country today, there are similar conflicts underway between police associations and their adversaries of the moment, and these association are applying the very same strategies and tactics that you will find in the following pages.

Some of the statistical information appearing in these case studies might be different or obsolete today, including economic benefits and demographic data. This discrepancy does not in any way detract from the significance of the accomplishments that each of these case studies clearly reflects within the context of the times and places they occurred.

The authors apologize in advance that there is a slightly southwestern flavor to these case studies—out of the ten articles, three of them come out of the Great Republic of Texas, and while the police versus Time Warner fight in 1992 ultimately became a nationwide campaign, it started in the Lone Star State. While the authors recognize that the world does not end at the boundaries of the Red, Sabine, and Rio Grande Rivers (and four states which many of us Texans have so much trouble remembering!), it is generally recognized in the police labor relations field that Texas has been the hotbed of police activism for many years.

At the beginning of each case study, there is a summation which connects the principles discussed throughout this book with the events in the study. The authors wish to gratefully thank each of the police association leaders who contributed these case studies.

Chapter 36

BUILDING POLICE ASSOCIATION POWER–THE SAN ANTONIO EXPERIENCE

HAROLD FLAMMIA

AUTHORS' NOTE: The San Antonio, Texas police collective bargaining agreement is regarded as one of the finest public sector contracts in the country with respect to both benefits and rights. This chapter shows how the San Antonio Police Officers Association built a powerful political machine which was then used for leverage at the bargaining table. Harold Flammia is a veteran sergeant with the San Antonio Police Department and is credited with being one of the few visionary police labor leaders who could shape his organization into one of the truly powerful local "players" on the local political scene- very few other police associations in the country can claim this status.

The San Antonio police collective bargaining agreement has become a famous document in police association circles throughout the United States. Between 1985 and 1989, San Antonio police officers rose from a mediocre wage and benefit package to one of the finest compensation plans in this country. This result was achieved through a little bit of vision, the application of basic principles of political organization, and a whole lot of hard work. I would like to pass on the keys to success in San Antonio, because every other police association has the potential to accomplish the same things.

Background

A little background about San Antonio, Texas would be helpful. Located in the heart of the Sunbelt, San Antonio has a rapidly-expanding population of close to one million people, and is the ninth largest city in the United States. The city's economy is supported mainly by the military (4 bases), tourism, and a fast-growing light industrial base. The city is governed by a council-manager form of government, with council persons being elected in single-member districts. The majority of the population is Hispanic (52%).

In Texas, municipal and county law enforcement officers may collectively bargain when the right is approved through local option referendum. San Antonio police won this right from the voters in 1974. At that time, the San Antonio Police Department wage and benefit plan was pathetic, ranked somewhere around 100th in the State of Texas. The exclusive bargaining agent for police officers–the San Antonio Police Officers Association (SAPOA), has approximately 1500 members today, and it began negotiating collective bargaining agreements for its members in 1975.

When I took over as president of the SAPOA in 1985, some improvements had indeed been made through the collective bargaining process on behalf of San Antonio police officers. Their relative standing in terms of wages and benefits had risen to around 30th in the state, and some significant gains had been made in terms of seniority and disciplinary rights. It was my feeling, however, that the contract was in a holding pattern, and in fact, that the San Antonio Police Officers Association could become the catalyst for making our police department one of the best paid and best equipped law enforcement agencies in the United States, and for increasing manpower to more acceptable levels. And I set out during my four years as president to accomplish this goal.

In Search of the Right Philosophy

It was self-evident that the key to going after better wages and benefits for the membership was to figure out how to make the city of San Antonio willing to put more money into the police department. And one of the first steps in solving this puzzle was to analyze why certain organizations and people who dealt with the city of San Antonio always seemed to get their piece of the pie, while others, like the SAPOA, always seemed to get no more than a lot of lip service from city council members and management staff.

It didn't take me too long to realize that there were certain people in the community, business and politically-connected individuals, who were major players in how decisions were made at city hall. These people were the "movers and shakers," the ones who knew what buttons to push in city government in order to get things accomplished either for an organization or private business.

And it did not take a rocket scientist to understand that the SAPOA had to move into the status of a major player if it was to get more than lip service from city hall. Specifically, we needed to become an organization that circulated among the community's major power brokers, and participated in their decisions. Only then would we have access to and influence on the ultimate decision-makers at city hall—the city council.

One of the attributes that all the power brokers seemed to have was **money**. They had money, and they used it wisely to gain influence in the political arena. It was obvious then that money equalled political power, and power equalled the ability to achieve the SAPOA's goals!

So the SAPOA set out on a course to amass money, and along with other political tactics, use it wisely to build organizational power.

The Game Plan

The SAPOA embarked on an ambitious political program to strengthen itself internally and develop its power in the community. Several factors in the political/ethnic climate of San Antonio contributed toward the success of the SAPOA's efforts. First, the city council's single-member district composition made it much easier for the association to politically influence local elected officials (as compared to at-large council members, where one organization's voice often seems to become less compelling). Also, the Hispanic population in San Antonio had a long history of political activism, so our efforts at building organizational power, while threatening and distasteful to some, at least fit into the political culture of our city.

Following are the major points of the SAPOA's political program between 1985 and 1989. Although some of these tactics might not work in other communities, they do, for the most part, offer a successful formula for police association power anywhere in the United States.

1. **Political Action Committee (PAC).** The SAPOA recognized that without a PAC to lawfully funnel money into politicians' election campaigns, we could go nowhere. The PAC started in 1986 with a voluntary contribution of $ 4 per month. City council members and staff

went into shock when more than 1300 SAPOA members began contributing over $5,000 per month to the PAC! The association then began taking this money and contributing it, along with an endorsement, to council members and state legislators who were supportive of our goals of better pay and equipment, and increased manpower. In 1987, the SAPOA contributed $10,000 to the city council races, and our association was the biggest contributor to the races that year. Needless to say, this one act got the council's attention, because council members suddenly became more attentive and wanted to be our friends. We were now being invited to political fund-raisers, where other business leaders, politicians and power players in the community wanted to be our friends too. The PAC was such a stunning success that we raised the contributions to $8 per member per month, and again to $16 per month. There are currently 1100 members paying $16 per month at a tune of more than $17,000 per month; and the SAPOA now has *the* major PAC in the City of San Antonio. This one step bought our organization **access** to the politicians—both on city council and the state legislature, who controlled the economic destiny of San Antonio police officers. Now, the SAPOA would not have to stand in line to have its proposals and concerns heard!

2. **Political Tools.** The SAPOA purchased thousands of dollars worth of computer equipment, and input every registered voter in the city and county, broken down by city council and state legislative district. Whenever a politician did not agree with our program of better pay and equipment, and more manpower, we would flood that person's district with material advising constituents about this antipolice position. This tactic seemed to get the offending politician's attention! We also gave our political friends copies of these voter lists free of charge, including who voted in the last election; and this contribution was invariably received with considerable thanks from the recipient. Another new tactic was to wire rooms in our two association buildings for 100 telephones, and to purchase the phones. We then made this phone bank available to dozens of politicians for their campaigns, and used it for telephoning voters in the city for issues that affected the SAPOA. Imagine the psychological effect on city council members who know that your association has up-to-date voter lists, the capabil-

Author's Note: After Mr. Flammia left office, the SAPOA subsequently reduced its PAC contributions back down to $4 per month.

ity of contacting voters in their districts through a phone room, and the will to contribute these political tools to your friends!

3. **Political/Bargaining Consultants.** The SAPOA retained a political consultant to advise it on many of the ideas being discussed here. The person hired wasn't just any political consultant—he was the same consultant that many of the city council members and Texas legislators used in their races, and a man who circulated comfortably among the power brokers of the community. Think about the message that our association sent when it hired this same consultant and made him a part of our political team! Through our affiliation with the Combined Law Enforcement Associations of Texas (CLEAT), we also had available the services of a top-flight labor negotiator, Joe Gilbreath, General Counsel of CLEAT, who acted as spokesman and advisor along the perilous path of contract talks. An experienced negotiator is just as important to a police association's success as a political consultant!

4. **Chamber of Commerce Memberships.** It was essential that our association have the respect of the business community, because these are the people that ultimately hold the greatest sway over city hall. The SAPOA joined the four different chambers of commerce (including the one for Hispanics), allowing our representatives to attend the chambers' meetings and social functions, and to be seen and heard. We compiled mailing lists of each chamber's membership, and then printed two different booklets on the crime, pay, equipment, and manpower problems facing San Antonio police officers. After these booklets were mailed, we received an invitation from a group of the most powerful (and very concerned!) group of San Antonio businessmen and women to speak about our problems. Looking back, this meeting was a pivotal moment in our drive for the goals we were seeking.

5. **Internal Membership Unity.** Many of the SAPOA's tactics between 1985-89 were controversial—we were attempting things that were new, and in many instances, untried in our part of the country. It was therefore imperative that the membership be 100 percent behind everything that was happening. **Communications** therefore became the watchword for the relationship between the SAPOA leaders and members. The association produced a first-class, hard-hitting magazine that talked about the many political activities and other accomplishments of the SAPOA. No money was spared in making this pub-

lication top-notch—it cost $10,000 per edition to publish! This magazine was sent not only to every member, but also to the business leaders, politicians, and other important persons in the city. The members were kept abreast of every development, every step, that the association was taking. When the PAC was created, every members received a 60-plus page explanation of why this program was so important. The booklets sent to business leaders (discussed in #4, above) were also sent to every member so each officer knew what the association was doing.

6. **Association Image-Building.** A part of achieving organizational power was having a good image among the community movers and shakers. This tactic concerns doing things for goodwill and for the betterment of the community. The SAPOA contributed thousands of dollars between 1985 and 1989 to charities for churches, the elderly, and children. We made certain that these contributions were well publicized, and often made such contributions to charities that were favored by political figures and business leaders. Although this last observation might seem a bit cynical, it was good business and left the association in a stronger position to accomplish its goals.

7. **Cooperation with City Officials.** Once the SAPOA established its PAC and other aspects of its political program, it began participating in support of many of the same goals that the city (and other power brokers) sought. In essence, once we had the city politicians' and business community's respect, we could then afford to be more cooperative and supportive of their goals—one of the responsibilities of having power is to use it for purposes that go beyond the immediate organizational interests. We supported city bond issues and made contributions to those campaigns, because a good city bond rating was good for the community. The association also became actively involved in and supported the city in its successful opposition to a tax cap referendum in 1988, contributing $5,000 to the city's political action committee in this campaign.

The Payoff

The big question in every reader's mind is: "What gains were realized from all of this effort and money spent by the police association?" The summary answer is that San Antonio police officer wages are now the highest in Texas ($33,660 for a 5-year patrolman, which is undoubtedly not as high as many other departments throughout the country, but becomes significant when added to the longevity pay and other benefits discussed below), and the fringe benefit package compares favorably to the highest paid law enforcement agencies in the country.

Here is a partial list of the benefits gained from two contract negotiations between 1985 and 1989 that were *not* in effect prior to that time. This enumeration does not include all economic/leave time benefits and personnel rights that were achieved in previous contracts.

1. Health insurance benefits for retirees, including 100 percent of premiums paid by the city for retirees and their spouses. Also, retirees and their spouses now receive the same benefits as under the current police insurance plan for regular officers (the contract had already provided for many years that the city pay 100 percent for all employee and dependent health insurance premiums).

2. Comprehensive dental and optical insurance, with officer and dependent premiums paid for 100 percent by the city.

3. Comprehensive prepaid legal coverage for virtually all personal legal matters, paid for 100 percent by the city.

4. $350 per month differential for officers working any night shift.

5. Six additional longevity pay steps of 3 percent over base pay for every five years of service. A 10-year patrolman makes $168 per month for longevity; a 30-year patrolman earns an additional $504 per month ($39,708 per year in total salary). The beauty of the percentage longevity pay is that it increases with any additional salary improvements!

6. Triple time-and-one-half for six major holidays (the double time-and-one-half for other holidays was also maintained).

7. An off-duty employment program under the chief's office which assigns off-duty, overtime work on city property on an equalized basis. This benefit has meant more than 3,000 off-duty jobs to San Antonio officers in FY 1990-91, and more than $450,000 in overtime payments during that time.

8. A requirement of double time for all Fiesta assignments (the 2-week annual festival in San Antonio). More than $600,000 was paid out this year for this benefit at the 1991 Fiesta.

9. Establishment of education pay at the rate of $150 per month for an associate's degree, and $250 per month for a bachelor's degree.

10. Specific equipment requirements in the contract, including a computer in every car, portable radios for every officer, and new patrol cars after 50,000 miles.

11. Field Training Officer of $250 per month, with a minimum of 80 officers receiving this pay.

12. Other benefits such as bonus pay for not using sick leave, and other forms of specialized unit compensation such as SWAT and the hostage team.

There were other noncontract benefits that accrued during this time because of the SAPOA's increased political power at the local and state level. We were able to *effectively* participate in the decisions to increase the manpower allotment by 400 officers and to commit 6 million dollars for a new police academy. Because of our new-found political influence, our SAPOA legislative lobby team was able to work a bill through the Texas legislature that improved our pension plan (governed by state law) to permit officers to retire after 20 years service irrespective of their age.

Long-Term Benefits of the Agreement

The benefits to association members, city officials, and most important, the public, have been tremendous. Other than retirements and forced terminations, the turnover rate in the San Antonio Police Department is virtually zero. For an academy class of forty officers, there are more applicants from all over the country than our recruiting unit can handle. This situation guarantees the citizens that experienced officers are being *retained*, and that new-hires will only be the highest quality officers available.

One of the elusive goals of all police officers is to reach an economic plateau where they feel that the job they do is truly appreciated by their employer and the public. It is so frustrating to hear politicians, bureaucrats, and yes, even police labor leaders, posture about how much cops deserve to be paid what they're worth; but no one is ever really able to deliver the goods! In San Antonio, the police association did in fact give its members what they really deserved. There is now a sense of professional pride among San Antonio police officers–they feel that their pay and benefits are commensurate with the dangers and stress of their jobs.

And finally, readers should take note of growing trends from across the country where police associations are battling it out with public employers over collective bargaining agreements. San Antonio is one the few major cities in the United States where a police association and city are not at war over wages and benefits. Everyone benefits when there is labor peace in the police department.

Some Final Thoughts

It is a truly wonderful feeling to be on top of the mountain. The view from up here is grand indeed! But always remember, when you are on top, there is only one place to go, and that is down.

The San Antonio police collective bargaining agreement has caused a great deal of controversy because of its many lucrative economic benefits. There are a few politicians and other community leaders who don't really want to share their power with the police association, and have spoken out negatively about the contract in an effort to reduce the SAPOA's influence. These persons must constantly be beaten back and defeated!

My successors have had to be vigilant to maintain the SAPOA's place as a community power broker. As a matter of fact, my successors has had to restore some of the association's goodwill that has been lost in the public controversy over the contract *and* continue to deliver respectable contracts to a membership which now expects nothing less than the best!

During the course of my tenure as president of the SAPOA, I had the opportunity to talk with a few police labor leaders from around the country who smugly boasted that they didn't need to be involved in politics because they had compulsory, binding arbitration as an impasse procedure. For those readers who think that they can accomplish what San Antonio did through *any* form of impasse procedure— FORGET IT!

The SAPOA and city have a form of final, binding impasse procedure if the parties can't settle a contract: fact-finding, followed by binding voter referendum (i.e., the "Colorado" system). However, under the San Antonio system, or even under the so-called "ultimate" state labor laws (e.g., Oregon, Wisconsin, Massachusetts) that provide for mandatory, binding arbitration in police contract disputes, there is absolutely no third-party neutral who would give the kinds of benefits that were achieved over two contracts in San Antonio between 1985 and 1989. As a matter of fact, I would even go so far as to contend something that 10 years ago would have been heresy in the police labor movement—a compulsory, binding impasse procedure is the kiss of death for a police association, because too much attention is paid to the mechanics of the bargaining process, and not enough attention paid to the political dynamics in the community that are taking place away from the bargaining table.

Tremendous economic gains can only come through the strongest political pressure and influence that can be mustered. So don't be lulled into thinking that you can break through to greatness with an impasse procedure—you are only kidding yourself!

There's a famous quote from social activist and community organizer Saul Alinsky that says: "Change comes from power; and power comes from organization." I learned about Alinsky's power principles from other great leaders in the police labor movement and applied them for the benefit of the San Antonio Police Officers' Association. I hope that other police labor leaders can benefit from the San Antonio experience, and use it on behalf of their membership.

Chapter 37

HOW A POLICE ASSOCIATION CAN MAKE THE CITY DELIVER A GOOD CONTRACT, AND STAY OUT OF ARBITRATION TOO–THE 1991 MADISON, WISCONSIN POLICE NEGOTIATIONS

JOE DURKIN

AUTHORS' NOTE: One of the points made several times throughout this book is the overreliance of many police association leaders on binding arbitration as the only way to achieve benefits at the bargaining table. Here's a case study from Madison, Wisconsin, a jurisdiction with one of the most sophisticated public sector collective bargaining laws in the country, and where police association leaders realized that confrontation, and not arbitration, was the best way to achieve bargaining-table goals. Joe Durkin is a career police officer with the Madison Police Department, and at the time of this article, was a member of the Board of Directors of the Madison Professional Police Association.

Wisconsin is a state which provides for final and binding, last-best-offer arbitration in the event of an impasse between a police association and public employer. The premise behind this arbitration system is that the parties can avoid serious conflict, and a neutral arbitrator can settle unresolved issues by accepting one party or the other's total package. The 1991 Madison, Wisconsin police negotiations, however, is an example of how a police association can avoid the arbitration process, and come out of negotiations with a *better* deal than would have been possible through arbitration.

219

A Little Bit of Background about Madison, Wisconsin

The city of Madison, Wisconsin has a population of 194,000, and is portrayed by the local business community as a pleasant, midwestern city of moderate size with a great quality of life. But like everything else, changes do occur.

Population and square mileage growth has been explosive in Madison over the past ten years. The result is no surprise—new criminal elements from other urban areas, increasing police workloads, higher crime rates, and of course, a spiralling drug trade.

The financial picture in the city of Madison has not been a positive one over the last decade. The Wisconsin property tax system penalizes growing cities such as Madison. And like so many other cities across the country, there has been an emphasis on government cost controls.

The Madison Professional Police Officers Association (MPPOA) and its 280 bargaining unit members (i.e., sergeants and below) felt the adverse impact of this situation. Wage and benefit improvements had been meager in recent years. Our assessment was that the Madison Police Department was 40-50 officers short of the per capita average ratio of other Wisconsin law enforcement agencies.

We watched as the police department was told during 1991 budget deliberations to make do with less. There would be no additional staffing, and the overtime budget would be cut by 30 percent!

The membership of the MPPOA was restless. When the MPPOA opened contract negotiations in October, 1991, the writing was on the wall for our organization to do something different.

MPPOA-City Contract Negotiations Are Turbulent from the Very Beginning

The opening bargaining session in October was a stormy one. The mayor and chief of police started off the day by unveiling to the public their "Blue Blanket" plan to attack the crack drug problem by allocating overtime funds to increase patrols in problem neighborhoods. At the same time, the mayor's negotiator came to the bargaining table behind closed doors with no wage proposal, a proposal for the MPPOA to give up our voice in health insurance carriers, and a variety of other concessions. The irony of the city's conflicting positions was not lost on the MPPOA leadership or its members.

The MPPOA came to the table with what we felt were very reasonable proposals. These included an 6 percent wage increase, and a minimum staffing level per shift, with premium pay when the shift wasn't filled, and a 1-year agreement.

Negotiations dragged on for the first two months, with the city employing stall tactics. During five bargaining sessions in October and November, there were no meaningful discussions. A month out from the December 31st contract expiration date, the city passed its budget, offered the MPPOA a 2 percent wage increase (and nothing else!) and seemed satisfied to wait us out.

As the contract expiration date loomed closer, we sought the services of a mediator appointed under the auspices of our state labor board, the Wisconsin Employment Relations Commission. We also called a membership meeting in December to devise a plan of action that would produce a settlement more favorable to our position.

The MPPOA Membership Goes into Action During December with a Three-Pronged Attack

In an effort to create a climate that would bring pressure to bear on the city for a more favorable settlement, the membership settled on three specific actions. These actions would be a "silent protest" at a city council meeting, the cashing in of overtime, and an informational picket at city hall.

The plan for the silent protest before city council was for as many members and supporters as possible show up at city council in uniform to deliver a letter to the council which addressed the MPPOA's concerns. As the council meeting day approached, MPPOA leaders telephoned all the members and encouraged their attendance. The media was contacted as well.

An issue arose prior to the meeting concerning whether officers could wear their uniforms. Rumors flew about the possible consequences for officers who did show up in uniform. At the last minute, we decided to remove our shirts to avoid conflict.

The silent protest turned into a great media event! The MPPOA vice-president removed his uniform shirt with television cameras present. More than 150 police officers and many supporters showed up, and entered the council chambers in a quiet, orderly fashion. The letter was accepted and our members left as quietly as they had come.

The protest seemed to have some impact at the bargaining table. At a mediation session two days later, our health care issue was resolved, with current benefits being maintained, and better language being adopted to protect health care benefits in the future.

Step two involved a "cash in" of overtime. The contract provided that officers could accumulate 150 hours of earned overtime, and take up to 40 hours a year in cash from this bank. The MPPOA felt that it could bring further economic pressure on the city as it struggled to balance the budget at the end of the year.

Our members were asked to complete "convert to pay" slips, date them for the last day of the payroll period of the year and allow the Association to hold them. We were able to gather more than $80,000 in convert-to-pay slips, and decided that if sufficient progress had not been made by the end of the year, we would turn the slips in to the city.

It turned out that the two major issues let on the table, wages and staffing, were not resolved by the end-of-year deadline. The slips were therefore cashed in. Our leaders believed that there was an economic impact on the city, but city leaders never gave an indication that there was a problem.

The last action took place two days before Christmas, which was also a day scheduled for negotiations. The MPPOA turned out more than 100 officers for an informational picket around city hall. Our members also walked throughout city hall, handing out leaflets which spelled out our concerns.

While trying to downplay the picket to the press, city representatives were visibly upset. Their negotiators refused to attend the scheduled bargaining session while the picket was in place. We did release the picketers after an hour, but the negotiations that day ended without any further progress.

The Contract Expires, and the MPPOA Turns Up the Heat

When the contract expired on December 31st, the MPPOA leadership had to explore our options. Final and binding, last-best-offer arbitration was a poor choice, even though it was readily available. Our conclusion to reject arbitration was based on these factors:

1. Our important proposal on staffing was a not a mandatory subject of bargaining, which meant that under Wisconsin law, it couldn't be considered by the arbitrator.

2. Other police wage settlements in Wisconsin were coming in around 4 percent; and wage comparables are a major criteria under Wisconsin arbitration law.

3. State of Wisconsin workers had already received 3 percent increases. This factor would also be looked at by an arbitrator.

It was clear that the MPPOA should continue to press for a negotiated settlement. We had a different set of problems than other employees (and other police departments as well!); specifically, staffing and safety were of utmost concern.

In an effort to settle the impasse, we proposed an association-city committee which would study and recommend to city budget-makers the staffing levels needed to provide effective police service to the citizens. This idea received an enthusiastic endorsement from the chief of police. The city, however, tried to tie our proposal to a two-year, 4-4 percent economic package, so it was rejected by the MPPOA because the offer did not include enough money for us to go back to the membership.

Now it was time to really go after the city with a vengeance. A number of actions were taken by our members, many of which were without MPPOA sanction or approval. Officers refused any voluntary work; all overtime earned was requested to be paid in cash; and many members found it difficult to find the time to write traffic citations, an action that caused considerable media attention and city finger-pointing.

The MPPOA took a number of official actions which highlighted our bargaining table dilemma. We took out an informational advertisement in our local Sunday paper which pointed out the mayor's budget cuts in the police department, and contrasted them to rise in violent crime and arrests, and visually showed how few police officers were actually patrolling the streets on a typical Saturday night. The ad requested that citizens contact local elected officials to voice their concerns.

The MPPOA Board of Directors visited with the editorial staffs of Madison's two local papers to discuss our problem. We were candid about our desire to reach a negotiated settlement. Within a week, both papers came out with editorials endorsing our staffing committee proposal, and also the need to reach a negotiated settlement so we could get back to normal business.

Another step the MPPOA took was to solicit the chief of police and other community leaders to approach the mayor and persuade him to move on our proposals. These contacts were important since the mayor was holding firm on his position and refused to move from it. One particularly important event was a memo from the chief to the MPPOA expressing his concern over the negative disruptions in the work place, and **his support of our position**! This memo was leaked to the press, much to the mayor's outrage.

All of these steps took place between January and March. During this same period, there were several more bargaining sessions; a number of exploratory ideas from the mediator, city, and MPPOA; and finally a proposal from the mediator that allowed both parties to save face and reach a settlement.

The MPPOA and City Settle the Contract–the MPPOA Learns Some Valuable Lessons from the Negotiations

The accumulation of all the MPPOA tactics finally resulted in further movement by the city. The mediator's last proposal, which was accepted by both the MPPOA and the city included a two-year package: 4-4 percent as originally proposed by the city; an additional 1 percent in shift differential pay that affected all the members; and the all important staffing proposal.

There were, as always, some disgruntled members who wanted more than what came out of the final agreement. But the MPPOA was able to achieve economic benefits greater than other city employee settlements, and achieve our most important goal, a step toward insuring greater staffing levels to protect Madison citizens from increased crime.

We learned many valuable lessons as we worked our way through this process:

1. Even when you have final and binding arbitration, it is not always the answer to a police association's contract goals. There are situations, like the Madison experience, where a negotiated settlement will reap more than arbitration will.

2. An association that gets into a conflict with the employer must be clearly focused on its goals, and be prepared to make a long-term commitment to achieving those goals.

3. In a conflict, communication with the membership is essential. You cannot depend on word-of-mouth. During the four-month fight,

the MPPOA sent out numerous mailings to the members, posted numerous updates on Association bulletin boards, and held three general meetings.

4. Our greatest accomplishment was to get a large number of members to participate. The ten-member MPPOA Board could not have done all the work that had to be done, and we would have failed if there had not been a larger network of members willing to assist us.

5. Public support of our position was important; unfortunately, it is difficult to measure the degree of support we did have. The MPPOA leadership felt that it did a good job of bringing the issues to public light—we received some letters and calls from people giving their support. Because of the serious crime situation in Madison, we had anticipated more vocal support from the community than was actually given.

6. At times, we allowed our momentum to slow due to behind the scenes maneuvering and the mediator's request for a "gag order." These delays caused conflict with some MPPOA members who wanted us to maintain a constantly aggressive posture. In a conflict, the leadership of the police association must walk a tightrope between keeping the membership on a war footing, and at the same time, using tactical methods that don't always appear visible to your members.

7. Our biggest failing was our inability to bring other city council members around to our position to counteract the mayor. We tried to lobby key city council members, but the mayor convinced them to stay on the sidelines and let him handle the negotiations. In hindsight, it is clear that we should have had the political contacts *before* negotiations began.

8. The lack of political contacts is why the MPPOA has decided to become more involved in the local political scene. We are now developing a Political Action Committee. We will be attending all city council meetings, budget meetings, and any other forum where our voice needs to be heard. We plan to establish much firmer press relations, so we're in a better position to voice our positions and concerns.

The MPPOA has learned that political action and public contact is an on-going process. These things can't just be put into place during contract negotiations. That's why when our next negotiations begin, we will be more connected to the political and media scene in Madison, Wisconsin.

Chapter 38

OBSERVATIONS ON A STATE AND NATIONAL ELECTION

RONALD G. DELORD

AUTHORS' NOTE: Through the illustration of a successful political endorsement in a governor's race, and one in a presidential campaign not so well done, this case study illustrates the steps that a police association must take to make an effective endorsement of a candidate, and the steps to avoid a catastrophe. Ron DeLord is one of the authors of this book, and in his capacity as president of the Combined Law Enforcement Associations of Texas (CLEAT), has been on both the winning and losing side of many political endorsements throughout his twenty plus year career.

For all practical purposes, local police associations should endorse in local races, state associations in statewide races, and national associations in national races. This would make it simple for everyone involved.

However, statewide and national candidates seek out police associations, especially larger associations, for endorsements. Oftentimes, these police associations endorse a candidate without understanding the overall impact of such an endorsement on down ballot candidates.

For example, the endorsement of a statewide Republican candidate can impact the down ballot Democrats you are also endorsing, or vice versa. State representative and senatorial candidates run locally, but they are tied to the statewide and national candidates of their party.

The dynamics of a statewide (governor, attorney general, or U.S. Senate) or national (presidential) race are different from those of a local race (statehouse, municipal, county, or congressional). Unless your association is large enough to influence voters or the media statewide, then your endorsement may be for naught.

Remember that every endorsement is a two-edged sword. When you endorse out of your normal range of candidates, you risk offending other candidates up and down the ballot. An association must seriously question whether the endorsement will increase or decrease the organization's ability to achieve its goals.

The 1988 Presidential Election

For the first time, the 1988 presidential election focused on crime and drugs as the centerpiece of the campaign. George Bush and the Republican Party capitalized on the issue early, thus forcing Democrat Michael Dukakis to defend his position on crime.

Police associations were courted and endorsements sought by both candidates. Virtually every day, the media covered another police endorsement for one of the candidates. The campaign became a game of one-upmanship on police endorsements.

The National President of the Fraternal Order of Police (FOP) and a group of FOP lodge officers from the Northeast went to the Rose Garden to endorse Bush. The Boston Police Patrolmen's Association and several large Massachusetts police unions also endorsed Bush.

Dukakis counterattacked with endorsements from the Combined Law Enforcement Associations of Texas (CLEAT), the Massachusetts State Police Association, and the Southern States PBA.

There is no doubt that Bush won the endorsement battle along with the hearts and minds of the majority of the country's police officers. Dukakis' position on the death penalty alone set him apart from the police. The endorsement contest was not helped by his weak campaign staff that refused to believe that crime and drugs were the number one priority of the voting public.

CLEAT was holding its annual convention in late July 1988 in San Antonio. The statewide police group was also the host for the National Association of Police Organizations (NAPO) convention immediately following our state convention. NAPO had invited both Bush and Dukakis to San Antonio to address the national convention.

The president of the State Police Association of Massachusetts and the State Public Safety Secretary came to San Antonio at the start of the CLEAT convention and requested an opportunity to seek the group's endorsement for Dukakis. CLEAT had never endorsed in a national election, and there had been no forewarning in the association magazine that such an action was contemplated.

Surprisingly, the CLEAT Executive Board voted to recommend an endorsement to the Board of Directors (presidents of each local affiliate). The discussion centered around whether CLEAT should endorse without any advance notice to the delegates or the general membership. The delegates voted overwhelmingly to endorse Dukakis.

The delegates to the NAPO convention were divided. Neither Bush nor Dukakis came to the convention; however, Dukakis did a live presentation via telephone. The northeastern unions that had collective bargaining rights and other benefits were strongly supporting Bush. Many southern unions wanted to make a statement that law and order rhetoric did not replace the need for a national comprehensive bargaining bill and other rights. The leadership of the western unions were pro-Dukakis, but did not want the backlash from their members.

The endorsement drew little attention until Bush got the endorsement of the Boston PPA. The Dukakis campaign then called and requested that I come to Boston for a police rally for Dukakis to defuse the Bush backyard attack. The speech that I gave attracted national attention.

The backlash in Texas was hot and fierce. The telephone lines lit up at the CLEAT office as scores of members called attacking me for endorsing that "liberal, communist, pinko Yankee." The mail was nastier. The roll call vote at the convention was overwhelmingly for Dukakis; however, board members started calling to see if I would "lose" the tally sheet.

I was forced to attend membership meetings throughout the state where angry officers tore into me. Friends refused to talk to me. The heat from the endorsement was worst than anything I had ever seen since assuming the presidency in 1977.

The key leadership in CLEAT did rally to my defense. Several major players wrote letters and defended me. Our position was that law and order sold newspapers, but it did not address our right to bargain.

During the last few months of the campaign, I requested that the National Democratic Party send me out of state on campaign tours to avoid further aggravation of the situation. I traveled in 21 states for Dukakis, attended the Winston-Salem debates, and flew with Dukakis on his jet for two days speaking at rallies.

The experience was invaluable to both CLEAT and me. If adversity builds character, then I should have enough for a lifetime. CLEAT was shaken to the rafters by the controversy. About five hundred members resigned, and a few small locals disaffiliated.

The 1990 Texas Gubernatorial Election

The lessons learned in 1988 were not lost on either CLEAT or myself. While CLEAT had endorsed Democrats for governor since 1978, we had not had two candidates seeking our endorsement. While the Mark White-Bill Clements gubernatorial campaigns in the eighties raised the ire of the police chiefs and some conservative police members, they did not shake the foundations of the organization like the 1988 presidential election between Bush and Dukakis.

When unknown Republican millionaire Clayton Williams won the 1990 primary with a strong law and order campaign, I knew we were heading toward another Bush-Dukakis battle. CLEAT had supported its long-time friend, Attorney General Jim Mattox, for governor, but State Treasurer Ann Richards beat both Mattox and former Governor White in a hard fought Democratic primary.

The Democratic primary race threw mud all over Richards. On top of being a liberal from Austin, she was accused of having used illegal drugs 10 years earlier. Williams emerged from the primaries untouched and riding a high tide of popularity.

The CLEAT Executive Board decided to avoid any unnecessary rush into the governor's race. We sent questionnaires to both candidates. While Williams hedged on bargaining, he did come off the normal antilabor positions of the Republican Party. Several locals met with Williams and Richards.

While Williams would meet in private with individual police association leaders, he refused to meet with the CLEAT Executive Board. Richards met with both the Executive Board and the eight largest affiliated groups. The survey questions were sent to each local.

By delaying the endorsement vote until the convention in late September, we were able to see what the polls indicated. The membership was educated about the endorsement at the convention through the magazine, and the board had been receiving letters on a regular basis about the progress of the campaign.

Each candidate came to the convention to seek the endorsement. It was a fatal error by Williams. Even though he was warned to avoid law and order rhetoric and concentrate on the labor issues, he gave the delegates a canned speech. Richards' speech the next day emphasized police officers' labor concerns—she overwhelmed the delegates and received a rousing ovation.

The vote was 37 for Richards, one for Williams, and seven for no endorsement. The delegates came to their own conclusion that Richards best represented the **goals of the organization**. A taped copy of the interview was overnighted the Monday following the convention to seventy-six affiliated groups—any member who complained about the endorsement could see the hard "evidence" as to why CLEAT has backed Richards rather than Williams. A four-page newspaper tabloid was also sent out in the next few weeks to all members announcing all endorsements.

The backlash was nonexistent. The education of the members and the perceived fairness of the endorsement process neutralized the opposition. I received only one nasty letter from a member.

Fortunately, Richards won. CLEAT would have survived anyway, but it reinforces the members to win a big one occasionally.

Chapter 39

"IN YOUR FACE" BARGAINING - HOW THE 1993 EL PASO COUNTY DEPUTY CONTRACT WAS WON THROUGH CONFRONTATION

RICHARD RATLIFF

AUTHORS' NOTE: Sometimes contract negotiations reach such a desperate point that the police association must go to an all out war, and take steps that raise the discomfort level of even some people the association regarded as allies and friends. At the time of this story, Richard Ratliff was a retired El Paso Police Department sergeant, an active deputy sergeant, and president of the El Paso County Sheriff's Officers' Association, and today works as a staff representative for several law enforcement locals affiliated with the Communications Workers of America, AFL-CIO.

As President of the El Paso County Sheriff's Officers Association (EPCSOA), I was centrally involved in a confrontation in 1992-93 between El Paso County, Texas and the El Paso County Sheriff's Officers Association (EPCSOA) over a collective bargaining agreement for more than a year. I would like to give readers a picture of what it takes to win a contract fight when the employer refuses to budge even an inch from its bargaining-table position. Our association engaged in hardball, "in your face" tactics which, while extremely unpleasant to our membership and the other side, turned out to be the difference between winning or losing our contract fight.

Some Basic Facts About El Paso County

El Paso is the largest city in west Texas. The population of El Paso County is 620,000 people; the million-and-a-half people in the contiguous city of Juarez, Mexico, makes for an enormous population center with the attendant border-city problems of illegal immigration, crime, and pollution.

The county population is almost 70 percent Hispanic, and voting patterns are predominantly Democratic. The county is governed by a county judge and four commissioners elected every four years from single-member districts.

The sheriff's department consists of 175 certified law enforcement deputies who enforce state laws (i.e., patrol, detectives, warrants). The 260 certified detention officers operate the county detention facility.

The Sheriff's Officers Association–A History of Struggle Prepares Us for the Fight in 1993

Texas is one of those unfortunate states where law enforcement officers must obtain collective bargaining rights through local option referendum. In 1978, the EPCSOA was formed solely for the purpose of obtaining bargaining rights *for deputies only.*

When the association turned in petitions in 1980 calling for a collective bargaining referendum, the county refused to call the election. With legal assistance from its state affiliate–the Combined Law Enforcement Associations of Texas (CLEAT), the association sued the county and won an appellate decision in 1981 ordering the county to call the election.

The association then won the local option referendum for the right to bargain in 1982, but the president forgot to turn in a written request to bargain over economic items within a specified time limit as required under the state law! The county then refused to bargain, and we had to use the court system once again–another appellate decision in 1984 ordered the county to negotiate, and our first contract for deputies was finalized in 1984-85.

After detention officers were brought under the Texas law enforcement licensing system in 1988, we sought to include detention officers into the bargaining unit with deputies. Predictably, the county refused and we had to go back to the courthouse a third time. And once again, an appellate court ordered the county in 1991 to bargain with detention officers!

We had three battles in the early days of our association. These confrontations taught us how to be patient, and how to take the longer view of organizational goals rather than focus only on immediate results. We were well prepared for the fight to come.

The Tumultuous Events Leading Up to the 1993 Confrontation

By now, I'm sure you have a picture of the general attitude we faced for years in achieving some form of meaningful bargaining rights for deputies and detention officers. Fortunately, we found a politically sympathetic climate for a short period between 1988 and 1992, when an enlightened commissioner's court recognized the problem of maintaining qualified law enforcement officers in the sheriff's department. The EPCSOA and county reached an agreement which put deputies in line with the best paid law enforcement officers in the state; there were 60 percent pay increases in certain job classifications, plus exceptional benefits.

But by the time we got around to implementing the appellate court decision which brought detention officers into the bargaining unit, the composition of commissioner's court had changed, and the political environment was more hostile to the idea of improved benefits for employees. Our 260 detention officers had some of the worst working conditions of any jail employees in the state: $14,200 starting salary (compared to the state average of $19,000); a mandatory six-day workweek caused by jail overcrowding and a personnel shortage; and a 30 percent turnover rate.

In April, 1992, the association began negotiations for a contract that expired in October, 1992. We were faced with the formidable task of making gains for some of the state's highest paid deputies, and getting an initial contract for one of the lowest paid groups of detention officers.

The contract talks dragged on through December, 1992, with the county demanding at all times that the deputies forfeit many of their hard-earned supplemental benefits (dental, vision, and pre-paid legal insurance, and a deferred compensation plan), *plus* forego a wage increase in return for a meager pay raise for detention officers. The association stood firm in its position that it was the county's, and not the deputies', responsibility to fund wage increases for detention officers.

When the contract expired in October, 1992, there was a one-year "evergreen" which gave our association some additional time to work out an agreement. Between October, 1992 and January, 1993, negotiations were sporadic and completely unsuccessful. In January, the association leadership realized that a majority of commissioner court members, lead by the county Judge, had every intention of letting the contract expire. We knew that more forceful tactics would have to be used.

The January to June War in El Paso County

The Israelis are known for their short wars (e.g., "the Seven Day War" in 1976). I'm sorry to say that the EPCSOA was not as lightening fast as the Israelis in taking on the enemy—it took us six months to win our fight, but fortunately, the results were similar!

Between January and June, we used a four-pronged attack to escalate our impasse with the county. The goal was to achieve our last offer made at the bargaining table: a 15 percent base pay increase for detention officers over three years; a career pay plan and benefits for detention officers like those already in place for deputies; and finally, a reasonable wage increase and maintenance of benefits for deputies.

Our tactics included the following: getting the members involved in the fight, using political/community alliances, defining the message so the public would understand, and picking out weak points in county government to attack.

1. **Membership involvement.** Membership involvement proved to be less difficult than I had thought it might be. Here are some of the ways our members pitched in during this campaign:

• The association held two different rallies in March, 1993, where deputies, detention officers, their families, and friends turned out to hear speeches from association leaders about the issues involved, and what the members would be expected to do. We were careful to define exactly what the issues were, and that we could only win through membership persistence and participation.

• The association provided deputies and detention officers with buttons stating "El Paso County Unfair to Deputies and Detention

Officers" which, thanks to Sheriff Leo Samaniego, were permitted to be worn at department facilities. We also found widespread support among other county employees (who had not had a pay raise in four years), and produced buttons for them to wear stating "El Paso County Unfair to All County Employees."

• Association members were also called upon to turn out for a commissioner's court meeting on April 14th, when a first vote was taken by the court on a contract that would have been acceptable to our members. More than 300 deputies and detention officers turned out for this meeting...*plus* other families, friends, and supporters of our cause. They handed out thousands of flyers to citizens about working conditions in the jail. We then marched into the meeting, which turned out to be a rowdy affair.

• One other form of membership participation was a core of 50+ deputies and detention officers who helped in the distribution of flyers and targeted demonstrations that we did throughout the campaign.

2. **Political and community alliances.** I have learned through reading and labor seminars about the importance of political and community alliances. And while I sought out these alliances, it wasn't until this contract fight that I really understood the importance of coalitions.

• The association had for several years worked on a close political relationship with Sheriff Samaniego. This relationship turned out to be significant, because he gave his complete support to our efforts, even when we had to use hardball tactics.

• We had a long-term relationship with our city counterparts–the El Paso Municipal Police Association (EPMPOA). Police officers from the EPMPOA publicly supported our cause, including wearing our buttons, putting up signs in the main police station (right by the County Building), and turning out at our rallies and demonstrations. The EPMPOA also had political and press contacts which turned out to be useful.

• We are members of the Communications Workers of America, AFL-CIO. This affiliation paid off when we requested the CWA and the Texas AFL-CIO call for a national boycott of our tourist-minded county. This boycott threat sent shock waves through the "tourist and convention" crowd. Not surprisingly, there was considerable resentment among convention, Chamber of Commerce, motel, and economic development representatives, but our message was firm—we weren't the ones causing the problem; instead call commissioners court and tell them to deal with our issues!

• Through the EPCSOA political action program, we had actively supported and campaigned on behalf of two commissioners. We turned to them for help during the contract fight, and it was through their behind-the-scenes assistance that we were able to line up the necessary votes to push our contract over the top.

• Over the past few years, the association had worked with civic groups and leaders on projects and matters of mutual interest. As the contract battle developed over the six-month period, we turned to the Central Labor Council (of which we were a part), Volunteer Fire Departments, VFW Posts, and several notable civic leaders, and asked them to contact the county judge and commissioners on our behalf.

3. **Defining the public message.** If there's one thing I've learned through my eight years of experience as an association leader, it's the fact that you can't win any kind of public confrontation unless you define your message in a way the citizens understand and are willing to support. You've got to keep your message simple, and use many ways to drive it home. Here are some of the things that we did:

• Our theme in the campaign was that detention officers needed a "living wage," that is, it was an embarrassment for county workers to be forced into a welfare environment of food stamps and rent subsidies. We also focused on the need for retention, and how much the high turnover was costing the county.

• We drove this message home through use of free press, which came about only because the association had taken the time to cultivate good media relationships. Coverage of our fight was therefore generally balanced. There were several sympathetic newspaper and electronic media editorials, and two radio talk show hosts receptive to the association played up our issue on their programs. We also issued numerous press releases concerning the contract.

• As a public service, our members placed door hangers on cars at malls, motels, and the airport advising the public to take auto theft and car-jacking precautions.

• Sheriff Samaniego had a weekly television program which covered local government issues. He was kind enough to invite CLEAT President Ron DeLord, EPMPOA President Mike Breitinger, and me to appear as guests on his program to talk about the contract dispute. The Sheriff appealed to the public for support, and asked citizens to call the county politicians in support of our contract.

4. **Attacking the county's weak points.** If you can pick out your employer's most vulnerable positions, you can truly make the people who have been trying so hard to be unfair to your members pay. Here are some of the things that we did to the county:

• The tactic of going after out-of-town dollars through a boycott can be effective in a tourist/convention-oriented community. When the AFL-CIO boycott was called, I wasn't prepared for the vicious attack from people who will give you a song-and-a-dance about "the best interests of the community." But I learned to deflect the attack, and to make the county political officials, not the association, the cause of the problem.

• We demonstrated at a public awards ceremony which the county judge and her husband were hosting for several of El Paso's elite leaders. We handed out handbills talking about the county judge's lack of sensitivity for law enforcement issues, and I had the satisfaction of personally giving her a copy.

• One of the big turning points in our fight was the joint effort by the Sheriff, CLEAT, the Texas AFL-CIO, and the EPCSOA to block the county from receiving a new state prison in El Paso. We argued to the State Department of Criminal Justice that the county's low wages could not compete with the state's higher correctional officer pay, and the sheriff's department would lose even more detention officers if a new prison was put into place. In May, 1993, the Department of Criminal Justice voted to award the new prison to a community other than El Paso!

• We also let county officials know that we would be demonstrating at the major Hispanic Chamber of Commerce Convention scheduled for July in El Paso. We were already lining up deputies from associations in Texas' six largest counties to bring our cause to the attention of 2500 delegates from around the country.

Our Pressure Became Too Much for County Commissioners–They Agree to Talk and a Settlement Is Concluded!

As our intense campaign wore on through the spring, the county commissioners asked in late April to have some work sessions with county negotiators and association representatives to discuss the contract. The association had four work sessions with commissioners to discuss the contract issues. During these sessions, I had to deliver a strong message to the commissioners that our position on all issues was final; that there would be no more concessions; and that their political nightmare would continue until we got a favorable settlement.

You never really know when you have hit the right pressure points to cause the opposition to cave in. But our *constant* pressure on El Paso County Commissioners become too much for them to bear.

In particular, I believe that the State Department of Criminal Justice's decision to award a new prison to a city other than El Paso was the final blow. County politicians had made an all out effort to land this prison, and their perception that the association had been the prime mover behind defeat of the prison made them realize just how committed our organization was to achieving our collective bargaining goals.

On May 26, commissioner's court voted 4-1 to adopt a new agreement to run through October, 1996. One of the ironies of this vote was that the county judge, who had been our biggest obstacle to a settlement, voted for the contract! Since the county judge had received considerable support from organized labor during her past campaigns, she felt compelled at the end to come over to our side rather than to be perceived as against her own labor organization.

The New Contract Maintains El Paso County Sheriff's Department Employees Among the Top Paid in the State

The new contract continued our deputies as some of the better paid Texas law enforcement officers. The agreement provided for 8 percent in wage increases spread over the term. By 1995, a top-step deputy was paid an annual base wage of $39,612. In Texas, this is premium pay for a sheriff's department.

Deputy supervisors fared even better. Sergeants topped out at $47,655, lieutenants at $52,539, and captains at $60,263.

There has been considerable improvement in deputy fringe benefits as well. Each deputy received $60 per month to be applied to dental, vision, and prepaid legal benefits. There was an increase in uniform and clothing maintenance allowances. Court time pay was improved

Author's Note: In Texas, law enforcement bargaining unit include all ranks except the top management official, in this case the Sheriff.

to a three-hour minimum at time-and-one-half, and field training offi-cers received $100 additional pay per month.

The most dramatic changes, however, were in the area of detention officer compensation. A 10-year, career ladder was created, with the salaries ranging from $18,693 to $29,298. Detention officers received wage increases over the next three years of a minimum of $4,000, and as much as $10,000! This salary scale put our detention officers at a higher wage scale than State of Texas correctional officers, and made the construction of a state prison less threatening in terms of retaining county detention officers.

There were other improvements for detention officers as well. A new rank of floor control officer was created, which provided a pro-motional position for intermediate supervisors. Also, many of the fringe benefits available to deputies were extended to detention offi-cers (e.g., workers' compensation at 100% salary rather than 75%), overtime computed on the basis of hours paid for rather than worked, and sell-back of sick leave up to 90 days upon resignation or retirement.

Important Lessons Were Learned from This Experience

I came away from this contract fight with a whole new perspective on what it takes to come out the winner in a labor-management con-flict. Following are some of the lessons which I want to pass on:

1. **When you're in a war, accept the fact that a certain num-ber of people are not going to like you.** Most of us have a very basic need—the desire to be liked by others, and any successful leader of a confrontation must overcome this need to be liked. When you lead a hardball, "in your face" fight against your employer, people will turn against you. Politicians and business people will tell you, either explicitly or by innuendo, that you will no longer be their friend. Even though I thought that many of these people were friends, they were never really friends or they would have helped me, and I wouldn't have had to go through a pitched battle to get benefits that our mem-bership deserved. So tune out negative static and keep focused on your goal.

2. **Always keep in mind who you're fighting for.** When the con-flict with your employer begins, the range and speed with which deci-sions are made is amazing; you must worry about what tactics to use,

when, where, etc. And it is very easy to become so immersed in these decisions that you can forget about keeping your members informed and involved in the fight. Remember: a battle without membership understanding and support cannot be won! While many members aren't going to devote a measurable amount of time to helping out in a campaign, these same members will be the first ones to complain if they don't know what is going on, or if they perceive that there is no opportunity to voice their opinions on the course the association is taking. So paint a clear and simple vision to the membership about the dispute, and then keep members up-to-date every step of the way.

3. **When politicians involved in your dispute have made prior promises, hold their feet to the fire.** I am firmly convinced that once elected, all politicians catch a disease, the primary symptom of which is memory loss–they can't seem to remember those promises that got them elected in the first place! In our case, the county judge had relied heavily on organized labor in her previous campaigns for office. The AFL-CIO had endorsed her and worked in her campaign because she purported to be a "friend of labor." But when it came to her own employees, the county judge dug her feet in against any fair compensation system. It was only after she was reminded by the many labor officials who had backed her during her campaigns that she decided to support our contract. Politicians want to have it both ways– get your support and then do whatever they want later, so don't be afraid to demand that they stick to their promises after the campaign is nothing more than a distant memory.

4. **It will be a lonely fight if you haven't taken the time to cultivate alliances beforehand.** Another lesson was that long-term relationships with other community groups and leaders really do pay off. It is so hard for police associations to see the need for this investment of time on a day-in-and-day-out basis. But the fact is that if you don't make the time to associate with other organizations and community leaders, you will have no one to turn to when you need help. Another way to put this important principle is that no matter how earth-shattering you believe the problems of the association to be, no one else really gives a damn about them unless you have worked hard at establishing strong ties to your community, and have been generous in your assistance to other groups and people. I would especially encourage ties between other police associations in your area. I found the assistance of the El Paso Municipal Police Officers Association to

be helpful, especially in terms of its press contacts, relationships with certain political leaders whom I didn't know as well, and the high community regard that it enjoyed. And even if your police association is not in the AFL-CIO, you should still maintain some form of contact with local labor groups—you share many of the same common issues with them, and most of these labor groups have considerable energy and enthusiasm when political issues are involved.

5. **Don't get sidetracked on issues that are secondary to the main dispute.** When you get into a dispute with your employer, it's all too easy to get sidetracked into fighting grass fires which are not central to the main issue. Let me give you an example from our recent fight in El Paso County. At the April 14th commissioner's court meeting, the one commissioner who had been our most staunch supporter over the years voted against the contract for reasons that were not at all clear to our association leaders. It would have been very easy to have become embroiled in a public fight with this one commissioner who seemed to have turned against us after we had supported him so strongly in his previous campaign, but if we had followed this course, we would have lost focus on our contract fight and have been less likely to win. So instead, we approached the commissioner out of public view, clarified why he was opposed to our contract proposals, and addressed those concerns in further negotiations.

6. **Saul Alinsky was right—you have to keep the pressure on until the enemy can't stand it anymore.** Saul Alinsky fans already know that one of his famous sayings is that you've got to maintain pressure on the enemy until it becomes unbearable. And if you're going to win the fight, you've got to keep the pressure on for long, sustained periods of time. One of the biggest failures I have observed with other law enforcement labor groups is that they think that one demonstration, one radio ad, or one flyer will, in and of itself, turn the tide and win the war. The fact is that your employer is prepared to wait you out, hoping that you will give up out of frustration and perceived failure. Your duty as leader of the group is to keep your members committed to a long-term view of the ultimate goal, and keep escalating the fight to the point where the other side just can't stand the heat any more. That kind of protracted fight might take a month, six months, or even a year, but there will be a breaking point where the politicians simply won't be able to take the pressure and will then be willing to negotiate sensibly.

If I Had It to Do over Again, There Are a Few Things That Could Have Been Done Differently

Even after such a dramatic success as the one in El Paso County, it is always valuable to evaluate what you have done and see if anything might have been handled differently. As I look back on our experience, one of the big stumbling blocks to a settlement was the considerable inexperience in labor relations matters of the newly elected county attorney and newly appointed first assistant who served as chief negotiator. They simply didn't have the fundamental skills of negotiation that might have moved us much faster to an agreement.

At the point that I saw their inexperience, I should have immediately gone to individual county commissioners and advised them of this impediment, and worked more closely with the commissioners on the points at issue. Instead, our association came to the commissioners at the point where the parties were really dug into their respective positions, and it was much more difficult for county political officials to back off without losing face.

Also, we took one of our close political allies on commissioner's court for granted (see above), and didn't keep him advised of what was going on in negotiations. This action proved to be a problem when he voted against our contract at the April 14th commissioner's court meeting because of a misunderstanding of our position. The moral, of course, is that you should never take your political friends for granted, just like you would never expect them to take you for granted.

Other than these two mistakes, I believe that our association ran a classic campaign which made an impression on the entire community. While there are many who might not have liked some of our tactics, I believe that we earned respect of even our most outspoken enemies.

Chapter 40

HOLDING ON TO CONTRACT BENEFITS AND AVOIDING LAYOFFS - THE 1991 PRINCE GEORGES COUNTY MARYLAND F.O.P. CONFRONTATION

DARRYL JONES

AUTHORS' NOTE: Sometimes the tremendous gains made at the bargaining table are jeopardized by events beyond the control of the police association—in the instance of this case study, it was the fiscal stability of the employer. Then it is up to the police association to take steps to preserve those gains. Since this 1991 conflict, Darryl Jones has gone to become president of the Maryland Fraternal Order of Police, and has been the recipient of a Kellogg Foundation fellowship.

In 1991, I faced the dilemma of leading my organization, the Prince Georges County, Maryland Fraternal Order of Police (F.O.P.), into a major confrontation with our county's political leadership. The battle involved holding on to our contract benefits and avoiding massive police layoffs. Here is our story.

A Little Bit About Prince Georges County and the Climate in 1991

Prince George's County, Maryland has a population of just over 750,000, and three sides of the county border Washington, D.C. The population has an even ethnic mix, with barely 51 percent being minorities. The police pepartment's personnel is 1250 officers, but there is considerable data to support a minimum strength of 1400. The county is primarily Democratic, and the government is run by a nine-member county council and elected county executive.

243

All officers are members of F.O.P. Lodge #89. A county law provides police officers with collective bargaining and binding arbitration rights, and the F.O.P. is the bargaining agent for the unit comprised of lieutenants and below.

In early 1991, the economy had begun to sour, and anticipated county revenue levels were not being met. The county executive "temporarily" suspended police officer recruitment and hiring, and froze all government hiring.

The County Makes an "Offer" to the F.O.P. Which Is Rejected

The F.O.P. was in the middle of a three-year agreement, with a 7 percent pay raise due on July 1, 1991 (which would be the start of the third year of our agreement). In January, the county executive and other government officials met with me and advised that the county would have to lay off police officers in order to fund our 7 percent pay raise! The county executive also stated that the fire fighters, who were under a similar agreement to the F.O.P., had already agreed to defer their 7 percent raise for a year and give up other monetary benefits in return for no layoffs.

When the F.O.P. leadership flatly rejected this "offer," the county stated that the 7 percent raise would be paid in July, but that as many as 200 police officers could be laid off unless some compromise was reached. Our leadership was outraged that the county would even suggest laying off police officers on an already understaffed police department.

A series of special meetings was called to advise the F.O.P. membership of what had occurred, to find out how the members felt we should proceed. Not surprisingly, the membership wanted to fight!

The F.O.P. Sets Up a "War Chest," Goes on the Offensive

The F.O.P. leadership anticipated a lengthy and costly battle, so we suggested a one-time $50 assessment per member to fund our campaign. One of our members, however, proposed that each member be assessed $100 a piece to be paid out over two pay periods. Two other stipulations were added to the assessment: any member who couldn't afford it could request the money be returned in a confidential letter to the F.O.P. President, and all unused money would be returned at the end of the battle. Only one member voted against the assessment, and the "War Chest" was born!

We then went on the offensive, taking our message to the community. Here are some of the things we did:

1. Retained a firm to produce TV spots and print ads.

2. Joined the Chamber of Commerce and mailed over 2,000 letters to business owners requesting support.

3. Bought full page ads in local papers denouncing the county for threatening layoffs in an already understaffed police department.

4. Lobbied our county council requesting that the police department be excluded from the county-wide layoffs.

5. Lobbied the Maryland state legislature, requesting "emergency aid" for our police department.

6. Produced and ran commercials on CNN and other local channels criticizing the county executive and soliciting citizen support for our cause.

Events Begin to Turn Against the F.O.P.'s Position

As we moved into our campaign, a number of factors developed that we found difficult to overcome. First, the county's budget deficit turned out to be $86 million, which was $16 million more than originally predicted. This deficit caused the county executive to lay off more than 200 employees and abolish another 700 positions. Because of the worsening economy, other jurisdictions were laying off employees as well. And the entire economic crunch was heightened even further when the state legislature reduced state aid to local governments.

Other public safety employee groups were going in a different direction than our F.O.P. The fire fighters union accepted the county's offer and was praised by the media. A large Maryland F.O.P. lodge deferred pay raises in its city to avoid layoffs. Another lodge lost an arbitration award which forced officers to accept concessions that were worse than our county was asking from us.

Other elements came into play as well. Year-end crime statistics actually showed a decrease in criminal activity. Our own accountant reviewed the county's books and determined that the deficit would be greater than the one actually predicted! Finally, the F.O.P. was continually criticized by the media, being labeled "stubborn and unreasonable."

The F.O.P. Sees the Handwriting on the Wall, Agrees to Negotiate, and Keeps the Pressure On

After looking at all of the factors piling up against us, the F.O.P. leadership decided in February, 1991, to negotiate a compromise with the county that would acquire enough benefits to offset the requested concessions, and at the same time, avoid layoffs. As you might imagine, the decision to renegotiate was not warmly received by some factions in our membership. But the price of leadership is always to do what you perceive as in the best interests of your group, even in spite of internal opposition.

Simultaneous to our agreement to renegotiate, the F.O.P. kept the pressure on the county. It was our belief that continual pressure would be our best chance to come out of negotiations with a fair settlement. We directed our campaign toward the concept that Prince Georges County citizens were not safe, and that the county engaged in wasteful spending practices.

We ran commercials portraying the county as "plagued with crime and unsafe to live in." We built coalitions with at least a dozen groups, including the Chamber of Commerce and Interfaith Action Community. Supporters called the county executive offices daily demanding that there be no police layoffs–some days the switchboard became so overloaded that it had to be shut down! We dug up examples of wasted revenue, sweetheart contracts, and lavish spending in the county government. Officers were advised to not take unnecessary chances and always wait for their backups, causing greatly increased response times.

The F.O.P. Renegotiates and Settles...Or So We Think

After some difficult negotiations, the F.O.P. brought back a package that contained some concessions, but also contained some major benefits. The most significant improvements were a 60% retirement pension after 20 years of service, a presumption that heart and hypertension illnesses were job-related, and a no-layoff clause. Merit pay and longevity steps were kept in place, annual leave carryover was increased, sick leave pay out on retirement was increased; and the number of allowable hours that officers could work secondary employment was increased. A reopener clause provided that if the economy improved, we could discuss economic issues. The 7 percent wage increase was deferred to April, 1992.

After the tentative settlement had been reached, the internal opposition became even more vocal. Open and anonymous letters circulated among the members denouncing the proposal and encouraging members to vote against it. The rank and file began choosing sides: the younger officers were afraid of being fired and supported the renegotiated package; the more senior officers wanted the 7 percent pay raise. There was a sentiment among many officers that the county was bluffing, and that the F.O.P. should call the bluff.

Fortunately, the F.O.P. kept our membership advised of what was occurring throughout the conflict. We held special meetings almost weekly, and sent out teletypes at least twice weekly. Since this issue was the most difficult and divisive one that our Lodge had ever faced, we didn't want to risk misinformation making the matter worse.

As we got closer to a vote, we bombarded our members with factual information about the county' fiscal situation, the recession throughout the country, and what was happening to police groups in the state and the country. We wanted our members to know that our renegotiated agreement was still far superior to what many other police officers were having imposed on them. In March, 1991, the ratification vote was 755 For and 203 Against—the first time in our Lodge history that a contract was ratified on the first vote!

After All This Work We Thought Our Difficulties Were Over, But Little Did We Know That....

After our settlement with the county, the economy turned even worse. By January, 1992, the State of Maryland was facing a $400 million deficit, which caused layoffs, reduced services, and drastically decreased local aid. In Prince Georges County, $60 million of state aid was withheld, and the local deficit grew even more. More County positions were then abolished, and a county-wide layoff and furlough program was put in place for all employees except police and fire.

Salaries of nonunion employees were unilaterally reduced by the county, and a hiring freeze was imposed.

Then the nonpublic safety unions and nonunion employees complained to the county executive and county council that they were bring treated unfairly, and that police officers and fire fighters were being given preferential consideration. These organizations and employees screamed for equity.

Because of this incredible pressure from nonpublic safety unions/employees and the perception of inequity, the county council proposed a bill, County Bill 13-1992 (CB-13), which would prohibit any county employee from receiving a salary increase. At the same time, legislators in the Maryland General Assembly were proposing a bill titled the "Neall Amendment" which would have mandated no pay increase for state employees. Additionally, the Neall Amendment punished any Maryland subdivision (county or city) which gave their employees any kind of pay raise; specifically, any local jurisdiction's state aid would be reduced by whatever amount was given as pay raises.

Now the F.O.P. Found Itself in a Bigger Battle than Before

Now we were in a battle for our lives! First, we had to concentrate on defeating the Neall Amendment. Fortunately, a massive lobbying effort with the assistance of police and fire fighter groups throughout Maryland and the threat of lawsuits defeated this horrendous piece of legislation.

The county council began another round of publicity maneuvers against the F.O.P., claiming that more than 600 nonunion employees would have to be laid off if we didn't renegotiate *again.* Also, the County asked us again to give up our 7 percent wage increase. We refused but did propose to renegotiate some our holiday pay and vacation leave benefits. The county council found our proposal unacceptable without eliminating the 7 percent pay raise, and six out of the nine council members continued to support the very threatening CB-13.

Now we were really at war with the county council, and in a perilous position. CB-13 could potentially have taken away our 7 percent wage increase, and we would then have had to roll the dice in court to find out whether our contract would prevail over this bill during these clearly perilous economic times. The F.O.P. battle involved attacks on many fronts:

1. We waged an all out radio campaign, running ads on 17 different stations which depicted the council members as a bunch of incompetents.

2. We staged the largest demonstration ever held in the county at the county administration building, and then packed the council hearing room, where F.O.P. speakers gave fiery speeches threatening to reward our friends and punish our enemies.

3. We printed 50,000 flyers criticizing the council generally, and the chairman and five other council members who supported CB-13, and distributed them in the neighborhoods of council members and throughout the county.

4. At the annual police/fire awards luncheon, a third of the audience walked out when one of the council members supporting CB-13 moved to the podium to speak. It was great publicity because it focused the media's attention to the issue, and the councilwoman was so shaken she could barely speak.

CB-13 was ultimately passed by five out nine county council members in April, 1992, but was vetoed by the county executive. The council then overruled the veto for the first time in the county executive's 10-year tenure.

The F.O.P. was then compelled to file suit against the county the very next day. The county was apparently fearful of the lawsuit, particularly since the F.O.P. kept the heat on publicly by equating money spent on the lawsuit to money wasted that could have saved the jobs of other county employees. An agreement was reached the next a few weeks later that if the F.O.P. dropped its suit, the police would be exempted from CB-13. And that is what happened.

What the Prince Georges County F.O.P. Learned About Labor-Management Conflict

Conflict is not a pleasant thing for any police labor leader to go through. But there is much to be learned from the experience. Here are three points that I would pass on to other police associations:

1. **When you are in a fight, you must keep the pressure on constantly.** The association must keep the issue in before the people

who matter in this fight, the politicians and the public, so that its message is received. And to accomplish this goal, there must constantly be some specific actions that get the message out—radio ads, flyers, telephone calls, etc. Otherwise, there can be no catalyst for a settlement of the dispute.

2. **One of the toughest parts of a battle is the internal struggle for leadership credibility.** Any time that a police association leader sees the need for a compromise, as was the case in Prince Georges County, there will inevitably be a segment of the membership screaming "sellout!" You are therefore compelled to walk a fine line between representing your members with the greatest vigor, and at the same time, educating them as to the harsh realities of how their economic well-being might be adversely affected if there is no compromise.

3. **You can never have enough money in a labor-management battle.** Money is critical when you're in a fight like the one in Prince Georges County! Without our "war chest," the F.O.P. could not have afforded to do many of the things that were crucial to our success.

Chapter 41

THE POLICE VS. TIME WARNER: THE STORY OF DAVID TAKING GOLIATH OUT TO THE WOODSHED FOR A GOOD WHIPPIN'

JOHN BURPO

AUTHORS' NOTE: Here's a case study about the biggest story in the American police labor movement since the Boston Police Strike of 1919–how police associations from across the country banded together in 1992 to fight the corporate titan Time Warner over the controversial Ice-T song, "Cop Killer."

For the past two months, the police labor movement has seen the biggest story in years–the Time Warner/Ice-T "Cop Killer" controversy. This conflict is the first known "corporate campaign" run by a coalition of police associations against a major American corporation. A corporate campaign is often used in private sector, labor-management conflicts, where a labor group launches selective attacks against a corporate adversary's most vulnerable points.

The "Cop Killer" controversy is a textbook example of how police associations can, regardless of their affiliation, work together toward a common goal; of how police labor leaders should frame high-profile issues; of how a police association media campaign can be effectively managed; and of how to recognize when the fight is over and it's time to settle the dispute. By virtue of geographical location and personal relationships, I had the good fortune to be involved from the beginning of the Time-Warner fight.

The First News About "Cop Killer" Comes Out of Dallas and Corpus Christi, Texas

Since the Rodney King incident and subsequent riots in Los Angeles, various aspects of the news media have been bashing law enforcement almost daily. This media abuse all changed after Dallas (Texas) Police Association Vice-President Glenn White published an article in the May 29th issue of the DPA newspaper, *The Shield,* entitled "New Rap Song Encourages Killing of Police Officers."

White's two column article reprinted the exact words to the rock song called "Cop Killer" from a Warner Brothers Records album named "Body Count" by rap artist Ice-T. White asked Dallas officers to write protest letters to Warner Brothers Records, and urged a boycott of all products of the parent corporation, Time Warner, such as movies, videos and amusement parks.

White's article became the catalyst for rousing what is an often half-awake (or is that predominantly sleeping?) police labor movement. His article was read by Corpus Christi Police Officers Association President Eric Wramp, who immediately called a press conference to express his disgust at Warner Brothers Records and the record. The June 4th issue of the *Corpus Christi Caller Times* was the first media piece about the pending boycott of Time Warner.

The Controversy Widens: The Largest Texas Police Association Jumps into the Fight

On Monday, June 8th, President Ron Delord of the 16,000-plus member Combined Law Enforcement Associations of Texas (CLEAT) met with key staff members to discuss the rapidly growing local media attention to the controversy over the "Cop Killer" song. A decision was made at this meeting to broaden the fight against the rap song and its ultimate producer, Time Warner Corporation.

Discussions centered around several important issues: how to act quickly and capture the high moral ground with the media before Time Warner realized the seriousness of the police opposition and regrouped with its massive corporate publicity machine; and how to effectively mount a nationwide media campaign against a $12 billion conglomerate with resources far outstripping every police association in America. Several decisions were made on June 8th that would prove to be critical to the later success of the police protest against Time Warner.

First, CLEAT realized the importance of acting immediately, before the national press discovered the story and the protest lost its newsworthiness. Almost every news story has a shelf life of about one day. If one of the major news networks aired the story before the others, it would be unlikely that the other news outlets would want to run a repeat of the story.

The next decision involved how to communicate opposition to the "Cop Killer" song. It was decided to schedule a press conference for Thursday, June 11th, in Arlington, Texas at a civic center directly across from the Six Flags Over Texas amusement park. The CLEAT staff was concerned about the lack of time to mobilize the police associations in Texas for a press conference in three days, but felt that to wait until the following week might be disastrous if other organizations began to oppose the song but followed a different course of opposition. In any conflict, **timing of tactical maneuvers is critical to success**!

Why was Six Flags selected for the site of the press conference? First, Time Warner owns 50 percent of the amusement park, so the location gave maximum media attention to the discrepancy between Time Warner's "family image" and Ice-T's vicious song. Second, the greater Dallas-Fort Worth metroplex has large numbers of police associations within close drive distance, an important factor to turn out a large number of uniformed officers for visual effect at the press conference. Last, the DFW media market is the largest in Texas, and offered the greatest potential for nationwide coverage.

How to Frame the Issue Correctly Now and Win the Fight Later

Before the corporate campaign kicked off against Time Warner, there were several important questions that had to be answered. Without structuring the battle lines the right way beforehand, there would be confusion among CLEAT members, other police associations, and the public. And confusion translates into the most destructive result in high-profile battles—**no support**.

The first consideration was to stake out a position that avoided any dispute over Ice-T's right to write or sing "Cop Killer"—nothing will bring a negative press reaction more than a demand for censorship of artistic materials. It was important to keep the issue away from Ice-T and instead, frame it around the corporate greed and immorality of Time Warner.

Another question was the "demand" that would be made of Time Warner at the press conference. What could a group of police associations realistically expect to achieve against one of the world's largest companies? The "demand" would be for Time Warner to apologize to America's police and the surviving families of slain officers, and to halt distribution of the song.

The question of whether or not to call for a boycott of Time Warner products at the June 11th meeting had to be addressed, particularly since the DPA was already asking its members to take such an action. The call for a consumer boycott is the ultimate act of corporate warfare. It seemed imprudent to call for a boycott until a better picture developed as to whether police groups, the public and media were willing to bring pressure on Time Warner to sustain such a fight. A wiser course seemed to be a *threatened* boycott, which would be a "wake-up" call to Time Warner without having to resort to a tactic of questionable long-term success.

CLEAT Gets Unexpected Help from a Time Warner Stockholder

As the local radio and papers began picking up the "Cop Killer" story in a few Texas cities, a Time Warner shareholder, living in Austin, provided a shareholder's packet, which contained a gold mine of information about the corporation, including its officers, corporate directors, and diverse subsidiary companies.

The packet included a letter from Time Warner announcing its upcoming shareholder's meeting in Beverly Hills on July 16th. Bingo! Beverly Hills was the obvious place to bring the conflict to a climax. The July 16th date gave CLEAT the time to effectively mobilize a nationwide campaign. This later date would also extend the media shelf life of the controversy by reopening the issue in another forum.

There's an old saying that the anticipation of a whipping far exceeds its reality. CLEAT hoped that as the date of the shareholders' meeting approached, Time Warner would weaken in its resolve to defend its position.

The Corporate Campaign Against Time Warner
Kicks into High Gear

On Tuesday, June 9th, the CLEAT staff started to mobilize Texas police associations and begin the corporate campaign nationwide. An announcement of the June 11th press conference brought a flood of calls from local, state, and national media.

About 500 "how to" information packets for police labor groups and other groups were prepared. These packets included: a CLEAT press release, a copy of DPA's article, a copy of the Concerns of Police Survivor's letter to Warner Brothers Records, a copy of the Time Warner announcement of the shareholders' meeting, a list of all Time Warner directors and major holdings, and a copy of a soon-to-be-used press conference visual that read like a movie announcement ("Time Warner...Now Proudly Presents...Cop Killer").

The press conference was a national media event. More than 75 uniformed officers were present. CLEAT President Ron DeLord and Glenn White of the DPA anchored the press conference. The press conference was started by playing the lead track to the song and distribution of the lyrics—the reality of the song hit the media like a ton of bricks. The visuals included a 3'x 4' movie poster ("Time Warner...Now Proudly Presents...") and a copy of the cassette with its graphic cop killer illustrations. **Always remember to bring materials to a present conference that visually reinforce the message you are delivering!**

Another important statement at the press conference was that CLEAT representatives would attend the July 16th Time Warner stockholders meeting and demonstrate against the record, and that police groups from across the country would be solicited to attend as well. CLEAT's position was that there would be no boycott until after the shareholders' meeting, which, as noted previously, gave the group time to determine how much opposition could develop against Time Warner and the record.

Time Warner Reacts and Gets Blown Away by Public
Condemnation

Time Warner executives took a hard line early on by stating that they would not cease distribution of "Cop Killer." In various letters and op-ed newspaper pieces, company officials took the position that Time Warner was not motivated by profits, and that it was concerned only with the free expression of ideas.

This response fell on deaf ears! The corporation's cynical defense of its position inflamed the police, the public, and the media. A *Fort Worth Star Telegram* writer noted that "It is hard [for Time Warner] to see through a dollar bill." *The Wall Street Journal* hammered the corporation with a hard hitting editorial entitled "Rapping With Time Warner."

In the weeks between June 11th and the July 16th shareholders' meeting, media attention surrounding the issue never ceased. Literally thousands of letters and phone calls pounded Time Warner. President George Bush called the song "sick," and Vice President Dan Quayle attacked Time Warner. Sixty members of Congress wrote letters to the corporation supporting the police. The governor of Alabama and attorney general of California unleashed on Time Warner.

Most important, other major police labor organizations threw their full weight behind the fight. These groups included the National Fraternal Order of Police, National Association of Police Organizations, New York City PBA and Detectives Endowment Association, Los Angeles Police Protective League, and Peace Officers Research Association of California.

Exciting Events Take Place Before the Shareholders' Meeting

Events proceeded at a furious pace on July 15th and 16th in Beverly Hills. On Wednesday night (July 15th), 65 police officers and family members from throughout the United States and families representing Concerns of Police Survivors attended a strategy meeting. Two Time Warner Executives came to defend their company's position to a very emotional, angry crowd, and the assembled police entourage left with no doubt as to the gravity of the controversy faced by the corporation.

Always expect the unexpected when you have a media circus. Whenever other groups become involved, leaders of the conflict lose a certain amount of control. The National Rifle Association joined the fray by having its front police organization, the Law Enforcement Alliance of America (LEAA), call a press conference for Wednesday also. LEAA captured some media attention by falsely claiming to have started the protest and boycott.

Another interesting premeeting development was a counterprotest by a radical organization. The police groups involved were concerned about having the shareholders' meeting disrupted by violence. As it turned out, only about 10 counterprotesters showed up, and their only contribution was shouting some slogans.

On D-Day, Thursday, July 16th, a smaller than expected group of about 50 police protesters marched outside the Beverly Hills Wilshire Hotel where the meeting was taking place. There were actually more media present than police officers! Remember: When confronted with a situation where you don't get the turnout at a demonstration that you expect, then restate your position—instead of the turnout being a "mass" demonstration, it becomes a "representative" group of the rank and file.

Here are a few other tips for holding a public demonstration that were illustrated by the Beverly Hills event: (1) always plan your protest for a time and place that will give maximum media coverage; (2) hold it for a relatively short period of time—your supporters will get bored quickly, and (3) whenever you have a smaller than expected crowd, keep everyone bunched together on one block to give the appearance of a much larger crowd.

The July 16th Shareholders' Meeting at the Wilshire Turns the Tide of the "Cop Killer" Controversy

Inside the Wilshire Hotel, more than 1,200 shareholders convened for the meeting. There were reports that Time Warner bussed in hundreds of employees so there would be a cheering section for the company's position. Chief Executive Officer Gerald Levin tried to hold the general shareholders' meeting before discussing the "Cop Killer" song, but he was constantly disrupted by shareholders demanding to address the issue.

The high point was Charlton Heston's dynamic reading of "Cop Killer" to the stunned crowd of wealthy investors. Heston was followed by impassioned speeches against Time Warner by many police labor leaders and other concerned people: Ron DeLord, CLEAT; Dewey Stokes, FOP National President; Tommy Velotti, New York

City PBA President; Tom Scotto, New York City Detectives Endowment Association; Bud Stone, PORAC President; Bill Violante, LA Police Protective League; Kansas City police widow Kathleen Young; Houston preacher James Dixon; Art Lymer, Metropolitan Toronto Police Association President; and more than 30 other persons. Their powerful message penetrated the very depths of the Time Warner corporation.

Like Most Disputes, the "Cop Killer" Fight Ends in Ambiguous Victory

On Tuesday, July 28th, Ice-T "voluntarily" removed his "Cop Killer" record from distribution. Whether Time Warner pressured Ice-T will never be known; however, it would seem likely that pressure was applied. Ice-T claimed that both Time Warner and he had received death and bomb threats from police officers. No apology was made by either Ice-T or the corporation.

It is puzzling that the principal adversaries agreed to withdraw the song from production but not apologize to the law enforcement community. The leaders of the protest fully expected the apology, but not the removal from distribution, and the reverse turned out to be the case.

By July 31st, several police organizations were ready to declare victory. CLEAT, the New York City PBA, LA Police Protective League, and New York State Sheriffs Association issued press releases calling for a cease fire in the war of words with Time Warner. It seemed to be the feeling of these groups that an effective boycott against the corporation was not justified and could not in any event be successfully sustained over a period of time.

Other police organizations vowed to continue the battle against Time Warner. What their objective was at that point seemed unclear, and their will to sustain the fight was also open to question. It would have seemed wiser to set this fight aside and move onto the pressing agendas that police associations faced throughout the country.

The following year, Time Warner cancelled its contract with Ice-T. The reasons for the cancellation were vague, but did bring the "Cop Killer" controversy to its final conclusion.

Chapter 42

THE 1992 POLICE CIVILIAN REVIEW BOARD CONTROVERSY IN SAN JOSE

MICHAEL FEHR

AUTHORS' NOTE: The Rodney King incident in Los Angeles precipitated a flurry of demands across the country for civilian review boards. Here's a case study where one police association neutralized the push for civilian review in 1992. Michael Fehr is a career police officer in San Jose who was the point man for this fight.

Since the Rodney King incident almost two years ago, police civilian review boards have become the battle cry among community activists. The San Jose Police Officers' Association was faced with a fight over civilian review in 1992, and as president of the 1,200 member association, it was my responsibility to lead the group during this conflict. Following is the Association's story.

A Little Background About San Jose, California

For many years, San Jose, California lived in the shadow of our internationally known neighbor to the north–San Francisco. In more recent times, however, the city of San Jose has matured. The population has grown to more than 800,000, making the city the tenth largest in the country. And it has attracted computer chip entrepreneurs, making it known worldwide as the "Capitol of Silicon Valley."

The San Jose Police Department has a personnel complement of 1,251 sworn officers. Our agency holds not only a statewide, but national and international reputation as well, for its field training program and other professional accomplishments. The 1,200-plus member police association is the recognized bargaining agent for all sworn

259

officers except the chief and one assistant chief, and is a major player in local political and community affairs.

As San Jose has continued to grow in the past few years, there have been the predictable growing pains. The most recent example of these growing pains was the 1992 push by the Santa Clara County Bar Association for a Police Civilian Review Board.

Mr. Rodney King Pays a Visit to San Jose

With all the coverage over what had become known as "the Rodney King Incident," it was inevitable that the issue of police conduct would be visited on San Jose. In the spring, 1992, the Santa Clara Bar Association climbed on the Rodney King bandwagon and made a recommendation for a police civilian review board in San Jose. The reasons cited for this proposal were that there was a need for trust of the police department, and this trust could only be established through an open process. This recommendation included a proposal that use of force complaints against San Jose police officers would be investigated by a civilian review board, which would hold open hearings and have full subpoena powers. The board would also have the power to dictate department procedure, policy, and disciplinary action.

This proposal by the bar sssociation presented a clear threat to the well being of the Police Association membership. Because of the police department's integrity in conducting internal affairs complaints, and the community's general acceptance of this investigative procedure, there was clearly no perceived need for an alternative review system.

The Police Association Tries to Mediate a Settlement with the Bar Association

As president of the police association, I also participate in another local organization known as the public affairs council, which is a conglomerate of business, labor and professional representatives working together to improve the "quality of life" in San Jose. Through a prominent representative of the council, a meeting was arranged in early October between Santa Clara Bar Association President Brian Walsh and me to determine whether common ground existed for resolution of this issue.

It became clear at this meeting that there would be no basis for a settlement of the dispute. Mr. Walsh was essentially under a mandate by his board of trustees for a police civilian review process, not only in San Jose, but in all law enforcement agencies throughout the county. In effect, the bar association was prepared to use San Jose as an example to force civilian review down the throats of the other county agencies.

There were some difficulties with compromise from the police association's point of view as well. There were two state laws, one concerning the confidentiality of police personnel records and the other known as the California Police Officers's Bill of Rights, which directly conflicted with the bar association proposal.

Also, I pointed out to Mr. Walsh during our meeting the conflict between the bar association's insistence on outside review for cops, and yet its resistance to the same concept when it came to civilian complaints against attorneys. I kept up this latter theme throughout the civilian review board fight, and the bar association continually side-stepped our demand for an explanation!

With Friends Like These, the Bar Association Didn't Need Enemies

The bar association was soon joined by an activist student group from San Jose State University. I believe that later events show that this alliance hurt the bar's position more than it benefited.

The city council placed the civilian review board on the October 19th weekly meeting agenda for discussion. The bar association opposed discussion of the issue at that time, because it had not had the opportunity to review a recently completed police department internal affairs study. This study examined internal affairs statistics in San Jose, interviewed participants in a typical internal affairs process, contained a literature search, and looked at other civilian review board processes in the Bay Area and throughout the country.

In an effort to be fair, the city council granted the bar association's request that the discussion be postponed to allow time to prepare arguments opposing the police department study. The student activists became infuriated and disrupted the meeting, taking over the council chambers and driving the mayor, council members, and city manager out of the council chambers and into a side conference room.

So the city manager's earlier decision to conduct a low key meeting by keeping away uniformed officers for security backfired! The unruly crowd must have seen the lack of security as a sign of weakness rather than compromise, and took advantage of the decision. Police personnel had to be summoned to secure the council chambers and protect council members. The entire situation clearly detracted from the bar association's attempt to project a professional position.

The Police Association and San Jose Police Chief Join Forces to Take on Civilian Review

As this issue developed, San Jose Chief of Police Lou Cobarruviaz had been the top administrator of the police department for less than a year. By virtue of his responsibilities to the police department, city, and community, he had occasionally taken positions at odds with the police association. As a result of several meetings with the chief, however, it was clear to me that he was in accord with the police association in opposition to civilian review!

Chief Cobarruviaz was adamant that he would not give in to the bar association demands. The chief felt that the department's internal affairs process was beyond reproach, and that if there was civilian review of department procedure, policy and discipline, then there would be no need for a chief of police in San Jose. The chief did not want to remain in his position as a figurehead, so he made it clear that he would simply resign if the civilian review board was put into place!

The local press created the usual media hype about the chief's position, reporting that the chief had given the city council an ultimatum if the council supported the bar association's proposal. The chief's statements were blown out of proportion. I believed, and told the press, that the chief was not threatening the council; instead, he was giving the council the "cold, hard facts."

The Civilian Auditor Alternative Is Raised By the Mayor and City Manager

There is no question that a considerable amount of political controversy had been generated by the bar association proposal. And city government, in an understandable attempt at being democratic and responsive, looked at an alternative to civilian review.

Mayor Susan Hammer, along with City Manager Les White, felt that a civilian review board was not a valid concept, but that something more than the present system was needed to satisfy the concerns of citizens who had made use of force complaints against San Jose officers and for various reasons had come away dissatisfied. After the October council meeting, they raised the alternative of a civilian auditor process, an idea that had come from the Seattle Police Department.

The civilian auditor process would allow a person dissatisfied with the outcome of a case to go to an outside auditor, who would then determine whether the complaint was legitimate. The basic parts of the original proposal would give the civilian auditor the authority to:

1. review and assess police misconduct investigations;

2. request the chief of police to further investigate cases which, upon review, the auditor did not believe were thorough and objective;

3. produce a semi-annual report to the mayor and council which would look at trends and patterns, and would recommend improvements to the process, training needs, and other preventive measures.

The Police Association Goes into High Gear to Fight Civilian Review

The city council set November 17th as the public meeting day to resolve the civilian review board dispute. The police association had a month to prepare for this confrontation with the bar association.

The association attorney and I met with the mayor, some city council members, city manager, and city attorney to explain our position. We pointed out our concerns, cited previously in this article, about state laws protecting personnel records and the officers rights. We also stressed that the San Jose Internal Affairs process was beyond reproach, that officers were open to being investigated by internal affairs, and that it was understood by the association and officers that internal affairs has a job to do. Our bottom line position in these meetings was that the police association DID NOT EXPECT special treatment for our members, but we DID DEMAND fair treatment.

Our next step was to make an appeal to our membership at the individual shift briefings and to all specialized units within the four police department bureaus. Association board members emphasized to our members the importance of their presence at the upcoming council meeting, and the importance of their professional behavior at that meeting.

The police association was active on other fronts as well. We produced public service ads outlining our position on the issue, made extensive use of the free press, and contacted various community leaders whom we had built coalitions with through the public affairs council and other community activities, soliciting their support.

November 17th Arrives, and the City Council Makes a Decision

More than 100 police association members showed up at the November 17th city council meeting. There were more than 500 people in attendance at the meeting, and they stayed for the entire six hours that the issue was discussed with city council.

I had the opportunity to address the council and present the police association's message of opposition to both the civilian review board and civilian auditor. During my presentation, I emphasized several points: the association's desire that all officers conduct themselves with pride, integrity, and professionalism; the embarrassment that is brought to our profession by the "bad cop;" the fact that the police department was committed to rooting out bad cops, as evidenced by a new department program to educate citizens on how to report improper police behavior; the success of the police department's self-policing, as shown by past suspensions, terminations and charges filed against San Jose officers; and that an internal, rather than external policing system, was the best method for accountability, training, follow-up, and self-scrutiny by the department.

More than 100 speakers offered their positions for and against civilian review and the independent auditor. People speaking for civilian review included bar association representatives and student activists. There were many opponents as well, including the chamber of commerce and a deputy district attorney.

After patiently listening to every speaker, the mayor and city council voted unanimously against a civilian review board, and instead, supported the civilian auditor process for the police department. The council did add other provisions to the original concept at the meeting: the auditor would be a paid position selected by the city council;

there would be timely updates of investigations supplied to complainants; the auditor would provide statistical breakdown of complaints; the auditor would have ability to interview complainants and witnesses; and the auditor could choose to attend, but not participate in, investigations/interviews of officers.

As Mayor Susan Hammer presented the council's position to the audience, she was booed and taunted by people in attendance in support of civilian review, mainly the student activists. But the mayor maintained her composure as she was continually interrupted throughout her presentation.

The student activists began standing on tables in the council chambers, chanting slogans, and rolling out banners opposing the council's decision. After allowing the dissidents approximately 20 minutes to express their disagreement over the decision, an order was read by the deputy chief in charge of the uniform bureau to disperse. Uniform personnel were then called to disperse the crowd and 24 people were arrested.

One final observation about the meeting is that our association members conducted themselves in a professional way during this six-hour, highly emotional council meeting. I am convinced that our behavior made this politically difficult decision much easier for the council in the face of a discourteous and at times unruly crowd of civilian review proponents.

In Summary, We Came Out Ahead of the Curve in the Civilian Review Fight

The police association would have preferred a complete endorsement of our current internal affairs process. But the city council was under the gun to make some gesture of commitment to the community activists. I do believe, however, that the mayor and council gave us a big show of support in recommending the civilian auditor over a review board.

And the fact is that the city cannot unilaterally impose the civilian auditor on the police association. The concept must be negotiated as a part of collective bargaining with the city. The police association therefore has a great deal of control over our destiny in this situation; on the other hand, we feel politically compelled to agree with the principle of a civilian auditor. Our major concern is over those parts of the process which might interfere with state laws protecting the confidentiality of personnel records and the Bill of Rights.

In the end, I believe there are five reasons why the police association won a political victory in spite of climate where a vocal part of the public was demanding a reform of police procedures involving the use of force. First, the mayor and city council had a great deal of trust in and respect for the San Jose Police Department and Police Association. Second, the incredibly professional demeanor of our members during the council meetings in October and November was significant, especially in contrast to the student activists who were demanding police oversight but couldn't control their own behavior.

Third, the police association has excellent relationships with local politicians, community leaders, and the chief of police. These relationships had been built up over a long period of time, and paid off when we needed help in the biggest political battle the association has faced in years.

Fourth was our labor attorney, John Tenant, who has assisted the police association on this issue over the past year. Mr. Tenant is an outstanding labor attorney who had faced a similar civilian review issue in Berkeley, California. He was able to give us guidance based on the troubling experience with Berkeley's civilian review.

And last, but most certainly not least, was the support of the police association's membership. For without the support of those who give us the reason to exist as a labor organization, we would have had no power base to fight this politicized issue.

Chapter 43

REPRESENTING POLICE OFFICERS IN JOB-RELATED LEGAL MATTERS - THE PORAC LEGAL DEFENSE FUND

LARRY FRIEDMAN

AUTHORS' NOTE: In an era where virtually every action of a police officer can result in disciplinary action, civil suit, or even indictment, there is an insistence among law enforcement officers for comprehensive legal protection. Here's a case study about one statewide police association, the Peace Officers Research Association of California (PORAC), which has established a top-flight legal program for its members. The author is the administrator for this program.

Suspect Sues Cops!" "Deputies Charged With Assault!" "Police Department Investigates Officers." Right out of today's headlines? Actually, California peace officers were the subjects of similar attacks back in the early 1970s. The Peace Officers Research Association of California (PORAC) realized that the traditional methods of representation were insufficient to meet the onslaught its members were facing.

PORAC is a statewide police association composed of member local associations which, in addition providing legal representation services, sponsors other insurance plans and provides services in the areas of political action, legislation, and education. It also publishes the monthly "PORAC Law Enforcement News."

In the early 1970s, many PORAC Associations were faced with an ever-increasing legal case-load, and were uncomfortable with their representation decisions. It had become more difficult to ensure consistency and to satisfy the duty of fair representation. And small and medium-sized police associations simply did not have the resources to adequately represent their members.

PORAC began considering various options for providing legal representation to peace officers who were faced with job-related legal problems. And after evaluating all of these options, the Legal Defense Fund (LDF) was born in 1974. It was set up as an insurance-type program, and it has remained as such to this day.

Here's How the LDF Works for Peace Officers

The basic concept of LDF is simple. Member associations pay quarterly contributions to the Fund based primarily on the particular claims experience (i.e., extent of plan usage). When a member needs representation, he or she calls the Fund and gets a referral to a panel provider (i.e., an attorney, law firm or for some administrative hearings, a field representative). The provider's bills are then scrutinized and paid by the Fund.

The LDF is administered by five trustees who are working police officers. Four are elected from the PORAC regions, and the fifth is appointed by the PORAC president. The day-to-day operations are managed by Delta Benefit Plans, a professional third-party benefits administrator.

This arrangement has been successful. Members get their claims handled smoothly and efficiently. They also know that their fellow peace officers have the final say on any benefits decisions.

LDF Covers Scope-of-Duty Claims

Members are insured for acts and omissions within the scope of their duties, whether the conduct gives rise to administrative action (i.e., discipline), a civil suit, or a criminal proceeding. Members are represented by experienced law firms or professional field representatives based on the type of plan their police association has chosen. Benefits begin as soon as a member learns of an investigation or lawsuit.

In addition to representation, members are provided with appropriate litigation support. This support service ranges from investigators and polygraphers, to accident reconstruction and use of force experts. Arbitrators and transcript fees are covered too.

Another important benefit is **conflict coverage**. The LAPD/Rodney King incident has made the issue of "bystander liability" a major issue for police officers. There is often a conflict between an officer who is the central focus of an investigation and one who is facing discipline for not reporting the incident. The LDF provides representation for both officers in this situation.

LDF Provides Special Coverage Features for Members

The fund also has two special features apart from the regular coverage. If members are disciplined as a result of their association's taking concerted labor activity, they are entitled to LDF benefits. When the entire membership of the Madera County Deputy Sheriff's Association was fired from their jobs, the LDF represented each and every deputy.

Another Fund feature provides for situations in which affirmative relief is required. If the trustees believe that a matter has statewide impact, or if there is a reasonable likelihood of an award and recovery of damages, attorney fees and costs, they may authorize litigation against the appropriate governmental entity.

Quality Control Keeps Plan Services Top-Notch

Quality control is assured by careful selection of attorneys. Only people who have demonstrated the ability to represent peace officers are allowed to handle LDF cases.

There are other parts of quality control as well. The fund has a complaint procedure that is widely publicized. And when a case is over, members get a survey so that we can monitor the level of service provided by the attorneys and representatives.

Here Are the Officers Who Participate in LDF

There are 27,250 peace officers in LDF, who belong to approximately 400 PORAC-affiliated associations in all parts of California and Nevada. In addition to police officers and deputy sheriffs, the LDF also represents public safety employees who work for a variety of agencies, including school, transportation, and park districts; universities; housing authorities; state agencies; hospitals; corrections departments; and district attorneys.

All ranks from officer to police chief are included in the program. Additionally, there are nonsworn personnel such as community service representatives and dispatchers.

And in Conclusion

LDF members take great pride in the fact that they have received high quality services for the past 17 years. They know that with more than an $800,000 war chest (i.e., cash reserves) we can go toe-to-toe with any police department, sheriff's office, prosecutor, or plaintiff's attorney. In 1991, the fund paid out more than $2.5 million in benefits.

Finally, the LDF attempts, along with its parent organization, PORAC, to educate its members. It recently conducted a three-day seminar covering many aspects of police representation. Education is a critical component of PORAC's overall program. For the LDF, it means that members are more likely to use services wisely and keep costs under control.

Chapter 44

HOW THE AURORA, COLORADO POLICE ASSOCIATION INCREASED ITS MEMBERSHIP IN ONE EASY ELECTION

MICHAEL SHANNON

AUTHORS' NOTE: Police departments in this country are traditionally understaffed for the tremendous workloads that law enforcement agencies face. Here's a case study of one police association in Colorado that did something about the problem through a referendum in 1993. Michael Shannon ran the campaign for the Aurora Police Association.

The Aurora Police Association (APA) entered the fall of 1993 facing a classic good news/bad news situation. The good news was that after months of behind-the-scenes work and negotiation, the APA had convinced the Aurora City Council to place a question on the November ballot calling for a sales tax increase to bring the department's staffing level to a minimum of 2.0 officers per 1,000 population.

The bad news was that the association had only two and one-half months to put a campaign together to win the election. The APA hired me as the general political consultant to construct a credible campaign during this very short foot race to election day.

The campaign situation was further complicated by the presence of a controversial city bond package on the same ballot and a negative political climate in Colorado. The bond package was potentially troublesome because of its size. Instead of a single question with a "yes" or "no" on the entire package, the "Capital Choice" bond package was split into a number of smaller pieces that added to ballot-crowding and complication. I was additionally concerned about the "reeling with the feeling" effect where taxpayers voting "no" on a number of the bond questions decide to vote "no" on the whole "shebang."

The cloudy political climate was mainly due to a high pressure constitutional amendment campaign that voters passed the year before. The amendment required voter approval of all local tax increases. It also put stringent limitations on what government could do in support of bond issues or tax questions and contributed to a negative perception of local government.

No Votes = No Bucks

Economically, the election was a high stakes venture for the APA because the next year, 1994, was a contract negotiation year, and a defeat at the polls would undermine any claims of citizen support the association might make at the bargaining table. In stories prior to the election, the local newspaper referred to the APA as "the powerful Aurora police union." Defeat would have transformed them into the pitiful Aurora police union at contract negotiation time.

The final variable in the mix was the conduct of the election itself. This was to be a ballot-by-mail, with no in-person polling places. Every registered voter in the city of Aurora would receive a ballot in the mail.

This variable automatically meant a more expensive election for the APA. Usually, municipal elections are characterized by a numbing combination of voter apathy, press ignorance, and low turnout. (In Aurora, only the press performed up to expectation during the election.) With a mail ballot, turnout would predictably explode. Our polling, done by Janet Grenske of Abacus Associates, predicted a turnout of between 35 and 40 percent, compared to the usual turnout of 11 percent.

The mail ballot also called into question who would vote, since the trip to the mailbox is much shorter than the trip to the polls. Targeting likely voters would be a by-guess-and-by-golly proposition. More voters and mystery voters combined to mean more expense for the APA effort, since we had to reach and convince a larger universe of potential voters.

Surprisingly enough, the mail ballot also meant a speedup in the entire electoral process, which is not something one normally expects from the United States Postal Service. Ballots had to be in the mail to voters by October 18. Since voting isn't like Christmas, and voters don't have to wait, election day for us was effectively October 23 through October 28, because polling predicted that most voters would complete their ballots within five days of receiving it.

Money: The Mother's Milk of Politics

Without money, you simply cannot run a campaign in American politics. The need for money is a problem. Another related problem is that police officers as a whole have zero experience in raising money. They are pretty good at making deals and getting in-kind donations from local business people, but you can't win an election on tire discounts and stop-and-shoot coffee.

That's why political action committees are so important for police associations: they supply a ready-made source of funds for conducting political and public relations campaigns. But the APA did not have a PAC, and you can't create and fund one in six weeks.

The APA had set out a fund raising plan with targeted potential donor groups. It also explored the possibility of a $100 per member assessment for the campaign. What the campaign finally settled upon was transferring $50,000 out of the APA legal defense fund into the campaign committee treasury.

This plan was good, because as the campaign's general consultant, it gave me a number from which to construct a budget; but it was bad in that it removed all the urgency from our outside fundraising. As a result, the only notable outside financial contribution was a very welcome $7,500 from the Colorado Police Protective Association.

Determining the Message

It is possible to run one of these campaigns on hunches, but the results can be extremely unpredictable, and your chance of success is reduced. With the contract negotiations approaching the following year, the APA couldn't afford to take any chances, so we hired Janet Grenske of Abacus Associates, to conduct a benchmark poll.

The preliminary numbers indicated that we had a good chance of winning the election–31 percent of the voters were in favor of the issue; but it was also obvious from the large undecided 44 percent, that we would have to persuade those undecideds too if we wanted to win.

Additionally, we had to keep in mind that many people who were listed as soft supporters of the issue in our poll might well change their minds when they voted, since a "yes" vote would mean agreeing to a tax increase. We had to make these leaners into solid supporters.

The basic theme of a manpower election is always crime, but it's important to tailor the particulars of the message to your specific audience. In Aurora, citizens were particularly concerned about the growth of gang crime. Both Denver newspapers and the broadcast media had recently run stories about the growth in gangs and gang violence. The job for our theme and message was to put all this gang fear and gang information into a package that put what the election would do to solve these problems into perspective for Aurora taxpayers.

The theme we chose was: **There's Safety in Numbers, Vote Yes on Question "A"'**. Safety In Numbers essentially took an existing cliché and applied it to our particular issue, which was increasing the number of police officers, who would in turn provide the safety.

Delivering the Message

The three main components of our message delivery system were the familiar: paid media, press events, and direct voter contact. There were subsets of these, which included a strong endorsement campaign and a speakers bureau.

Our paid media was limited to direct mail because we had to target fewer than the total universe of voters. Broadcast media will only let you talk to everyone (unless Regis and Kathy are making house calls), and we could only afford a few electronic media spots.

The mail effort would be a larger initial mailing to a larger list, in this case voters who had voted in either the '88, '90, or '92 elections; and a follow-up, get-out-the-vote (GOTV) piece to a smaller list that was a subset of the initial mailing. When it came to writing the first piece, I felt a bit like Lucille Ball: "You got a lot 'splaining to do." Our issue was complicated: we had to explain where the 2.0 per 1,000 ratio came from, prove to residents in the richer parts of Aurora that gangs weren't confined to the ghetto, and justify raising taxes.

Because of the detail required to cover all these bases, I decided to make the first mail piece a four-page tabloid newspaper called the *Aurora Defender*. This format would allow room for pictures, a map of gang activity, an editorial cartoon, and an endorsement by the paper of our issue.

The GOTV mailing was an endorsement postcard that would list our endorsements from newspapers, civic groups, and anyone else we could persuade to go on record as supporting us. This postcard would be a short, punchy piece that would simply recap the longer message of the tabloid.

Press Coverage: No Car Wreck, No News

Usually a campaign that has even the least bit of organization can expect two stories from the media concerning the race: the first story is the announcement story, and the last one is the just before the election wrap-up. Unfortunately, in Aurora, we didn't even get that.

Our first press conference was to announce the formation of the Citizens for a Safe Aurora steering committee, and to proclaim that gangs were our message. The site for the conference was the unfinished jail, which would be opened as a result of the election. The local weekly (which gave us reasonable coverage during the election, in contrast to the so-called major newspapers), a fringe TV station, and one radio station showed up.

Our next news conference was to release the results of our poll. Here, again, we went to the trouble to make it visual–this time at a "gang gate," a concrete barrier placed in the streets to discourage drive-by shootings. This time only one TV station and the weekly came out.

Our final press conference was canceled because we weren't able to get the volunteers necessary to make the extensive preparations it required. Rather than have a poorly prepared conference, I opted to eliminate the risk and do without.

When the sleepy electronic media finally did wake up, it wasn't to do us any favors. The last few days before November 2, two of the stations decided to do a series on government waste, and used the unfinished jail as an example. Fortunately, because of the mail ballot, the election was over before these guardians of the public purse woke up and decided to cover it, so these stories did us no harm.

How Endorsements Can Cause Invisibility

Endorsements were important to the campaign, because I wanted to show the voters the APA had broad-based support for the issue, instead of it being a vote to benefit a labor union. Representatives of the APA board made presentations to the editorial boards of all the major newspapers and all the weeklies that would meet with us. They made a strong case for the issue and asked for an endorsement. They also informed the media representatives that an endorsement the weekend before the election would do their readers no good, since the mail ballot would be over.

This effort was time well spent. *The Denver Post* and the *Aurora Sentinel* both gave strong endorsements that we were able to use in the campaign. Locally, getting endorsements from civic groups was much harder. Groups like MADD and AARP, with members who benefit from increased police protection, didn't have either the time or the gumption to give an endorsement. Fortunately, local district attorneys and sheriffs were supportive, as were booster clubs, the Chamber of Commerce, and individual elected officials.

The APA also worked hard to neutralize potential opposition at the same time they were gathering support. Unfortunately, CANT: Citizens Against New Taxes, didn't have enough intellectual integrity to return phone calls, so the APA never was able to make a case for them.

Manpower: Another "M" Word That Spells Trouble

One good thing about the mail ballot was that it removed any need for poll workers the day of the election. But it didn't remove the need for volunteers for the direct voter contact campaign, to work at campaign headquarters, to answer the phone, run errands, address envelopes, walk door-to-door, and to build and install yard signs.

In addition, the one volunteer-intensive portion of our campaign was a door-to-door canvass of targeted precincts. The post office would handle both mail pieces, but it would take literally hundreds of volunteers to contact voters in person to deliver our message just prior to the receipt of the mail ballots, and to display a physical presence in the neighborhoods.

But the volunteer portion of the campaign never happened because the campaign never achieved volunteer critical mass, that is, the time in a campaign where volunteers begin to snowball and recruit other volunteers without your active, daily supervision. Under the critical mass scenario, volunteers are supposed to materialize almost out of thin air.

Before critical mass is reached, most of the campaign staff is on the phone trying to recruit people to come in and work at headquarters. Once critical mass is reached, there are enough people working each day to handle recruitment on their own, leaving paid staff and the association board time to plan the big events.

Our only success mass volunteer events were yard sign construction. All other tasks normally done by volunteers were instead completed by APA board members in their spare time.

Dialing for Voters

Without volunteers for the final GOTV efforts, the campaign had to scramble. Midwest Publishing, the telemarketing firm that does the APA fundraising, agreed to run a phone bank for the association at a very reasonable cost. We were able to phone 7,000 households in four days with a persuasion message in the few days after they got the mail ballot. This endeavor was less than the number of households we wanted to walk, but it was infinitely better than doing nothing.

Message Delivery One-On-One

The board members of the APA carried the campaign to the grassroots civic level. During the course of the campaign, APA representatives participated in over 50 town meetings, candidate forums, and neighborhood get-togethers, spreading the message to each one.

They also delivered literature, passed out brochures at fairs and events, and generally provided the backbone of the campaign effort. It was hard work, but it paid off on election day.

The Fat Lady Sings

When all the ballots were finally counted, the APA had won the election by a landslide 68 percent. Turnout was a very heavy 35.9 percent, well within the polling prediction. It was a victory for law enforcement in Aurora, and we were hopeful it would provide the momentum for successful negotiations at the bargaining table in 1994.

The APA won the election and deserved to win because the organization did its homework. From the early days of meeting with the city council and city manager to get them on board for the vote, to the public campaign effort, the APA leadership tried to be organized, systematic, and professional. When they could do a job themselves, they did it; when the task required outside help, they hired it. And when they won on election day, they enjoyed it.

20/20 Hindsight in Aurora

You wouldn't think that when a police association wins an election with record turnout by 68 percent, there would be much room for second guessing, but some folks—me for instance—are picky. Although the APA won its minimum staffing election, there are three areas where the campaign could have been even more effective, and the problems we encountered contain a lesson for other politically active law enforcement associations. These three areas are: campaign finance, internal campaign management structure, and connecting with the electorate.

You Can Never Be Too Rich

Raising money for campaigns is hard. You will invariably hear, "So-and-So dried up all the money, there isn't any more to raise." Or the economy's bad, or it's too close to the last election, or something or someone prevents raising any money.

If you don't want to deal with these excuses, then I suggest forming a political action committee (PAC) for a source of ready campaign funds. Aurora did not have a PAC, and the campaign was almost stillborn. Captains of industry suddenly became privates of fundraising when the APA asked them to help raise money for the election!

Fortunately, the association membership approved a sizable transfer from the legal defense fund, and the campaign was able to get underway. But even with a PAC, you may need to raise outside money, and the APA learned it must control its own fundraising fate and be prepared to do its own asking.

You must know who has donated to law enforcement projects in the past, either through the department or through the association. Go to these people first. Be aggressive when approaching outsiders for funds, have a specific amount in mind, and don't collapse if you are rejected.

If one target says no, move on to the next. Remember those whom the association has done favors for in the past (if you don't have this information on a list you can get within five minutes, you are failing as an leader!), and ask them to return the favor with a check.

When you approach a potential donor with your hat in hand, you will leave holding only your hat. Cops aren't accustomed to functioning in a sales environment, but that's what political fundraising is: SALES. Without selling ability, your alternative is a PAC or a bake sale.

Once you have the money, be prepared to spend it. In a couple of instances, we wasted irreplaceable days saving pennies. In a campaign you can raise more money, but you can never get more time.

Staying Out of the Ditch

Associations that have a full-time staff have a real advantage during a campaign. The full-time staffers can make the campaign their job for the few weeks until the election. Most associations, however, are like the APA with an unpaid president and board of directors, which is a great disadvantage.

In that situation, beware of board meetings where there is plenty of general agreement as to campaign goals and timetables, but no specific responsibility. Jobs must be broken down into manageable parts and assigned to board members who agree to take specific responsibility for completing the task by a specific deadline.

A meeting where all assembled nod their heads, but no one taps his or her chest and says that job is mine, is a meeting that will get nothing done.

All the board must participate. You can't have a handful of members trying to do their police job plus all the election tasks, and then expect jobs to be done, much less done in a timely fashion.

Reach Out and Recruit Someone

Here I think our campaign had two big oversights: we didn't draw on the membership, and the paid campaign office manager didn't start soon enough.

I never felt during the campaign that the average officer had an emotional stake in the contest. It could have been that we were so concerned about the voters that we didn't take the time to fully involve the rank-and-file. If I had it to do over, I would send a special newsletter to the membership, and would have had more early membership meetings to explain what was at stake. As a result, the campaign office never had the volunteers from APA members, family, and friends that should have been working to pass the issue.

Had the office manager been on the ground a couple of weeks earlier, this might have changed. During the first few weeks of any campaign, most of the day is spent lining up bodies to get the headquarters functioning. Once you reach volunteer critical mass, you have enough people on the phone to turn over recruitment to them, and the leadership can turn to other tasks.

In Aurora, we never could sustain that volunteer reaction. As a result, all the volunteer-intensive activities, door-to-door canvassing in particular, were canceled.

APA board members worked overtime going to neighborhood meetings and candidate forums, allowing at least some voters to see police supporters in the flesh, but this didn't have the mass impact of two-person groups blanketing blocks of the city wearing APA T-shirts and caps, and handing out literature.

Another recruitment area that proved very tough was endorsements from community leaders. Face it, some people are wishy-washy. They want your help, but when they have to put themselves on the line, it's a different story.

Don't let them off the hook. God gave us arms for twisting, so don't be reluctant to do it. You can make up and be friends after the election. When you've won, you'll be gratified as to how popular you are, and how glad Mr. Wishy and Ms. Washy were to be part of the campaign team.

In spite of these small shortcomings, the Aurora Police Association won it's election in a big way and it deserved to win. The board worked hard and the membership risked the money. What they accomplished and what they learned can be useful for law enforcement groups everywhere.

Chapter 45

HOW YOUR POLICE ASSOCIATION CAN MAKE THE DIFFERENCE IN A MAJOR POLITICAL CAMPAIGN

Mark Clark

AUTHORS' NOTE: This case study is a classic demonstration of how a police association can make the ultimate difference in which candidate wins in a hotly-contested political race. The author is a lobbyist for the Combined Law Enforcement Associations of Texas, and has worked for the Houston Police Department for 17 years.

A police association can play a major role in a political campaign, and this participation can reap major rewards for the organization. This chapter will take you step-by-step through one police association's contribution to a recent major political campaign in Texas and discuss some of the things the group did that contributed to the re-election of a long-time, political friend and ally. The lessons of this campaign can be used by any police association in the country.

Senator John Whitmire–A Candidate Who Was in Real Trouble

This 1992 primary campaign involved Texas State Senator John Whitmire, who was the current Chairman of the Senate Intergovernmental Relations (IGR) Committee. The IGR Committee is *the* most important committee in the legislature for working law enforcement officers and fire fighters in Texas, because it presides over all local government labor and pension issues in the senate.

In his 20 years as a Democratic house member and senator, John Whitmire had always been supportive of police officer rights and benefits. The necessity of his re-election, especially in light of his powerful position as a committee chairman, was absolutely imperative for the success of future law enforcement employment law legislation.

Senator Whitmire's re-election was in serious trouble in large part because of a federal court's controversial interference in the reapportionment process. The court had severely gerrymandered the senator's district in early 1992 to include large blocks of Hispanics. The best estimate was that the district was 60 percent Hispanic.

This situation led to a challenge in Texas spring Democratic primary by a well-known and heavily financed Hispanic state legislator, Roman Martinez. Whitmire's troubles were further aided by a large amount of negative media attention in his home district concerning his involvement with some successful land developers.

This senate district is predominantly Democratic, so it was clear that the victor in this primary race would be the anointed senator for the biannual 1993 legislative session.

The Police Association Goes into High-Gear for the Senator

It became clear early in 1992 that my police association, the Combined Law Enforcement Associations of Texas (CLEAT), would have to work extra hard for Senator Whitmire. CLEAT is "an Association of Associations," representing approximately 75 different local law enforcement labor groups and more than 16,000 members across the state in various legal, labor relations, and legislative matters.

It was in the best interests of our organization, and the labor movement of our state, that we become involved in Senator Whitmire's race. As CLEAT's Director of Governmental Relations, it was my responsibility to serve as a volunteer advisor to the campaign.

CLEAT began working at the very first stages of the campaign. Our group was able to get on the campaign team early because of our past relationship with Senator Whitmire. And because of our organization's previous reputation as a serious player in political campaigns, we were made a part of the important strategies that would be developed during the campaign.

We knew from previous political campaigns that if there is a trade secret in this business, it is **early involvement**. Major decisions that dramatically shape the direction of a campaign are always made early–that is the point at which critical decisions are made on staff personnel and consultants, and on policy positions.

And this work at the beginning of the campaign brings up LESSON #1: **The earlier you get involved in the campaign, the more you can do for the candidate and the more you become a part of the trusted inner campaign circle, and the more the candidate will remember afterward what you did for him or her.**

Deciding What Our Association Could Bring to the Campaign

CLEAT took a look at what it could actually do for the campaign. For this particular case, we felt most comfortable raising political contributions, and organizing a get-out-the-vote program (GOTV), particularly in telephone work and large scale law enforcement block walks. We did not make the mistake that many campaign volunteer organizations make of exaggerating their organization's skills and making themselves appear too ambitious.

This analysis and decision as to the extent of our organizational commitment to the campaign brings up LESSON #2: **Make a realistic appraisal of what your association can bring to the candidate's campaign, and promise the candidate only what you can deliver.**

Early Campaign Work That Makes the Difference Between Winning and Losing

Before the campaign formally began, I took the time, along with other campaign advisors, to study the senator's district prior to the court-ordered reapportionment, as well as all the new areas that had been added to his district by the federal court. We all felt that it was important to understand the new district and to determine the political nuances of the area.

I also met with local party officials (state and county committeemen, precinct captains) to discuss the newly aligned district, and with current office holders from the new district. These meetings enabled the campaign to identify some of the key opinion leaders in the district, and to solicit their assistance.

These meetings had a tremendous value to my police association as well. The process of meeting with the senate district "movers and shakers" raised their level of trust and respect for my organization. The personal contact gave our group a political credibility that would carry over long past the Whitmire campaign.

And this last observation brings us to LESSON #3: **Heavy participation in a campaign develops political alliances which are significant for long-term political goals of the police association and which go well beyond the immediate election.**

Giving Help to the Senator's Campaign

The first rule in politics is that money drives political campaigns. Many of the CLEAT-affiliated groups have their own Political Action Committees (PACs), and I was able to raise more than $5,000 from these PACs. In a Texas Senate campaign, $5,000 is a great deal of money, and is always appreciated by the candidate.

I was also immediately responsible for finding and assigning volunteers to the campaign office; and as some may know, finding police officers to help out over a sustained political campaign can be a very difficult task indeed!

Two important goals were accomplished by having volunteers in place at campaign headquarters. First, the presence of volunteers in the headquarters gives your organization a "feel" for the campaign, that is, you can better monitor the ebb and flow of the candidate's operation, and what your group might be able to do that is being overlooked by other campaign advisors and/or volunteers.

Second, it insured that the GOTV telephone and blockwalking commitments that our police association had made would in fact be carried out. GOTV work is considered by political operatives in Texas to be the heart of a campaign, because this activity concentrates heavily on voters who take advantage of our state's "early voting" (i.e., formerly called "absentee voting") system. And in close elections, early voters invariably make the difference between winning and losing.

I am particularly proud of the role our police association played in the GOTV telephone and block walking work. Once a professional polling firm determined the voters who were most likely to be supportive of our candidate, then our volunteers worked on the telephones and talked to voters personally at their homes on a precinct-by-precinct basis in order to secure a commitment on behalf of the candidate.

This activity, also referred to in political terms as "voter canvassing," involved many different features. These features included targeting the areas to be canvassed by phone and by block-walks, recruiting additional law enforcement volunteers, designing the volunteers' message to be used in the canvassing, scheduling the canvassing effort, making transportation arrangements for block-walks, and making sure that the canvassers did their assigned tasks.

Our canvassing operation was a major effort performed by large numbers of volunteer law enforcement officers. And I'm proud to say that they all did yeomen's work on behalf of Senator Whitmire.

This last point brings us to LESSON #4: **The old adage—"if you're going to do something, be sure to do it right" - really applies to any police association in an election campaign.** If you follow this important principle, your organization's political reputation will always keep you far ahead of the usual crowd of political hangers-ons who talk a good game, but can't deliver when the campaign is on the line.

The Value of Having a Volunteer Aide to the Candidate

In any election, it is always valuable for the police association to assign a loyal, attentive, and street-wise volunteer to accompany the candidate when he or she is out in the district. Our association scheduled several volunteer law enforcement officers to fill that highly sensitive position during the campaign.

The result was that Senator Whitmire was able to develop a trusting, long-term relationship with our volunteer members during the campaign. And equally important, this situation gave our police association complete access to the candidate at all times.

The End Result of Hard Work—Victory!

The Whitmire campaign turned out to be a two-phase affair. Due to the presence of three candidates on primary day in March, 1992, no one received a majority of votes. John Whitmire received 46 percent, and his chief opponent, Ramon Martinez, received 48 percent. Then a nail-biting run-off followed in April!

In the toughest election of his 20-year political career, Senator Whitmire defeated his challenger. The margin of victory was 1800 votes out of 30,000 cast (a 53 to 47 percent margin of victory). He will now return to the Texas Senate next year for what will hopefully be another good political year for our organization in the legislature.

The significance of our police association GOTV campaign specifically targeted at early voters can be seen from the statistics: the Senator received almost 2,000 more early votes than his opponent and his margin of victory was 1,800 votes. It is clear that the emphasis on early voting was **the key factor** in this campaign!

Some Parting Thoughts About Police Associations and Success in Election Campaigns

Major campaigns like the Whitmire race are hectic, complex, and stressful. I would like to make some parting observations about this and other campaigns. Some of these thoughts might seem obvious, but all too often, volunteer groups like police associations, and even political professionals, overlook these most basic of principles!

1. The police association should never overestimate its capacity to perform the campaign duties that it has committed to perform—failure to deliver will lead to serious disillusionment and loss of credibility from the candidate and his campaign staff.

2. Always remain cooperative with the professional and volunteer staff of the campaign—**no campaign wants unmanageable, complaining people around!**

3. Do not act independently of the campaign, question the campaign strategy, or criticize its management. Your association is not the be all and end all of the campaign; you are only one small part of a much larger team.

4. Treat your work assignments with a "can do," productive attitude. *Do not* leave them unfinished or treat them frivolously.

5. Refrain from *any* negative comments and conduct in a campaign. Negativism is definitely contagious. Your volunteers must simply stay focused on their assignments, and treat each day like it is the day before election day.

Police association leaders and members have real opportunities in political campaigns. They can gather a wealth of political experience and information—about candidates and issues, about the strategies and tactics of campaigning, and about the techniques of voter contact. There are opportunities to build working coalitions with other organizations, make political friends and allies, participate in a team effort, and understand the challenges and rigors of closely contested races.

But above all, there is a chance to make a real political impact on your members' lives and destinies. Your police association's participation in the political process *can* make the difference. Indeed, political awareness and involvement are the key to effectively representing your membership's interests in a world that revolves entirely around by politics.

Part VII - SPECIAL ADDITION

**DISORGANIZED LABOR:
A HISTORICAL PERSPECTIVE AND
ANALYSIS OF THE POLICE LABOR
MOVEMENT IN THE UNITED STATES**

Chapter 46

SOME GENERAL OBSERVATIONS ABOUT THE POLICE LABOR MOVEMENT IN THE UNITED STATES

The authors did not intend at the outset of writing this book to include any analysis of the police labor movement in this country, either past or present. Our primary, if not complete focus was less on academic information than on the real power, politics, and confrontation issues facing police labor leaders every day.

As we neared completion of this book, however, we realized that there has been no credible or comprehensive work done in more than twenty years on the historical perspectives or a current analysis of the police labor movement. There have been substantial changes in the field in the past twenty years which have not been chronicled, and a whole new generation of police labor leaders has come on the scene with little or knowledge about the historical roots of the police labor movement, and its connection to what is going on today. Also, some of the issues discussed in this book—association business rivals, for example, are impacted by past history and current conditions in the field.

Some General Comments About Public Sector Unionization

Private sector unionization reached its peak of 35 percent of the work force in 1947. With the total nonagricultural labor force increasing at a greater rate than union membership, private sector union membership has been declining since 1955, when the American Federation of Labor (AFL) and Congress of Industrial Organizations

(CIO) merged. Total union membership declined from 23 percent of the work force in 1968, to 19 percent in 1978, to 16 percent in 1989, and is about 12 percent today.

During the same period, however, public sector unionization has increased. Although the rise in the number of public employees joining labor unions and collectively bargaining is not as dramatic as it was during the 1960s and 1970s, public employee unionism is still the strongest area of growth for labor unions, with about 35 percent of public employees unionized. It started with the signing of Executive Order 10988 by President John F. Kennedy in 1962. The unionization of the federal sector continued thereafter into state, county, and municipal governments.

The largest federal union is the American Federation of Government Employees (AFGE, AFL-CIO). AFGE is the bargaining agent for patrol officers in the U.S Border Patrol. Two of the other large federal unions are the National Treasury Employees Union (NTEU), which is not affiliated with the AFL-CIO, and the National Association of Government Employees (NAGE), which affiliated in 1982 as an autonomous division of the Service Employees International Union (SEIU, AFL-CIO). NAGE has a division called the International Brotherhood of Police Officers (IBPO) which will be discussed later.

Unionization and collective bargaining are often inappropriately used as synonymous terms. Public employees represented by a sole and exclusive bargaining agent are unionized. Public employees represented by a labor union or association who are without a collective bargaining contract are also still unionized.

By 1978, the Bureau of Labor Statistics reported that unions had signed up 1.4 million federal employees and 2.2 million state and local government workers. AFL-CIO unions with growing public sector memberships include the American Federation of State, County and Municipal Employees (AFSCME), American Federation of Teachers (AFT), Service Employees International Union (SEIU), and Communications Workers of America (CWA). The nonaffiliated National Education Association (NEA) has grown from 1.1 million members to 1.7 million. With NEA and AFT discussing a merger, a new national teachers' union may emerge with over 3 million members.

The police have become an important part of the general public sector labor movement. It is estimated that three-fourths of the police officers in the United States now belong to employee labor organizations, although many of these officers do not have the right to engage in collective bargaining.

Some More Observations About Firefighters, Police Associations, and Words

For almost a century, firefighters in this country have enjoyed a relative peaceful labor environment under the banner of one national AFL-CIO union. For peace officers, the organizing and unionization environment has always been turbulent, hostile, volatile, disruptive, and virtually devoid of any organizational loyalty. There are no signs that the future of the police labor movement looks any better.

As a whole, the law enforcement community is politically conservative, and for the most part apolitical, at least, insofar as the white male officers who at present are the majority. With 80 percent or more of the nation's law enforcement officers in employee organizations unaffiliated with the AFL-CIO, the use of the term "union" causes many law enforcement officers to bristle and try to explain how their employee organization is really an association. Since the overwhelming majority of all paid firefighters belong to local unions affiliated with the International Association of Fire Fighters (IAFF, AFL-CIO), the firefighters seem to be more attuned to the use of union when describing their employee organizations. It is just a matter of semantics because associations, unions, and lodges are all labor organizations if they are formed by dues paying employees desiring to improve their wages, hours, and working conditions through collective bargaining or collective begging.

In the private sector, the term "union" is used almost exclusively by labor organizations. Private sector workers started organizing into unions in the late 1800s. With the passage of the Railway Labor Act and Wagner Act in the 1930s, unions have been actively organizing private sector employees into unions. With 93.0 percent of certification elections in the private sector involving AFL-CIO affiliated unions, the private sector workers feel more comfortable with the term "union."

In the public sector, especially among law enforcement labor organizations, the terms "association or lodge," instead of "union," are more likely to be attached to the name of the organization. The Fraternal Order of Police (FOP) uses the word "lodge" to describe its affiliated groups. Some organizations use "association" in their name and are also FOP lodges. Affiliates of the International Union of Police Associations (IUPA, AFL-CIO) and the International Brotherhood of Police Officers (IBPO/NAGE, AFL-CIO) tend to use the term "union" more often in their organizational names. Independent law enforcement labor organizations, not affiliated with FOP, tend to use combinations of the terms "police officers' association," "police association," or "police benevolent association." Independent labor organizations in sheriff's departments generally use "deputy sheriff's association," "sheriff's officers' association," or "deputy sheriff's benevolent association." As you will see, there is no one common denominator when it comes to organizational names or affiliations. The term "association" or "union" will be used interchangeably throughout this part of the book.

While the fire service has a number of job titles, the term "fire fighter" generally applies to everyone. "Law enforcement officer," "police officer", or "peace officer" are the generic terms. The law enforcement community is inclusive of police officers, deputy sheriffs, state police, detention officers, park rangers, airport police, constables, and so forth. The term "police" or "police officer" will be used hereafter to mean any law enforcement officer in a labor organization.

All unions puff up their membership numbers. All membership figures used in this part of the book must be taken with a grain of salt. More accurate membership numbers are only found when the union is representing a designated department where the authorized strength is publicly known. On the national, state, and regional level, "membership inflation" is not only common, but accepted. The membership figures that come from the association's literature, other reported sources, or the authors' best estimate will be used.

Associations and unions affiliated with organized labor will be identified with the name or initials of the national union and term "AFL-CIO." Police employee organizations not affiliated with the AFL-CIO will be called nonaffiliates or independent. On the national scale, the Fraternal Order of Police (FOP) and National Association of Police Organizations (NAPO) are the major independent umbrella organizations. NAPO is not a labor union as such. While composed primarily of independent local and statewide organizations outside of FOP,

NAPO will allow member organizations who are affiliated with both the FOP and AFL-CIO unions. The major AFL-CIO unions with sizable police memberships include: American Federation of State, County and Municipal Employees (AFSCME), International Brotherhood of Police Officers (IBPO/NAGE), International Union of Police Associations (IUPA), National Coalition of Public Safety Officers (NCPSO/CWA), International Brotherhood of Teamsters (Teamsters), and Service Employees International Union (SEIU).

Chapter 47

THE HISTORY OF THE POLICE LABOR MOVEMENT

The general public sector union movement follows a distinct pattern; however, it does not parallel the police labor movement, although their paths do cross during various time periods. The police labor movement differs greatly from the overall trade union development. The police labor movement can generally be divided into six distinct periods: pre-1919, 1919, 1919-1960, 1960-1979, 1979-1996, and 1996 to the present.

The Early Years: Pre-1919

The pre-1919 period begins in the late 1800s when fraternal benevolent associations began developing in many police departments, but these were controlled by high ranking officers who were more concerned with pleasing the political machine than bettering the policemen's lot in life. Every large city had one of these benevolent societies to assist the lowly-paid policemen with burial insurance as well as sponsoring social events. Policemen's associations were formed as early as 1892 in New York; 1894 in Buffalo; 1904 in Washington, D.C.; 1907 in Rochester; 1908 in Milwaukee; and 1915 in Pittsburgh.

The late 1800s also saw the advent of trade union militancy, and the policemen in some parts of the country began to copy their methods to bring about much need changes in working conditions. Police labor strife can generally be traced to 1889 when five policemen went on strike in Ithaca, New York over having their wages reduced from twelve to nine dollars a week. The American Federation of Labor (AFL), founded in 1886 by craft unions, was approached by the policemen in Cleveland for a charter in 1897, but they were turned down because union leaders felt that the police broke up labor disputes and would come into conflict with the union's aims.

The use of police officers by politicians and corporations to break up labor strikes, and in some cases kill and maim union members, did not go unnoticed by labor union leaders and their members. This resentment of police officers as strikebreakers caused organized labor to miss a number of opportunities to bring police officers into their fold under one police charter. In fact, this resentment of police officers is the reason it took eighty-two years after Cleveland requested an AFL charter for the AFL-CIO to finally issue a police charter in 1979 to the International Union of Police Associations (IUPA).

The other public sector employees were not prohibited from AFL charters. In 1917, the Federation chartered a national union for federal employees, and accepted into its ranks the independent National Association of Letter Carriers and Railway Mail Association. The teachers were organizing in rapid fashion, and the firemen were unionizing to such a degree that plans were being made to charter them as an international union.

In 1918, police labor unrest erupted in Ohio when Cincinnati policemen went on strike for three days over wage demands. Policemen began to approach the AFL more and more for assistance. In 1919, the Federation rescinded the ban on police union charters that had originated in 1897. The applications for police union charters flooded the AFL, and by September, 1919 it had chartered thirty-seven locals. This caused AFL president Samuel Gompers to comment:

> I have been President of the American Federation of Labor for thirty-six out of the thirty-nine years of its existence. In all those years I have never seen or heard nor has there come under my observation in any form so many appeals so many applications for charters from any given trade or calling, business or profession, in so short a time as were received by the American Federation of Labor from policemen's unions.

The Fall of Police Unionism: 1919

The United States entered the war in Europe in 1917 as Russia collapsed into chaos. When the war ended in November, 1918, Germany and its allies were left in a state of disorder. The United States and the world was gripped by a fear of the red menace. Many unions were influenced or controlled by the communists, socialists, and anarchists. On August 2, 1919, police in London and Liverpool went on strike and troops were used to crush the protesters.

The growing police union movement reached its peak in 1919, and then the movement collapsed in one failed strike by Boston police that same year. It started in late 1918 when a threatened strike by Boston's firemen who had affiliated with the International Association of Fire Fighters (IAFF, AFL) caused the city to increase pay for firemen and policemen. Labor unrest continued the next year as the Boston Social Club (policemen's association) was refused recognition by the new police commissioner, who after hearing threats of mass resignations, announced:

> Any member of the police department who is dissatisfied that he cannot perform his work faithfully, honestly, and cheerfully, pending the decision regarding the requested salary increase may resign.

The policemen appealed to the AFL for a charter and were accepted, but when they sought recognition and bargaining rights, the city took action by firing the nineteen leaders of the new police union. The policemen went on strike on September 9, 1919, not over the original complaints of poor wages and working conditions, but to protest the city's attempt to prevent them from joining organized labor. The four day strike by 1,117 of the 1,544 policemen caused widespread looting, hundreds of injuries, and seven deaths before it ended with the state guard being called out to restore order.

All the striking policemen were fired and never rehired. This strike became one of the overriding factors that prevented policemen from having one national police union today. It also stifled most public employee unionism until the 1930s. The often-quoted statements by Massachusetts Governor Calvin Coolidge and U.S. President Woodrow Wilson about the Boston Police Strike have been used ever since to justify restricting or prohibiting police unionization.

Governor Coolidge stated:

> There is not right to strike the public safety by anybody, anywhere, anytime.

President Woodrow Wilson declared:

A strike of policemen in a great city, leaving that city at the mercy of any army-of thugs, is a crime against civilization. In my judgment the obligation of a policemen is as sacred and direct as the obligation of a soldier. He is a public servant, not a private employee, and the whole honor of the community is in hishands. He has no right to prefer any private advantage to the public safety.

It seems strange to have the police labor movement collapse in 1919 over one strike when both public and private employees were striking in record numbers, and these unions survived. The Boston Police Strike, in 1919, was a defining moment for the AFL. The indecisiveness of the AFL leadership to call a general strike of all workers to aid the Boston policemen on strike was based primarily on their resentment and hatred of policemen as strikebreakers. Police unionism practically ceased to exist again until the 1960s.

The Fraternal Years: 1919-1960

After the Boston Police Strike, the police labor movement was effectively crushed. The next 41 years saw policemen's associations being dissolved by bitter city officials and an outraged public, and many officers gave up their associations without much protest. Although organized labor withdrew from organizing police officers, fraternal and benevolent associations prospered because many police chiefs and city officials did not feel threatened by these organizations.

One such fraternal organization founded during this period of labor strife that has survived until today is the Fraternal Order of Police. FOP was founded in 1915 in Pittsburgh, Pennsylvania. FOP has remained vehemently antiunion, and its constitution states that it "shall have no affiliation, directly or indirectly, with any labor union, congress, federation, or committee of like nature." FOP was one of the few police organizations to grow during the 1930s, and it tried to work toward better wages and working conditions.

The 1930s saw the revival of police unionism as certain AFL affiliates started looking toward police officers as recruitment targets as the fears of 1919 died down. The American Federation of State, County and Municipal Employees (AFSCME) was given a national charter by the AFL in 1936 after feuding with its parent organization, the American Federation of Government Employees (AFGE), over an autonomous division. AFSCME wasted little time in reviving organized labor's attempt to recruit police officers by chartering a police local in Portsmouth, Virginia in 1937. AFSCME started organizing drives aimed at police officers throughout the 1940s, and established affiliates in Denver, Hartford, New Britain, Flint, Springfield (Illinois), Tacoma, Portland (Oregon), Omaha, St. Paul, and Duluth.

The lessons learned by city administrators and police officials during the Boston police strike about policemen joining organized labor caused them to resist these unionizing attempts. AFSCME's organizing of policemen was stopped short by litigation and prohibitions against union membership by police departments in such cities as Detroit in 1943, Los Angeles in 1943, Chicago in 1944, St. Louis in 1945, Wichita in 1946, and Jackson (Mississippi) in 1946.

With the private sector labor movement peaking in the 1950s, AFSCME was joined in organizing the public sector by such unions as the Laborer's International Union of North America (LIUNA, AFL-CIO), Service Employees International Union (SEIU, AFL-CIO), and the independent International Brotherhood of Teamsters, Chauffeurs, Warehousemen and Helpers (IBT). The Teamsters, who were expelled from the AFL-CIO for corruption in 1958, created a public outrage when they announced that they were going to organize the nation's policemen. In January, 1959, Teamsters' president Jimmy Hoffa publicly stated he was sorry he ever suggested organizing the police, because of all the bad publicity and governmental investigations that erupted.

The Militant Years: 1960-1979

The Wisconsin legislature enacted the first public employee collective bargaining statute in 1959. That event was followed by the signing of Executive Order 10988 by President John F. Kennedy which granted federal executive branch employees the right to organize and bargain collectively. The police labor movement started a resurgence as public employees at the federal, state and local levels flocked to unions. This period was also marked by growing police union militancy as police officers drifted toward trade union tactics, including strikes, pickets, and work stoppages to increase wages and benefits.

During the period 1958-1976, the private sector unions declined from 24 percent to 16.9 percent of the total work force, while public sector unions rose from 1.3 percent to 6 percent of that total work force. The feelings of the late 1960s were best summed up by Baltimore Police Commissioner Donald Pomerleau when he warned the delegates to the 76th Annual Conference of the International Association of Chiefs of Police (IACP) in 1969 that:

> In my opinion employee organizations as they exist today represent the greatest deterrent to the professionalization of law enforcement...The old chain of command, lines of authority, will not meet our needs in the last quarter of the twentieth century...Arbitrary and capricious personnel management no longer will be tolerated by the masses of employees in government and rightly so.

Police Commissioner Pomerleau also reminded the delegates that he had warned them in 1967 to "take a hard look at our departments," and stated:

> I suggested then and I reiterate now; employee organizations are inevitable in law enforcement.

This use of trade union tactics by police to achieve their goals was not lost on the nation's police chiefs. The 1960s witnessed numerous reports, commissions and investigations of the causes of police labor unrest. The IACP delegates to that 76th conference in Miami Beach in 1969 heard the "bad news" about police unionization. The Report of the IACP Special Committee on Police Employee Organizations clearly presented the arguments against unionization:

> The most potent and compelling argument against the unionization of policemen is, of course, the strike—organized labor's most important and effective tool. A strike is the ultimate weapon of any labor union, and it is foolish and naïve to believe that, when all else fails, non-strike laws, clauses and agreement will hinder its implementation.

The Boston police strike delayed the creation of one national police union under the AFL-CIO banner for five decades. Perhaps the second most important benchmark in the police labor movement occurred in 1969. The upheavals of the late 1960s within society and police departments overrode the fears of organized labor created after the Boston police strike. The largest police employee organization in the nation, the New York City Policemen's Benevolent Association contacted the AFL-CIO in February, 1969 about receiving a national police union charter. A special committee in the AFL-CIO agreed to let Federation president George Meany charter the new national police union under certain conditions:

1. a suitable constitutional structure would have to be drawn up on a national basis, with commitments of affiliation of police organizations in a representative number of cities;
2. satisfactory assurances are received that such an organization will confine itself strictly to its jurisdiction and will not encroach upon areas of employment represented by existing AFL-CIO affiliation.

The months following the tentative approval by the AFL-CIO of a national police union charter created a wave of excitement among large municipal police associations and generated fear and concern by competing fraternal police organizations and city officials. A meeting was called for November 2, 1969 in Omaha to draft the organization's constitution. The aims of the new national police union were:

1. to create a common philosophy and communication among many police groups in the United States,
2. to present a united front in negotiations with municipalities,
3. to give police officers a strong voice in legislation, and
4. to maintain a continuous dialogue between the union and the community.

The delegates adopted the name International Brotherhood of Police Officers (IBPO); however, there has been some confusion about the name since it has been reported that the new union's name was the International Association of Police Officers. The drive for AFL-CIO affiliation was led by former New York City PBA president John Cassesse, who was named chairman of the constitution drafting committee. The following cities were reportedly represented at the Omaha meeting: New York, Chicago, Kansas City (Missouri), Salt Lake City, St. Paul, San Jose, Portland (Oregon), Auburn (New York), Quincy (Massachusetts), Shreveport, and New Britain (Connecticut).

The newly created IBPO started to grow and probably reached 10,000 members at its peak. The new police union appeared to be gaining support from the AFL-CIO affiliates during the period 1969-1970. Unfortunately, IBPO raided several AFSCME police locals, and they were having trouble winning support from other independent police associations. In February, 1971, the AFL-CIO rejected IBPO's charter request, and President Meany commented that there was no "demand or real desire for a policemen's international union throughout the country." It is probable that Meany, like many older labor union leaders, held resentments against police officers because of their role in controlling strike and picket line violence. Secondly, AFSCME was concerned about a new police charter encroaching on their desire to bring police officers into their local government employee umbrella.

To compound IBPO's problems, an independent police union based in Rhode Island also called itself IBPO, and protested the use of its name. In 1969, the Rhode Island-based IBPO had merged into the independent federal employees union, National Association of Government Employees (NAGE). Cassesse changed the name to the National Union of Police Officers (NUPO), and in 1972, NUPO affiliated with organized labor by becoming an autonomous division of the Service Employees International Union (SEIU, AFL-CIO). Membership was last reported as 3,000 in 1977, and NUPO was probably officially disbanded after SEIU president George Hardy wrote all SEIU police locals a letter on April 23, 1979 giving them permission to join the newly-chartered AFL-CIO police union, the International Union of Police Associations (IUPA).

The Missing Years: 1979-1996

The National Conference of Police Associations (NCPA) was founded in 1953, and changed its name later to the ICPA when Canadian police unions joined. The International Conference of Police Associations (ICPA) was officially disbanded on December 4, 1978; however, the controversy over its rise and demise has not ceased. Although ICPA no longer exists, it is important to know its history and leaders because they have surfaced again in ICPA's splinter organizations.

ICPA functioned as a loose confederation of autonomous police associations that conducted wage surveys, published a newsletter, and conducted national lobbying. They existed on a very low per capita that was only $3.00 per member per year in 1978. ICPA was initially formed by associations in such cities as Detroit, New York, Chicago, Los Angeles, San Francisco, Milwaukee, Minneapolis, Cleveland, New Orleans, Houston, and state associations from California, New York, and New Jersey.

The exact membership of ICPA will probably never be known, but various sources report 275,000 members in 1971, 158,000 members in 1972, 160,000 members in 1975, 182,000 members in 1977, and 200,000 members in 1978; however, the most realistic figures were reported by a former member as never more than 60,000 members actually paying dues. ICPA grew steadily during the 1950s and 1960s, but started losing members in the early 1970s.

It is ironic that ICPA should later split over affiliation with organized labor. At their mid-winter conference in 1969, ICPA had the opportunity to save John Cassesse's bid for a national police union charter. Cassesse attempted to convince the ICPA delegates to support the AFL-CIO charter bid, but they voted 31-2 to continue their opposition to affiliation with organized labor. New York City PBA president Edward J. Kiernan supported Cassesse, but he later served on a joint ICPA-FOP Council that issued a statement that said, "the public can best be served by the police organizations by distinctly separate and not affiliated directly or indirectly with labor unions." ICPA and FOP later discussed merging into one huge organization but differences between national leaders caused it to fail.

Edward Kiernan retired from the NYPD and was elected president of ICPA in 1972, and he served until its demise in 1978. The delegates to the ICPA Convention in Toronto in August, 1978 were evenly split on question of affiliation with the AFL-CIO, and President Kiernan broke the tie in favor of affiliation. Kiernan and ICPA secretary-treasurer Robert Gordon had allegedly been meeting with the AFL-CIO since 1977 without consulting with the other ICPA leaders. At the mid-winter ICPA board meeting in Phoenix in December, 1978, Kiernan and Gordon were followed out of the meeting by sixty-seven police associations. They crossed the hall to another meeting room and formed the International Union of Police Associations (IUPA), and filed for a national police union charter from the AFL-CIO.

The division of those supporting AFL-CIO affiliation and those opposed destroyed ICPA that day. Heated words were exchanged and accusations concerning the collapse of ICPA still linger over the heads of those leaders involved. ICPA's president and secretary-treasurer left the organization with a reported debt of at least $280,000, and both former association officers faced civil litigation asking for $900,000 in damages by the Attorney General of New York for an alleged kickback scheme during an ICPA magazine solicitation in that state. Local

ICPA affiliates resigned to avoid the indebtedness, and when Kiernan was asked who was responsible for the losses he replied, "[w]e resigned from (ICPA). Those remaining in the organization would have to take the responsibility." The hard feelings over the collapse of ICPA were best expressed by Al Scaglione, president of the Police Conference of New York, when he said:

> I'm surprised that the AFL-CIO would want to issue a charter to any organization run by Kiernan. I guess George Meany knows best, but why do they think that Kiernan, who destroyed a national organization and left it in debt, is the right man to organize nationally? Does a man change his stripes?

This period saw continued growth by independent police organizations. Both NAPO and FOP expanded their membership base into new states. Statewide police employee organizations in Texas, California, Florida, Michigan, and Wisconsin were also growing. The development of these statewide groups is significant because it marked a growing recognition by local police association leaders that they could not fund costly labor and legal services independently, and that the pooling of dues money into a larger collective statewide pool gave greater economic strength to each local affiliated association.

The AFL-CIO was still stagnant during this period, and that stagnation was intensified when the PATCO strike was crushed by President Reagan. The breaking of the PATCO strikers was viewed as another example of the weakness of the AFL-CIO.

The Resurgence of the AFL-CIO and Its impact on the Police Labor Movement: 1996-Present

A decade after the PATCO strike, the AFL-CIO seems to have to stalled its 40-year decline. The election of a Democratic president in 1992 who was less antiunion than Reagan and Bush softened the pressures of the federal government on cleaning up corruption in many of the unions. While Congress went to a majority of Republicans in 1994, organized labor has been able to pass several pieces of legislation.

More critical to the police labor movement was the ousting of the old guard AFL-CIO leadership. President Lane Kirkland was literally forced to step down by a coalition of primarily public sector unions led by SEIU and AFSCME. AFL-CIO secretary-treasurer Tom Donahue assumed the presidency and appointed CWA's secretary-treasurer Barbara Easterling to the same national post. At the AFL-CIO convention, SEIU president John Sweeney and United Mineworkers president Richard Trumka created a slate as president and secretary-treasurer, respectively. The new slate won overwhelmingly and created a new position of executive vice president for AFSCME vice president Linda Chavez-Thompson. The "new" AFL-CIO immediately allocated millions to organizing and political action.

How does the AFL-CIO's millions impact the independent police employee organizations? IUPA received a grant from the New York State AFL-CIO to launch a raid on the independent PBA of the New York State Troopers. IUPA had earlier decertified the PBA for 900 state criminal investigators, and now IUPA had decertification cards on the bargaining units for troopers and supervisors. While the PBA ultimately defeated the raid, the PBA spent in excess of $100,000. The Teamsters Union is raiding FOP and independent associations in Maryland, District of Columbia, Maryland, and Florida. The Communications Workers of America is involved in major police organizing drives across the entire Sunbelt. Just about every AFL-CIO union is trying to organize public employees, and many are seeking police officers.

NAPO has formed a committee to study the impact of the AFL-CIO unions raiding independent police associations. After raids by the Teamsters, and threatened raids by IUPA, the Florida PBA voted to allow some affiliated chapters and charters to seek voluntary affiliation with the National Coalition of Public Safety Officers (NCPSO, CWA, AFL-CIO) to protect themselves under the Article XX "no raid" provisions of the AFL-CIO Constitution. The time may finally be right for the various national police organizations to discuss mergers and coalitions so that there is one major national voice for all law enforcement officers.

Chapter 48

THE NATIONAL ORGANIZATIONS REPRESENTING POLICE OFFICERS TODAY

The police labor movement is extremely fragmented today as many unions and associations claim to be the spokesperson for the nation's police officers. To the uninitiated, it has become difficult to identify the major police organizations representing substantial numbers of police officers. With mergers, affiliations, and name changes over the last twenty-five years, it is important to examine which police employee organizations are viable and which are merely "paper organizations." The turmoil surrounding the police labor movement was probably best expressed by SEIU president George Hardy, who had used the resources of his union to help police in 1972. Hardy's comments in November, 1997 to the AFL-CIO Public Employee Department were:

> There isn't a police organization in the entire country that belongs to a real labor union-not New York, Or Detroit, Or San Francisco. Not a damn one belongs to an (AFL-CIO) union, and we have to live with this image the public has...of irresponsible police strikes and job actions.

Although SEIU released its police locals and the AFL-CIO finally chartered a national police union, the police officers in the United States belong to just about every imaginable labor union, association, fraternal organization, and professional group. Since dual membership in many organizations is very common among police officers, it is impossible to accurately determine the actual strengths of most groups. In many locations, the police officers will belong to one organization that negotiates the contract and another organization that acts as a social group. And in another city the same two organizations may play a reverse role. The following is a brief analysis of the major police employee organizations in the United States.

Fraternal Order of Police

The Fraternal Order of Police (FOP) is the oldest and largest of the major police organizations, having been founded in 1915. Although accurate records are not available, FOP has shown a steady growth over the years with reports of membership as 30,000 in 170 lodges in 1943, 80,000 members in 730 lodges in 1969, and 157,000 members in 930 lodges in 1975. The Bureau of Labor Statistics (1980) reported FOP at 140,000 members in 1,200 lodges. In 1982, National FOP president Leo V. Marchetti proclaimed 160,000 members after victories in Chicago and Washington, D.C. Current FOP literature claims 230,000 members. FOP claims to have more labor contracts for police officers under their name than any other police employee organization in the United States.

Membership is open to all police officers with associate memberships available to civilians for a fee. FOP does not exclude supervisors from membership as many public and private sector unions have done. FOP holds biennial conventions composed of one delegate for every fifty members of the lodge and three delegates for each state lodge.

The Grand Lodge offices moves with the National Secretary. When the past Secretary passed away, the office was moved from Louisville (KY) to Nashville (TN). FOP does maintain a legislative office in Washington, D.C. Several years ago, FOP started paying the Grand President a salary. Except for the administrative employees at the "floating office," FOP does not employ on staff any attorneys, business agents, or labor relations personnel.

FOP has not significantly altered its original structure since its inception eighty-two years ago. It has remained a loose confederation of lodges which are autonomous of the national organization, and this autonomy is maintained by having the National Lodge charter new affiliates that formulate their own constitution as long as they are not in conflict with the national lodge. FOP lodges range from passive to militant; however, each hesitates to accept trade unionism as a goal.

FOP does not consider itself a union and claims to have chosen the "professional" route over "trade union" methods. FOP opposes police officers joining organized labor for two reasons: philosophically it wants to follow the path used by doctors and lawyers of being a "professional" organization; and pragmatically, it believes that it has a sound reputation with the public, so it uses subtle, soft-sell tactics on the national level while allowing local lodges to be militant.

One of the major weaknesses of the FOP is its selling of associate memberships to non-police officers and soliciting advertising from local merchants. FOP has one of the lowest per capita taxes of any major police organization at $10.00 per member per year, and that poor financial base probably creates the need to raise funds through alternative methods on both the national, state, and local level. In 1982, FOP's national publication contained a column by National Treasurer Richard A. Boyd that complained about the financial problems of FOP, the need for a higher national per capita, and ways to raise the needed money. Boyd commented on the various fund raising functions FOP lodges could use:

> (1) review your own local dues structure...make dues the percentage of the starting salary...(2) review the possibilities of metropolitan and regional cooperatives for the purposes of pooling your resources in money making programs (3) review and improve your Associate Lodge membership (4) Bingo-probably the most exciting and fulfilling money making project which any lodge can have (5) ...professional Haunted House in a store front (6) ...have an annual fish fry in their community (7) Lodges run firecracker stands in States which allow them (8) Lodges run day care centers for their membership and the public.

The rise of police militancy in the 1960s and 1970s, and the push for organized labor affiliation by various groups caused FOP to lose lodges to more aggressive police employee organizations. In 1979, the FOP lodge in Hollywood, Florida was decertified by IBPO Local 621. One Hollywood police officer was quoted as saying, "[t]hey are strictly fraternal, a fund-raising organization with no legal or contractual skills to offer." In 1980, Cleveland's 1,883 patrol officers represented by the Cleveland Police Patrolmen's Association voted to affiliate with IUPA under the AFL-CIO banner and not FOP which represents, but does not bargain for, 561 patrolmen and 288 supervisors. Local FOP president William Gallagher cried foul, and stated, "[s]ay you had a labor dispute and called the police. What if the people on strike also belong to the AFL-CIO?"

FOP has survived since 1915 against heavy odds, and in recent years, FOP appears to be gaining strength in some parts of the country, particularly the Midwest. A good example was in 1981 when Chicago's mayor and police commissioner agreed to allow the city's police officers to be represented by one union in collective bargaining negotiations

A major confrontation among the various unions and associations within the department became evident. Each organization had traditionally received dues deduction for the small group of officers that it represented, with no one group having anywhere near a majority to represent the 10,200-member police bargaining unit. The contenders were the FOP, Law Enforcement Division of the Teamsters Joint Council 25 (Teamsters were not affiliated with AFL-CIO at the time), Chicago Police Officers Association Local 1975 (affiliated with the United Paperworkers International Union, AFL-CIO), Chicago Patrolmen's Association (independent local group), and the Confederation of Police Local 5 (affiliated with the International Union of Police Associations, AFL-CIO).

FOP's newspaper reported that on October 16, 1981 the election took place after heavy lobbying by all groups. The "no single representative" position on the ballot placed first and FOP placed second. In the runoff election on November 10, 1981, FOP won exclusive recognition by a seven-to-one margin. The FOP National President proclaimed, "These police officers believed and proved that the Fraternal Order of Police could oppose the Teamsters and the AFL-CIO in bargaining elections and that the FOP would be the winner."

Although FOP won some major representation elections against the other police organizations, the 1980s were clouded by uncertainty about the direction of the National Lodge. At the 45th Biennial Convention in 1981 the delegates voted down a much needed per capita increase. FOP's leadership was faced with having to accept the principles of more aggressive labor unions in order to maintain a competitive position, while at the same time, FOP was burdened by the traditions and practices of the past. To survive against tremendous pressures from both inside and outside the organization, FOP is faced with deciding if it wants to be a labor union or fraternal group, and then to move forward with that decision. Former FOP president John Dineen summed up the problem facing FOP when he stated:

Do the members want a Fraternal-Social Organization or do they expect strong effective leadership to produce improved salary, fringe benefits and working conditions for them? We must organize the Fraternal Order of Police into the effective spokesman for the police officers and law enforcement officers in these United States.

FOP represents nearly 50 percent of all law enforcement officers in the nation. It is an old fraternal organization with a rich history. FOP is trying to stay on top in a very competitive market. Whether FOP continues to thrive and grow will depend upon the decisions it makes in the next few years. The lack of an adequate per capita and too much dependence on outside fund raising will obviously hamper its ability to compete against well-funded AFL-CIO unions. With its decentralized national staff and dependence upon State Lodges and Labor Councils to provide all services, attention must be made toward strengthening these units.

International Union of Police Associations (AFL-CIO)

Former New York City PBA and ICPA president Edward Kiernan issued a news release on February 20, 1979 stating that AFL-CIO president George Meany had approved the first charter ever for police officers, and the first major charter by the Federation in over a decade. Now IUPA president Kiernan claimed that police employee organizations were joining in droves. Kiernan predicted 60,000 to 70,000 members by the summer convention, and an eventual membership of 350,000. The *San Francisco Examiner* (July 18, 1979) reported during the first convention in that city that IUPA had 55,000 members. The article stated that IUPA's goal is national legislation requiring collective bargaining and binding arbitration of disputes for police, sheriff's deputies, state police, and other law enforcement officers.

The glowing reports of rapid growth were largely distorted for media consumption. Quarreling and bitter in-fighting among the leaders hindered growth in the early years. IUPA's first secretary-treasurer, Robert Gordon, was involved in several controversies. In the early 1980s, Gordon was sued for $5 million by American Federation of Police president Gerald Arenberg when Gordon allegedly libeled Arenberg in *Police Magazine* in a story on police solicitation practices. In mid-1981, Gordon got into a heated letter writing exchange with the leaders of their affiliated Local 28, San Francisco Police Officers Association, over the progress, or lack of progress, of IUPA. This eventually led to SFPOA voting to disaffiliate from IUPA.

After attempting to get Gordon to step down voluntarily, a coalition of younger IUPA vice-presidents decided to run a candidate against him at the July 1982 convention in Las Vegas. Former Memphis Police Association president David Baker, who incidentally led the 1978 police strike in that city, was picked to challenge Gordon and easily defeated him to become the new secretary-treasurer.

In 1980, the *AFL-CIO News* reported IUPA's membership at 16,500, and not 50,000 as reported to the Bureau of Labor Statistics that same year. In its own literature, IUPA honestly states that it had a peak membership of 20,000 in 1981, and fell to about 8,000 members in 1983. Recently, IUPA was quoted as claiming 80,000 members; however, those numbers do not match with IUPA's LM-2 report to the BLS for the period ending in March, 1995. Best estimates are that IUPA has about 35,000 members today.

IUPA's organizational structure is little different from that of the defunct ICPA, FOP, or NAPO. It is an "association of associations" that consists of loosely bound autonomous police locals. In the 1980s, the per capita was raised from $1.00 per member per month to $1.55, but that was still the lowest per capita of any AFL-CIO affiliate. During this time period, IUPA was reportedly in debt at least $200,000, and asked the AFL-CIO to waive its national per capita. IUPA eventually raised its per capita to $2.25 per member per month, but without telephone solicitations, IUPA could not keep its doors open.

IUPA has a paid staff consisting of the president, vice president, secretary-treasurer, two staff representatives, and some clerical employees located at a small office outside Washington, D.C. Similar to FOP and NAPO, IUPA primarily provides federal legislative representation. State and local affiliates charge their own per capita for most labor and legal-related services.

IUPA has had success in recruiting police officers in towns with an organized labor base, such as Milwaukee, Tacoma, Long Beach, Houston, Las Vegas, Omaha, Toledo, Jackson (Mississippi), and Baton Rouge. IUPA has had some major disaffiliations since 1982, including associations in Phoenix, Memphis, Cleveland, and Anaheim.

IUPA does not appear to be getting the assistance it needs to compete on the national level from the AFL-CIO or its affiliates. On paper, the AFL-CIO chartered a national police union to have jurisdiction over all police work, but as early as 1980, President Kiernan complained to AFL-CIO president Lane Kirkland about the lack of cooperation by Federation affiliates, particularly AFSCME. He also asked the Federation president to speak to the Teamsters Union who were at the time discussing re-entry into the AFL-CIO, about their continued efforts to organize police officers. The request obviously fell on deaf ears as the AFL-CIO readmitted the Teamsters, and the Teamsters promptly started mobilizing its Public Safety Division in competition with IUPA.

In reality, the 89 unions comprising the National AFL-CIO have not only refused to release their police locals to IUPA, but most of these AFL-CIO unions are also actively competing against the much smaller IUPA. Only SEIU released its police locals to IUPA in 1979, but after the primarily Louisiana SEIU police locals joined IUPA, the door closed. Today, SEIU is actively recruiting police officers, and its affiliated NAGE/IBPO is also competing against IUPA.

Instead of trying to market the IUPA program to other police employee organizations, IUPA has spent needless time attacking rival police groups. In 1980, Kiernan went to the winter board meeting of the AFL-CIO and requested a boycott against FOP. He hoped to use the AFL-CIO boycott to dry up the fund-raising activities of FOP by claiming they were antiunion. One top AFL-CIO official was quoted as saying, "[t]he guy's (Kiernan) declaring war on his own people and can't see it. If Kiernan has what it takes and can offer a good labor program, he should have no trouble enlisting members. I am not going to ask my labor members to boycott the FOP or any other local police association that is trying to raise funds."

The future is cloudy for IUPA if the current trends continue. The 35,000-member IUPA is a very small national union trying to compete against AFL-CIO unions with 500,000 to over 1 million members. Unlike the IAFF which entered the AFL in 1918 and has exclusive jurisdiction over fire services for 80 years, IUPA only entered the AFL-CIO in 1979 after many unions already had police locals. With a large staff of organizers and millions to spend, AFSCME, CWA, SEIU, IBPO and the Teamsters are aggressively seeking independent associations. IUPA wants to be "the national AFL-CIO police union, but neither the National AFL-CIO or its big national unions are impressed.

IUPA will have to find a merger partner who can supply it with organizing money to spread its message. Otherwise, FOP and the big AFL-CIO unions will continue to out muscle them for members. IUPA is the only AFL-CIO union dependent upon telephone solicitations, and that source of money is not guaranteed.

National Association of Police Organizations

In 1979, the delegates to the ICPA convention that opposed affiliation with organized labor formed a steering committee to organize another national police organization. Robert Scully, co-chairman of the steering committee and a vice president of the Detroit Police Officers Association, described the new organization in these terms:

> Our intention is to become what the ICPA was supposed to be. We have nothing against the major unions. We support them, their goals, their achievements. But we feel nobody can represent police officers like police officers. Kiernan used to support that belief, but he seems to have changed his views overnight.

While NAPO does not bargain for its affiliates or attempt to act as a bargaining agent, the third annual convention on August 23-28, 1981 voted to support a legislative program to remove the bar by state government to collective bargaining by public employees. At the fourth annual convention in Dallas on August 17-21, 1982, NAPO's legislative counsel stated "that much of what NAPO is able to do is to prevent laws that adversely effect law enforcement from being passed."

NAPO literature sells the organization as a national lobby group for police officers. NAPO claims to have grown from 30,000-members in 1978 to 175,000-members in 1996. Since NAPO does not report to the Bureau of Labor Statistics as other labor unions are required to do, it is impossible to verify their membership claims. The per capita is $1.50 per member per year with a sliding scale after 3,000-members. NAPO maintains a full-time executive director and general counsel at its Washington, D.C. office. Like FOP and IUPA, NAPO raises funds from outside solicitations and licensing of its name for products. NAPO also has created a National Law Enforcement Officer Rights Center to file briefs on behalf of police officers in national cases.

NAPO is a federation of autonomous, independent state and local police associations who, for the most part, seek a safe haven from the FOP and the AFL-CIO. NAPO affiliates include a number of New York City police unions, Portland (Oregon), Detroit, Dade County, Los Angeles, Nassau County, Suffolk County, and statewide police associations in such states as Texas, California, Wisconsin, Michigan, Minnesota, New York, Ohio, and Florida.

NAPO's weakness is that it will probably never emerge as a threat to any of the other police labor organizations since it has chosen to straddle the fence as a "legislative federation" and not to compete as a labor union. NAPO's legislative track record is impressive, especially after NAPO endorsed Bill Clinton and FOP endorsed George Bush. NAPO has had great access to the White House since 1992. The rivalry between FOP and NAPO for power in Washington probably led FOP to join NAPO in endorsing Bill Clinton over Bob Dole in 1996.

The question is whether NAPO can sustain itself when FOP and the AFL-CIO unions are raiding their member organizations. Since NAPO is not a labor union, it lacks the resources and mission to fight back. NAPO and FOP are both decentralized national lobbying organizations with limited resources and services, and combined they claim to represent 3 of every 4 police officers in the nation. If NAPO cannot reach an accord or merger agreement with FOP, then NAPO will have to eventually seek some protection from AFL-CIO unions. The next decade will sort out the weaker organizations. The greater question may be whether an independent nonunion like NAPO can survive.

International Brotherhood of Police Officers (AFL-CIO)

The International Brotherhood of Police Officers (IBPO) was founded in 1964 by police officers in Rhode Island, and in 1969 IBPO affiliated as a separate division with the independent National Association of Government Employees (NAGE). IBPO reportedly had about 2,000 members when it affiliated with NAGE. Reliable membership figures are not available since NAGE reports IBPO's membership figures in with its nonpolice members.

In 1980, the Bureau of Labor Statistics showed NAGE had 200,000 members in 595 local unions; however, independent sources as to IBPO's membership vary such as 35,000 members in 175 locals,

30,000 members in 500 locals in 1977, and 37,000 members in 280 locals. NAGE is primarily a blue collar, federal employees' union. In the federal sector, employees are not required to pay union dues, so many federal sector unions report high numbers of employees under contract while having very low numbers of members actually paying dues. NAGE reportedly pays per capita on 50,000 total members to SEIU, of which maybe 10,000 or less are police. Recent newspaper articles reported NAGE membership at 40,000.

IBPO's organizational structure is different from other police employee groups in that it does not have officers elected solely by its police members. NAGE is composed primarily of federal workers, and was founded in 1961 as the Federal Employees Veterans Association. NAGE's constitution establishes seven separate divisions, namely the Federal Aviation Science and Technological Association (FASTA), the International Brotherhood of Police Officers (IBPO), the International Brotherhood of Correctional Officers (IBCO), the National Association of Municipal Employees (NAME), the Massachusetts State Employees Association (MSEA), the National Association of Nurses (NOAN), and the National Health Care Union (NHCU).

Each division has an advisory board that is elected at the convention. The national officers include the national president, executive vice president, secretary, treasurer, and nine vice presidents. IBPO literature reports that each national officer is elected to a three-year term at the convention, and each delegate can cast one vote for each ten members represented. Kenneth T. Lyons is the founder of NAGE and the only president the union has ever had. Unlike NAPO, FOP and IUPA which have police officers elected as their president and national officers, IBPO has one police officer as the elected vice president serving on the NAGE national board.

NAGE/IBPO is unique in other ways because it has the largest staff of attorneys, organizers, and employees of any competing national police employee organization. IBPO's per capita is substantially higher than FOP, NAPO, IUPA, and AFSCME, with only the Teamsters Union probably having a higher dues structure. IBPO is structured similar to private sector unions where the national union issues the local charter and can place the local union into trusteeship.

IBPO literature describes their membership benefits as full-service legal protection in job-related criminal and civil cases, a $10,000 acci-

dental death and dismemberment insurance policy, professional negotiators, national representatives for grievances, and lobbying representation in Washington, D.C. The national headquarters is located in
Boston, but the union maintains fully staffed offices in Washington,
D.C. and some satellite offices in other cities where they have con-
centrations of members.

IBPO's membership has been primarily concentrated in the New
England states with locals in Springfield, Worcester, Cambridge and
Middlesex County in Massachusetts; Cranston (Rhode Island);
Lewiston (Maine); Manchester and Nashua (New Hampshire); and
numerous local unions in Connecticut. IBPO has other local unions in
Atlanta, Fort Collins, Boise, and in Virginia and Florida. IBPO has
had its share of disaffiliations with all of its Texas locals leaving in
1983, and locals dropping out in such cities as Orlando, Salt Lake City,
Santa Barbara, and Lincoln.

Prior to December, 1982, when NAGE affiliated with SEIU, its
aggressive raids on AFL-CIO affiliates and other independents kept
them embroiled in controversy. NAGE waged a 3-year raid to unseat
the incumbent International Brotherhood of Firemen and Oilers
(IBFO, AFL-CIO) for the right to represent 4,000 noninstruction
workers in the Philadelphia School District. The comments by the
IBFO's president in 1981 probably typify the feelings of organized
labor toward NAGE:

> Time after time organized labor has experienced ruthless, attempted raids by
> this parasite organization…Instead of organizing the unorganized, NAGE tries
> to steal the members of legitimate labor unions.

Raiding by IBPO unseated AFSCME as the bargaining agent for a
number of police departments in New England. In 1979, IBPO challenged the American Federation of Government Employees (AFGE,
AFL-CIO) which had represented the U.S. Border Patrol since 1966.
IBPO won the election to decertify AFGE as the bargaining agent for
the 2,500 border patrol officers. AFGE filed unfair labor practices
against IBPO and the Federal Labor Relations Authority (FLRA)
ruled against IBPO and ordered a new election. IBPO sued in federal district court to have the order for a new election thrown out and
IBPO certified as the new bargaining agent. When NAGE affiliated
with SEIU in December 1982 and joined the AFL-CIO, NAGE

dropped the lawsuit and certification challenge, and thus AFGE remains the bargaining agent for border patrol officers.

Perhaps the gravest blow came in late 1981 when IBPO Local 442, representing 3,300 District of Columbia police officers and sergeants, was challenged by FOP. The battle over exclusive recognition of D.C. police was a hectic one. The police were initially represented by a social organization called the Police Association of the District of Columbia (PADC) until it was ousted by IBPO in 1974. In May 1977, the PADC defeated IBPO, but as beaten by IBPO again in March, 1978.

Unrest over a new contract that the officers felt did not provide enough wages, gave IBPO agency shop provisions, and the high IBPO dues structure caused IBPO to drop from 2,600 to 1,500 members in a matter of months. The bitter election that resulted in the predominately black IBPO calling the predominately white FOP a bunch of racists ended with FOP defeating IBPO by 1,555 to 1,084.

Traditionally, IBPO has concentrated its organizing in small-to medium-sized cities and counties with collective bargaining rights. Except for organizing the police in Atlanta, IBPO has not organized a major metropolitan police agency in more than a decade. IBPO is a centralized national union with all services being provided by the national union out of Boston, and there is no elected police president. This structure does not appeal to major police associations accustomed to providing their own services or receiving them from a statewide association. Unlike FOP, NAPO, and IUPA, NAGE does no telephone solicitations or other fund-raising, and has a sizable cash flow from dues.

IBPO's most serious problem will arise when founder Kenneth Lyons retires or dies in office. No successor exists and the SEIU service agreement allows for NAGE locals to be absorbed into SEIU. SEIU has several police locals outside IBPO, including Wayne County (MI) and the Iowa state police. Perhaps the IBPO and SEIU police locals will be merged when Lyons is gone.

International Brotherhood of Teamsters (AFL-CIO)

The most controversial national union representing police officers is the International Brotherhood of Teamsters. Expelled from the AFL-CIO in 1957, the Teamsters were readmitted in 1987. The Teamsters had been expelled over charges that their leadership was corrupt and involved with organized crime. Since their formation in 1899, the union has had a reputation for centralized power, secrecy, nepotism, violence, and lucrative amenities for its executive board members. Past presidents Dave Beck, James Hoffa, and Roy Williams were sent to prison.

Why did the AFL-CIO readmit the Teamsters? The AFL-CIO has suffered from a declining membership since expelling the Teamsters, and they needed the members and dues from the 1.6 million member Teamsters Union. The AFL-CIO also wanted to stop the nation's largest and most powerful union from raiding AFL-CIO affiliated unions. The Teamsters' political action fund is the largest union PAC in the country with over $6 million in the bank.

What did the Teamsters want from reaffiliating with the AFL-CIO? The Teamsters wanted some legitimacy and they needed the AFL-CIO to pressure the federal government to lighten up on its trusteeship of the international union. The Teamsters Union is in a catch-22 with its reputation. One of the biggest attractions of the Teamsters is their reputation as a union with muscle and their willingness to use that muscle to achieve its goals. On the other hand, the federal government and union members committed to cleaning up the organization are making headway in displacing some of the corrupt officials.

The Teamsters peaked at 2.3 million members in 1978, and since then they have lost 500,000 members primarily due to trucking deregulation. The International lost $58 million in 1992, and the total net worth of the union is roughly $60 million, down from $154 million in 1991. People tend to think only of truckers when they hear the word "Teamster," but the union has over 600 locals representing private and public sector workers in just about every conceivable occupation.

Although no accurate figures exist on how many police officers are card carrying Teamsters, in 1980 a Teamster official was quoted as claiming 20,000 police members throughout the United States. More reliable sources place the Teamster police locals at about 10,000 members, but they may bargain for a total of approximately 15,000 officers in 225 suburban and rural law enforcement agencies.

Police officers joining the Teamsters, whether in a police only local or as a part of a larger local, are a small fraction of the union's total membership, and therefore, likely have very little voice in the union's affairs. The actual dues paid by police officers belonging to the

Teamsters are reportedly two times the hourly wage with $4.00 per member per month returning to the International Union. Teamster dues are substantially higher than all other unions competing for police, with only IBPO's per capita being close. In 1981, Anchorage police dropped out of Teamsters Local 959 to form an independent police union after the per capita was increased to $1.46 per hour.

The Teamsters have been able to recruit police officers and sheriff's deputies in many parts of the country. In 1980, the Teamsters had locals for Sioux Falls police, Flint deputies, Des Moines police, Albany (NY) sheriff's supervisors, and Boston highway and park officers. The Teamsters are strongest in Michigan, Minnesota, Wisconsin, Iowa, and Alaska. Since the 1980's, the Teamsters have had organizing drives aimed at recruiting police in Florida, Louisiana, Virginia, California, Maryland, Illinois, and the District of Columbia.

The Teamsters formed the Minnesota Public and Law Enforcement Local 320 and claim 1,800 police officers in 64 bargaining units. Although they are facing heavy opposition in the antiunion southern states, the Teamsters organized Winston-Salem (NC) police; however, state law prohibits collective bargaining and the city sued to stop affiliation. The same story occurred in Lawton (OK) when police officers dropped FOP for the Teamsters. The city threatened to sue to block the affiliation, so the local police affiliated with IUPA. Police officers in several northern Virginia cities and counties joined the Teamsters, but protests from cities and counties and the lack of a bargaining law ended the affiliations.

Georgia prohibits bargaining by public employees, but that did not stop the Teamsters in 1978 from getting dues authorization cards from 55 percent of Atlanta's police officers after the black mayor allegedly refused to "meet and confer" with the predominately white FOP. The city refused to grant the Teamsters dues deduction even though they gave that privilege to the fire fighters' union. In a decision of the U.S. District Court for the Northern District of Georgia, the court enjoined the city from denying the Teamsters the use of the city's check-off ordinance. The organizing drive faltered and the Teamsters never received dues check-off.

When the Illinois state legislature passed a comprehensive collective bargaining law for all public employees in 1986, the Teamsters set their sights on suburban police departments in the northwestern part of Chicago. Teamsters Local 726 secretary-treasurer Carlo "Chuck"

Spranzo said, "I'll be frank with you, this is a business. The only place there's anybody available is the public sector and that means police officers, public works and firemen." The 1,750 members of the Cook County Corrections Department joined the Teamsters, as did scores of small police departments.

FOP continues to represent the majority of police officers in Illinois. But long-time FOP supporters like Officer Roy Desmond believe that the Teamsters can organize police officers in that state. He stated:

> I have nothing against FOP, but I feel the Teamsters can do a better job. They're a more professional organization. That's why you're going to see more towns going with them. If some people want to take it personally, we can't help it.

Not everyone in Illinois was happy with the Teamsters' organizing efforts. Schaumberg's village manager, Stephen J. Atkins, said, "[t]he bottom line is the Teamsters have alleged connections with organized crime and they don't belong as representatives of our police department." Art Stone, executive director of the Illinois FOP Labor Council, commented on why some police officers have sought out the Teamsters because of its image of muscle and a powerful organization:

> We've got a different job. We're in the business of preserving law and order, not creating havoc. The reason they [police officers] wanted to look at someone else is not because they would be better represented, but because their intimidation may get them more. I believe the Teamsters have a few people who believe muscle will get them more than professional negotiation.

In 1979, San Diego police dropped their contractual agreement for bargaining with the Teamsters after admitting they only used the Teamsters to get leverage with the city. In 1978, St. Petersburg police contacted Teamsters Local 444 when the Pinellas County PBA could not get a contract out of the city. Local 444 already represented the Bartow police and had the Teamsters charter for all public employees in Florida. The resulting turmoil in the media caused the city to give the police a substantial raise to avoid Teamster affiliation.

The Teamsters drive through the South probably suffered a severe setback after the 15-day strike by New Orleans (LA) police that ended on March 4, 1979. The Teamsters organized the Police Association of New Orleans (PANO) which had dropped out of the Service Employees International Union after SEIU could not negotiate a contract with the city. Teamsters Local 253 was just as unsuccessful as SEIU because the mayor refused to negotiate with the 800-member local, but instead chose to talk to the 300-member FOP lodge. The resulting strike caused the city to recognize PANO, but talks collapsed over the unit designation. The furor over cancellation of Mardi Gras turned public opinion against the union and resulted in no contract, 200 disciplinary actions, fines of $600,000, and the disbanding of the Teamster local.

There is little published data concerning exactly what services the Teamsters Union offers police affiliates outside of their reputation as "tough" negotiators. The Teamsters Union will continue to organize police officers in spite of their reputation of having organized crime connections. Police officers who are having trouble negotiating contracts or resolving grievances will continue to seek out the Teamsters to frighten police administrators and elected officials. Although the Teamsters have failed to recruit any large municipal departments, they have come close enough on several occasions and they are not easily discouraged.

In a newspaper article on the Teamsters and police organizing, one Teamster official was asked to explain the union's bad reputation. He commented, "[a] bunch of garbage! Sure we have our bad apples, no more than you'll find in other unions and in corporations." A Rolling Meadows, Illinois police officer best summed up the pro-Teamster attitude of some police by saying, "[t]he guys said they wanted somebody big enough to kick the city in the ass." And, Chicago Teamsters Local 714 president Bill Hogan commented, "[w]e can do a lot for police...cities and states do not listen unless you've got some muscle."

The Teamsters Union has members and money. With a dwindling membership base in the private sector, the Teamsters want public employees and police officers. No one believes the Teamsters will become the dominant police union, but they may force other police labor organizations to merge or seek alliances to protect themselves from the Teamsters.

National Coalition of Public Safety Officers (CWA, AFL-CIO)

In 1996, the Communications Workers of America (CWA, AFL-CIO) entered the national police labor movement by creating a sector called the National Coalition of Public Safety Officers (NCPSO). CWA is a 600,000-member union that has traditionally been composed of telephone workers. Today, CWA's membership is about 25 percent in the public sector. Like other AFL-CIO unions, CWA has faced a shrinking private sector as the telephone industry has deregulated. This has caused CWA to reorganize as a white collar union seeking affiliations partner. The International Typographical Union, the Newspaper Guild, and the National Association of Broadcast Employees and Technicians are some of the recent affiliations.

CWA has been organizing state workers and corrections officers in such states as Texas, Mississippi, Oklahoma, and West Virginia since the early eighties. In 1992, the 16,000-member Combined Law Enforcement Associations of Texas (CLEAT) approached CWA after affiliation discussions with IUPA broke down. CLEAT negotiated an affiliation agreement that allowed CLEAT to remain autonomous.

In 1995, NCPSO assisted several New Mexico sheriff's and police departments in winning bargaining recognition. These local unions formed a statewide association–the New Mexico Coalition of Public Safety Officers Local 7911. New Mexico has a collective bargaining statute that was passed several years ago, but many departments had not been active in attempting to unionize until Local 7911's formation. Local 7911's main focus is negotiating collective bargaining agreements and providing legal services.

Police officers in Tucson and Peoria, Arizona have recently affiliated with NCPSO, and there are serious discussions in Arizona about a statewide local. The Tucson affiliation was significant because the local NCPSO affiliate beat an FOP lodge in a representation election for the right to negotiate a contract for almost 800 Tucson police officers. The FOP had been the exclusive representative for Tucson officers for more than 25 years. Tucson officers has previously rejected an IUPA attempt to decertify the FOP in the eighties.

A statewide association has also been formed in Georgia–G-COPS, Local 3200, primarily offering legal and legislative services to Georgia police officers. This group is concentrating its efforts in the Atlanta metropolitan area, but is expected to branch out to other parts of the state.

The Florida Police Benevolent Association is comprised of 34,000-members in charters and chapters, including the state corrections and probation officers in one unit. The independent Florida PBA had raided AFSCME several years earlier and decertified them. Now, the former president of the state PBA had formed a rival organization and was trying to decertify the PBA as the bargaining agent for these 18,000 corrections and probation officers. In addition, the Teamsters were raiding PBA locals and had recently decertified the PBA in Daytona Beach. IUPA and the Marine Engineers Beneficial Association (MEBA, AFL-CIO) entered into a joint organizing agreement to raid the PBA and FOP in Florida.

The Florida PBA voted to negotiate an agreement with NCPSO to allow its charters and chapters to voluntarily affiliate. This affiliation would provide these charters and chapters with protection under the AFL-CIO's Article XX "no raid" provisions, and these local unions would have the resources of a much larger national union. The combined NCPSO and PBA campaign defeated the decertification attempt for state corrections and probation officers. The Coastal Florida PBA Charter of the Florida PBA recently affiliated its 1,100 plus members with NCPSO.

In July, 1996, leaders from various CWA-affiliated police and corrections unions met in Tampa to develop a strategy for NCPSO. It is too early to determine the future of this organization. The general consensus from the meeting was that there was a restlessness among public safety labor unions. The causes included politically-correct chiefs, reinventing government mayors and governors, public demand for television perfect police forces, mounting social ills, and overcrowded prisons. Training and education of public safety officers was considered a primary issue. Only time will tell if the NCPSO strategy will work. There is no governance structure and the per capita is the $2.00 per member per month paid to CWA.

American Federation of State, County and Municipal Employees (AFL-CIO)

The American Federation of State, County and Municipal Employees (AFSCME, AFL-CIO) is the largest public sector union in the AFL-CIO. AFSCME is an industrial type union that accepts all employees of the state and local government except teachers and fire fighters, and they will charter employees of agencies who do business with the government.

In 1980, the BLS reported that AFSCME has 1,020,000 members in 2800 local unions, but no figures are given for police members or police locals. Various sources estimate AFSCME's police membership at 10,000 to 15,000. Since the AFL-CIO chartered IUPA, there has been very little activity by AFSCME in police organizing. There does not appear to be any evidence that AFSCME has increased its police membership in the last few years, but there does seem to be evidence that they are slowly losing police members to rival independent unions.

In 1978, the Waterville (Maine) police dropped AFSCME for the Teamsters, and the Oakland County (Michigan) deputies decertified AFSCME for the independent Police Officers Association of Michigan (POAM). The same year AFSCME gained the affiliation of the Civil Service Employees Association (CSEA) of New York that increased its membership from 750,000 to the one million mark. In the early 1970s, AFSCME's largest police local was the 1,500-member Baltimore police, but they have since joined FOP. AFSCME's largest police concentration is in Connecticut, Illinois, and some western states.

Although AFSCME was the motivator behind organized labor and the independent unions reentering the police labor market during the 1940s to 1960s, they have concentrated their organizing efforts among other government workers in collective bargaining states instead of the police. Prior to 1970, AFSCME had a no strike ban and punished police locals that went on strike. At various times, AFSCME has tried to revive its police organizing, and at a conference of AFSCME police locals, the late AFSCME president Jerry Wurf said, "[w]e want policemen in AFSCME...and we're going to get them."

AFSCME is not pushing its police organizing at this time, but they have not released their police locals to IUPA either. Although AFSCME has been involved in continuous jurisdictional disputes since its birth in 1936, they will probably maintain the status quo unless IUPA collapses and reopens the police market to AFL-CIO affiliates. AFSCME president Gerald W. McEntee is talking tough and has a reputation for "building coalitions of like-minded groups." Unless the present situation changes, AFSCME will be involved in too many problems with governmental units suffering from budget crisis to bother with raiding independent police associations.

Conclusion

Although it appears that the opportunity for one national police union has passed, the indicators may appear again in the future. The other public sector unions started organizing early before anyone else within their jurisdiction had formed rival unions. In addition, the salaries for public employees were low and there was little adverse reaction to public employee unionism. Many reasons have been put forth as to why the police have failed to have one united national union when other employee unions have succeeded. There are professions and trades still basically unorganized that will probably achieve one national voice before the police.

The secret may lie in the leaders of the national police organizations setting aside their egos and personal agendas long enough to determine how best to merge the various competing lodges, associations, and unions into one national police organization. The foundations are in place with many autonomous local and state police organizations providing bargaining, legal, and legislative services in the their state. All national police organizations provide the same federal legislative lobbying and political action. The key is to get the local organizations to join one state organization, and in turn have each state organization affiliate with one national organization for federal legislative services. The money and time wasted competing for the same pool of members does nothing but divide and conquer rank and file police officers.

One of the best reasons for why police officers have been unable to form one national union came in 1974 from the president of the New York City Sergeant's Benevolent Association, Harold Melnik, who said:

> There is no single individual who has openly come forth with the ability, acceptability and platform to rally all or most police organizations for merger into a national police union...It can be said that while the police association leaders of the major cities recognize the awesome power that could be obtained through a national body properly led, a fear of assimilation with a loss of identity still exists in the minds of many of these leaders. Until the day comes when police officers readily identify themselves as part of labor, only local and statewide groups will suffice and prosper.

ENDNOTES

Chapter 1. There is a reference in this chapter to the excellent book by Bennis and Nanus, *Leaders-The Strategies for Taking Charge.* Harper and Row (New York, 1985).

Chapter 3. The materials in this chapter have been taken liberally, and in some instances verbatim, from the excellent book, *Rules For Radicals*, by Saul Alinsky, Vintage Books, New York, 1989. These materials have been used and reprinted with the kind permission of Random House, and the authors wish to thank the publisher for extending this courtesy.

Chapter 4. The materials in this chapter have also been borrowed, in some instances verbatim, from *Rules For Radicals*, Saul Alinsky, Vintage Books, New York, 1989. These materials have also been used and reprinted with the permission of Random House.

Chapter 7. The ideas from this chapter are taken almost exclusively from the excellent book by David Weil, *Turning the Tide: Strategic Planning for Labor Unions.* The definition of strategic planning found on page 41 of this book are found on pages 6-7 of *Turning the Tide.* The subjects on strategic planning in this book on analyzing the environment, setting priorities, resource allocation, and organizational structure can be found at various places of *Turning the Tide*; for example, resource allocation can be found in Chapter 7, and organizational structure can be found in chapters 8 and 9. The authors are vary grateful to Mr. Weil for his authorization to use the materials from his book. He is a recognized authority on the subject of labor organization strategic planning and has made an immense contribution to the American labor movement through his work.

Chapter 8. Many of the ideas in this chapter were taken from an excellent resource book on the subject of prepaid legal plans—*A Lawyer's Guide to Prepaid Legal Services*, published in 1988 by the American Bar Association. The principal author is Alec Schwartz. It may be obtained by contacting the ABA at: 750 North Lake Shore Drive, Chicago, Illinois 60611.

Chapter 9. The portion of this chapter discussing Third Party Administrators is taken from an excellent booklet published by the Society of Professional Benefit Administrators entitled "Everything You Wanted to Know About TPA's But Were Afraid to Ask," publication date not indicated. This information can be obtained by writing to the Society at 2 Wisconsin Circle, Suite 670, Chevy Chase, MD 20815.

Chapter 23. There is a reference in this chapter to legal authority for a local referendum to alter the provisions of a state collective bargaining law which mandates an impasse procedure. This authority can be found in the case of *City v. Association of Portsmouth Teachers*, 597 A2d 1063 (N.H., 1991).

Chapter 26. This chapter was originally written by Jim Lynch, who works for the Arkansas Institute of Government, University of Arkansas as Little Rock, as a feature article appearing in *The Police Labor Leader* in November, 1992 related to a City of Little Rock bond issue. Since this information on bond issues fits well with other issues on confrontation, the authors decided to place this material into this part of the book rather than the part where the other case studies appear. The authors have made some revisions from the original article. Jim Lynch has given his kind permission to reprint the material, and the authors are indebted to him for his assistance in past ventures and support of this book project.

Chapter 43. PORAC Legal Administrator Larry Friedman advises that since this article was published in *The Police Labor Leader* in 1993, that the PORAC Legal Defense Fund has increased to a membership of 34,900 members, and paid out more than four million dollars in legal benefits in 1996.

Chapters 46, 47, and 48. The material appearing in these chapters has been, unlike all the preceding chapters, meticulously researched. Following is an alphabetical bibliography of all source materials used for these chapters.

REFERENCES

AFL-CIO Approves New Kiernan-Gordon Union. *Police Magazine*, May, 1979: 46-48.

AFL-CIO Official Criticizes Police Unions. *Police Magazine*, March, 1978: 49.

AFSCME Becomes Largest AFL-CIO Affiliate. *Police Magazine*, July, 1978: 9.

American Federation of Police Files $5 million Libel Suit Against Gordon, IUPA (AFL-CIO). *Police Chronicle*, February, 1981.

Are Unions Dead or Just Sleeping? *Fortune*, September 20, 1982: 98-112.

Ayers, Richard M., and Thomas L. Wheelen, eds. *Collective Bargaining in the Public Sector*. Gaithersburg, Md.: IACP, 1977: 40-41.

Bargaining Notes. *The FOP Journal*. January, 1981.

Barry, Bob. President's Report. *The San Francisco Policeman*, July, 1981.

Behar, Richard. A Reformer and the Mob. *Time Magazine*, November 22, 1993: 54-55.

Behar, Richard. How Hoffa Haunts the Teamsters. *Time Magazine*, December 21, 1992: 60-61.

Bergsman, Ilene. Police Unions. *Management Information Service Report*. VIII (March, 1976): 1-19.

Bernstein Aaron. The Teamsters and the Mob: It may really be over. *Business Week*, June 17, 1991: 102-103.

Bernstein, Aaron. The Teamsters Try Something New: Democracy. *Business Week*, December 9, 1991: 34.

Bopp, William J. *The Police Rebellion*. Springfield, Ill.: Charles C Thomas, 1971: 15-16, 78-84.

Bopp, William J. *Police Personnel Administration: The Management of Human Resources*. Boston, Mass.: Holbrook Press, Inc., 1974: 336-337.

Bornstein, Tim. Police Unions: Dispelling the Ghost of 1919. *Police Magazine*, September, 1978: 25-29.

Boyd, Richard A. Report of the National Treasurer. *The FOP Journal*, February, 1982.

Bronfenbrenner, Kate, & Tom Juravich. Union Organizing in the Public Sector: An Analysis of State and Local Elections. ILR Bulletin 70. Ithaca, New York: Cornell University Press 1996.

Bureau of Labor Statistics, 1980: 29, 40, 45-46.

Burpo John. *The Police Labor Movement: Problems and Perspectives*. Springfield, Ill.: Charles C Thomas, 1971: 3, 6-8, 10, 34-35.

Castlio, Glen. Rise and Demise of the ICPA. *PORAC News*, October, 1979.

Cleveland Police Union Joins IUPA. *Police Magazine*, November, 1980: 19-20.

Collins, Duane. I.U.P.A. - Chicago. *The San Franciso Policeman*, October, 1981.

Cone, Russ. Police Union's Chief Convinced Public Will Like It. *San Franciso Examiner,* July 18, 1979.

Critical Issues in Police Labor Relations. Gaithersburg, Maryland: IACP, 1974: 50-51.

Davis, Keith. Labor Unions. *Collective Bargaining in the Public Sector.* Edited by Richard M. Ayers & Thomas L. Wheelen. Gaithersburg, Maryland: ICAP, 1977: 25.

D.C. Police Switch From IBPO to FOP, But Accept IBPO's Contract. *Police Magazine,* March, 1982: 38.

Denying Georgia Police Dues Checkoff Violated Equal Protection. *Public Employee Bargaining,* November 14, 1979.

Dineen, John. Now is the Time to Organize. *The FOP Journal,* October, 1980.

Dineen, John. FOP Wins in Chicago. *The FOP Journal,* January, 1981.

DPA News, October/November, 1982.

FEDNEWS, June, 1982.

3 Florida Counties Join IBPO. *Police Chronicle,* August, 1982.

The FOP Journal, November, 1981.

Frank, Allan Dobbs. The Wages of Frustration: "When All Else fails, Call the Teamsters." *Police Magazine,* September, 1978: 21-22, 30-32.

Future of Unionism in New Orleans in Question After Failed Strike. *Police Magazine,* May, 1979: 45-46.

Gammage, Allen Z., and Stanley L. Sachs. Police Unions. Springfield, Ill.: Charles C Thomas, 1972: 30-33, 37, 44-47, 50-51, 56-57.

Gentry, Margaret. Union Signs Police: Mob Ties a Concern. *Houston Chronicle,* June 23, 1980.

Government Employees, National Association. *Constitution and By-Laws,* 1980.

Government Employees, National Association. Why You Need Professional Representation and Why It Should Be...IBPO. Published with no date.

Helburn, I.B. *Public Employer-Employee Relations in Texas: Contemporary and Emerging Developments.* Austin, Tx: Institute of Public Affairs, The University of Texas at Austin, 1971: 24.

Hilligan, Thomas J. Public Employee Organizations: Past Developments and Present Problems. *Labor Law Journal,* XXIV (May, 1973), 288-305. Labor Relations Yearbook, 1981: 289-294.

Hollywood Police Choose IBPO Over FOP. *Police Chronicle,* April, 1979.

Hudson, Robert. What's A Nice Cop Like You Doing in a "Big Bad" Union. *Police Product News,* May, 1979: 18-27.

Hudson, Robert. What A Nice Cop Like You Doing in a "Big Bad" Union, Part II. *Police Product News,* June, 1979: 18-25.

IBPO Clobbers AFGE in Border Patrol Election. *Police Chronicle,* June, 1979.

IBPO Gets Final Certification in D.C. *Police Magazine,* September, 1979: 20.

ICPA Bid to Join AFL-CIO in Trouble. *Police Magazine,* January, 1979: 69.

Introducing the Fraternal Order of Police and the International Brotherhood of Police Officers-The Anti-Union Unions You Should Know About. *The Enforcer,* October/November, 1980.

Juris, Hervey A., and Peter Feuille. *Police Employee Organizations.* Evanston, Ill.: Center for Urban Studies, Northwestern University, 1973: 14-15.

Juris, Hervey A. and Peter Feuille. *Police Unionism: Power and Impact in Public Sector Bargaining.* Lexington, Mass: D.C. Heath and Company, 1973.

Kiernan, Edward. "An Open Letter to the Members of the San Francisco Police Officers' Association from Ed Kiernan, President of the International Union of Police Associations, AFL-CIO." *The San Francisco Policeman,* January, 1982.

Kiernan Hits Raiding by Teamsters, AFSCME. *The Empire State Investigator,* July, 1980.

Levi, Margaret. *Bureaucratic Insurgency: The Case of Police Unions.* Lexington, Mass.: D.C. Heath and Company, 1977: 7.

Maddox, Charles. *Collective Bargaining in Law Enforcement.* Springfield, Ill.: Charles C Thomas, 1975, 9-10.

Marchetti, Leo V. From the President. *The FOP Journal,* February, 1982.

McCarthy, William P. Key Issues in Police Unionism: Another Viewpoint. *National Symposium on Police Labor Relations.* Washington, D.C.: Police Foundation, 1974: 65-75.

Melnick, Harold. Key Issues in Police Unionism. *National Symposium on Police Labor Relations.* Washington, D.C.: Police Foundation, 1974: 59-64.

NAGE Files Certification Suit. *FEDNEWS,* August, 1982.

NAGE Raid Stuffed By Firemen and Oilers. *In Public Service,* February, 1981.

NAPO Report. *PORAC News,* November, 1981.

National Association of Police Organizations. *DPA News,* August/September, 1982.

Noble, Kenneth B. AFL-CIO council admits Teamsters. *Austin American-Statesmen,* October 25, 1987.

Parenti, Ron. Petition to Withdraw From IUPA. *The San Francisco Policeman,* December, 1981.

Police Associations, International Union, AFL-CIO. *Constitution and By-Laws,* 1996.

Police Associations, International Union, AFL-CIO. Letter from President Edward Kiernan. February 20, 1979.

Police Associations, International Union, AFL-CIO. Informational Brochure, 1979.

Police Employee Organization. *The Police Chief,* December, 1969: 51-55.

Police Labor Monthly, July, 1982.

Police Organizations, National Association. *Constitution and By-Laws,* 1996.

Police Organizations, National Association. Recruitment Pamphlet, 1979.

Police Union Elects Baker New Secretary-Treasurer. *AFL-CIO News,* August 14, 1982.

Pomerleau, Donald D. The Eleventh Hour. *The Police Chief,* December, 1969: 40-42.

Progressive Coalition Wins Big at IUPA Convention. *The Arizona Law Officer,* Summer, 1982.

Pugh, Michael P. The Effect of Unionization Versus Non-Unionization on Wage Determination in Municipal Police Agencies With One Hundred or More Sworn and Non-Sworn Personnel. Ph.D. Dissertation, Sam Houston State University, 1980: 36-38.

Salerno, Charles A. Overview of Police Labor Relations. *Collective Bargaining in the Public Sector.* Edited by Richard M. Ayers & Thomas L. Wheelen. Gaithersburg, Maryland: IACP, 1977: 5-7.

Serrin, William. Union Chief Plans to be Aggressive, Allow Wide Latitude. *Houston Chronicle,* December 30, 1981.

Serrin, William. Teamsters Union Faces Major Challenges. *Houston Chronicle,* June 1, 1982.

Service Employees International Union, AFL-CIO. Letter from President George Hardy. April 23, 1979.

Spero, Sterling D., and John M. Capozzola. *The Urban Community and its Unionized Bureaucracies: Pressure Politics in Local Government Labor Relations.* New York: Dunellen Publisher, 1973: 14, 28-29.

Spizman, Lawrence M. Public Employee Unions: A Study in the Economics of Power. *Journal of Labor Research,* I (Fall, 1980): 265-273.

Stieber, Jack. *Public Employee Unionism: Structure, Growth, Policy.* Washington, D.C.: The Brookings Institution, 1973: 2, 6-7, 56-57, 91, 105-106.

Teamsters Look to Roll Up Police. *PORAC News,* June, 1986.

Teamsters Still Desperately Want Police in Their Union. *The Arizona Law Officer,* September, 1980.

Teamsters Take Over in Minnesota and New Orleans. *Police Magazine,* May, 1978: 28-back cover.

Teamsters Trying to Organize Two Southern Police Departments. *Police Magazine,* November, 1979: 56-57.

They'll Get Their Chance to Go Teamster. *The International Teamster,* September, 1980.

U.S. Department of Labor, Bureau of Labor Statistics. *Directory of National Unions,* 1979.

U.S. Office of Personnel Management. *Union Recognition in the Federal Government.* Washington, D.C.: Government Printing Office, 1980.

Warren, James. Necessity, Not Choice, Moved Teamsters. *Chicago Tribune,* Sunday, October 25, 1987.

Wright, Connie. New Police Union Brings Contrasting Reactions. *Nation's Cities Weekly,* May 14, 1979: 9.